CW00971391

Hostage Spaces of the Contemporary Islamicate World

Suspensions: Contemporary Middle Eastern and Islamicate Thought

Series editors: Jason Mohaghegh and Lucian Stone.
This series interrupts standardized discourses involving the Islamicate world by introducing creative and emerging ideas. The incisive works included in this series provide a counterpoint to the reigning canons of theory, theology, philosophy, literature, and criticism through investigations of vast experiential typologies—such as violence, mourning, vulnerability, tension, and humour—in light of contemporary Islamicate thought.

The Poetics of Mourning in the Middle East, Alina Gharabegian
The Politics of Writing Islam, Mahmut Mutman
The Writing of Violence in the Middle East, Jason Bahbak Mohaghegh

Hostage Spaces of the Contemporary Islamicate World

Phantom Territoriality

Dejan Lukić

Suspensions: Contemporary Middle Eastern and
Islamicate Thought

B L O O M S B U R Y
LONDON • NEW DELHI • NEW YORK • SYDNEY

Bloomsbury Academic
An imprint of Bloomsbury Publishing Plc

50 Bedford Square
London
WC1B 3DP
UK

1385 Broadway
New York
NY 10018
USA

www.bloomsbury.com

Bloomsbury is a registered trade mark of Bloomsbury Publishing Plc

First published 2013
Paperback edition first published 2014

© Dejan Lukić, 2013

Dejan Lukić has asserted his right under the Copyright, Designs and Patents Act, 1988, to be identified as Author of this work.

All rights reserved. No part of this publication may be reproduced or transmitted in any form or by any means, electronic or mechanical, including photocopying, recording, or any information storage or retrieval system, without prior permission in writing from the publishers.

No responsibility for loss caused to any individual or organization acting on or refraining from action as a result of the material in this publication can be accepted by Bloomsbury or the author.

British Library Cataloguing-in-Publication Data
A catalogue record for this book is available from the British Library.

ISBN: HB: 978-1-4411-9484-8
PB: 978-1-4725-7086-4

Library of Congress Cataloging-in-Publication Data
Lukić, Dejan.
Hostage spaces of the contemporary Islamicate world :
phantom territoriality / Dejan Lukić.
p. cm.—(Suspensions, contemporary Middle Eastern and Islamicate thought)
Includes bibliographical references and index.
ISBN 978-1-4411-9484-8—ISBN 978-1-4411-6035-5 (ebookpdf) 1. Political kidnapping.
2. Terrorism. 3. Hostages. 4. Terrorism—Religious aspects—Islam. I. Title.
HV6431.L855 2012
364.15'4091767—dc23
2012019252

Typeset by Newgen Imaging Systems Pvt Ltd, Chennai, India
Printed and bound in Great Britain

Contents

Series Foreword

Poets, artists, theologians, philosophers, and mystics in the Middle East and Islamicate world have been interrogating notions of desire, madness, sensuality, solitude, death, time, space, etc. for centuries, thus constituting an expansive and ever-mutating intellectual landscape. Like all theory and creative outpouring, then, theirs is its own vital constellation—a construction cobbled together from singular visceral experiences, intellectual ruins, novel aesthetic techniques, social-political-ideological detours, and premonitions of a future—built and torn down (partially or in toto), and rebuilt again with slight and severe variations. The horizons shift, and frequently leave those who dare traverse these lands bewildered and vulnerable.

Consequently, these thinkers and their visionary ideas largely remain unknown, or worse, mispronounced and misrepresented in the so-called western world. In the hands of imperialistic frameworks, a select few are deemed worthy of notice and are spoken on behalf of, or rather *about*. Their ideas are simplified into mere social formulae and empirical scholarly categories. Whereas so-called western philosophers and writers are given full leniency to contemplate the most incisive or abstract ideas, non-western thinkers, especially those located in the imagined realms of the Middle East and Islamicate world, are reduced to speaking of purely political histories or monolithic cultural narratives. In other words, they are distorted and contorted to fit within hegemonic paradigms that steal away their more captivating potentials.

Contributors to this series provide a counterpoint to the reigning canons of theory, theology, philosophy, literature, and criticism through investigations of the vast experiential typologies of such regions. Each volume in the series acts as a "suspension" in the sense that the authors will position contemporary thought in an enigmatic new terrain of inquiry, where it will be compelled to confront unforeseen works of critical and creative imagination. These analyses will not only highlight the full range of current intellectual and artistic trends and their benefits for the citizens of these phantom spheres, but also argue that the ideas themselves are borderless, and thus of great relevance to all citizens of the world.

Jason Bahbak Mohaghegh and Lucian Stone

Preface: Diagrammatic Intensifications

A line of pure methodology: "It is impossible to think or write without some façade of a house at least rising up, a phantom, to receive and to make a work of our peregrinations."[1] The entire interplay of violence, war, and torture that occurs in the militant sphere between what we call the East and the West could be viewed as a battle of façades rather than of ideologies or civilizations. In fact, one side is nothing more than a façade of the other.

A phantom appears disappearing. This is its divine character, so to speak, since God too, especially in Islamic thought, manifests himself in his withdrawal from the world. This book is concerned with the space of phantomality, the space of separation, the space of withdrawal. In addressing the divine character of violence through militancy, or terrorism, I certainly do not want to sacralize it. The relationship between violence and the sacred has already been established by numerous authors, and the role of the theological in political terminology has also been rigorously, albeit controversially, unveiled by Carl Schmitt. Rather, I want to point out the convergence of the theological (that which belongs to the enunciation of God) with the political (that which belongs to the enunciation of the sovereign) in the construction of militant space, or what can now be called the hostage space. In this respect, hostage taking is a fractal detail in the history of conflicts on our planet. It is a detail around which powers of war, law, and sovereignty circle like a planetary constellation around a black hole—or, hostage taking is the event horizon in the cosmos of sovereignty.

In the Fall of 2007, I took a boat along the Adriatic coast from the old town of Dubrovnik in Croatia to a coastal village in the Lezhë district of Albania. Once on the beach, I first entered into an abandoned bunker, a courtesy of the ex-president and communist sovereign Enver Hoxha and his attitude toward the world: protection by hyper-insulation. (Indeed, during his presidency the entire nation was nothing but a crowded bunker, sealed off from the outside world.) But then another half-domed building invited my eyes. I walked into a small mosque with only one man inside. He was old, and spoke broken Serbo-Croatian. In a short conversation without a linear thread, he told me two things: (a) that throngs of medusas (also known as jellyfish) have swarmed the coast close to the village, as part of their yearly visitation each September, giving hardship to local fishermen since they eat large quantities of anchovy plankton, and (b) that his son has disappeared on his way to the Italian side of the Adriatic (direction: port of Bari) in the venture of illegal human trafficking. Through these two stories I began to think of the phantom territories, hostage spaces, witnessing, war, politics, theology, the East/West divide, and conspired toward a reality that underlies this book.

The inside of the insomniac trajectory. Consider the experience of the stowaway. Enclosed in the entrails of the ship, he becomes resistant to dreams—pure somnambular being. The stowaway travels secretly and in this way invents the most original space by his trajectory. Here the night of travel becomes the time of illumination and wakefulness, a crepuscular immanence. This experience cannot be disentangled from the writing that performs it, just as the spell of a violent fairytale cannot exist outside the body which it envelops. The stowaway invents a new dimension of space: that of phantom territoriality, which is contiguous with terror, exhaustion, survival, that is with bare passions. The stowaway is solitary and yet he forms a secret group that proliferates by risk alone. In other words, it is only a matter of time before a solitary polyp turns into a thousand medusas.

Moreover, the presence of borders is exasperating for a stowaway since they mark the highest point of intensification in the duration of a travel; they are lines of exhaustion, of both the territory and the passenger. The stowaway darkens the horizon of the whole world by making all borders dissoluble. Everything becomes a passage when everything becomes a secret. This is why I travel within this image given to me by the old man. It is not so much the borders that we pass, but the edges that generate another kind of sound, another kind of memory, solely liquid. The fairytale's geography suffuses us. The events I write about are indistinguishable from the bodies of the jellyfish, events that are nothing but the crystals of pulsations.

Stowaway writing. Writing that is itself like a stowaway can only generate jettison texts where traveling in minor steps means traveling in giant steps, and where the speed of these steps is no longer a physical unit but a form of thought: how to travel through the world and its insults at once undefeated and alive? For writing is not so much an exorcism of hostile powers as much as an invitation of these powers (so as to then step into their hostility). A clandestine writing. The word "clandestine" comes from a blend of "secret" (Latin *clam*) and "intestine" (Latin *intestines*), as if the concept was invented for hidden travelers alone. Here we can also mention its further parallels with writing, one positioned precisely in-between the secret and the guts. To be clandestine is to be swallowed up like a secret inside the entrails of a ship.

The outside of the insomniac trajectory. The book in your hands should be seen as a diagram (rather than a history of terms), a constellation of lines referring to varying figures of a hostage space. This analysis marks the intertwining lines of affects, militancy, locations of impact, details within a detail (the veil, the cloak, the beard, the incantation, etc.), for these same details reveal outlines of more abstract notions regarding the law, sovereignty, and terrorism.

The table of contents can be seen as an enumeration of nine axioms (there could be many more) of hostage spacing. Each one operates as a landscape of concepts with its own consistency. Each has its own vibratory inflections, its own impossible resolutions. The consistency of the entire book thus resembles a cipher. This composition is not meant to valorize cryptic writing; on the contrary, my hope is that the writing here proves clear and transparent. But to write is to think and to compose, it is to set into movement, and ultimately to produce a message (i.e. the inscription, the command, or the law). Cipher, on the other hand, is a simple word whose genealogy is worth addressing: it comes from the old French term *cifre* (in Bosnian this sounding is retained in the word *šifra*), which in turn comes from the Arabic *şifr*, which means "zero." Zero is a nothing, or something of no importance, yet it is also a zero degree of intensity, the middle of consistency where everything starts (to use Gilles Deleuze's image of the middle). In other words, ciphering is the leveling of profundity (of thought and ideas). This notwithstanding, the cipher—the violence of its implementations, the disaster of its results, and the exuberance of its ideas—asks for a work that will meet it on its own terms.

Here appears a proliferation of definitions and ideas, multitude upon multitude. If there is a main argument, it is this one: the hostage taker (also a type of stowaway) invents and constructs a peculiar territory—a phantom territoriality. This she does through secrecy, biopotentiality, illegality, irregularity, relics, delirium, animality, strange forms of political economy, etc. Thus there are many digressions within these pages. I take this methodological zigzag from a lived experience. During the siege of Sarajevo in the mid-1990s, when the entire city was taken hostage, the inhabitants had to move through the streets in constant zigzag trajectories, since this was the only way to avoid being shot by snipers. Writing too is a combat (with oneself, with texts under consideration, with events under discussion, with images, etc.) and a hostage space. And if it is to be treated as such, in all its visceral quality, then metaphors are inappropriate; one rather does as one would in a real-life situation—that is, one must zigzag.

A note on the problem of context: this work traverses an elusive geoscape, one that traces primarily the conditions of postcommunist East European societies such as Bosnia, Albania, and Chechnya. My engagement with Islamic thought is thus generated through this singular prism. For certain, the contemporary Bosnian, Albanian, and Chechnyan reading and appropriation of Islamic history, philosophy, poetics, and iconography is like no other, at once peripheral (within the Muslim world) and thoroughly embedded in the project of modernity (often without connection to the monolith of a classical tradition). As such, they remain at a far distance from mainstream discourses that have circulated for millennia in more central locations of the Middle East. Most of these Balkan revaluations, whether of sacred texts or existential codes, would not be validated or endorsed by the reigning institutions of Islamic theology, politics, or scholarship (they go elsewhere, seeking strategic inaccuracy, and often treading beyond the long-standing truths). This is precisely what lends them their intricacy as reinventions of concepts, as impressions born out of necessity.

Moreover, militant Islam is obviously quite different from nation to nation, from community to community, from individual to individual, and from one historical period to the next. Consequently, the militancy of global Islam is not homogenous, nor does it belong to any essentialist principle; rather, it is diverse in degrees of applications, affects, and convictions. I am seemingly somewhat indiscriminate in my rendering of this typology of radical thought. The reader should note that this project is envisioned, above all else, as a conversation between myself and the hostage taker. It is a conversation that shifts between agony, joy, and indifference. The scholarly references are there only to push this engagement further. The book itself is an extraction of the main intensities that emerge in this confrontation. What surfaces is a theory of a hostage taker, one in particular (when there is a specific name) and no one in particular (when there is no name), but never a story of everyone. For this to be evident, one has to be attuned to a "subterranean coherence" sketched time and again in the text. In this sense, the book is a blueprint rather than a built model of the hostage space.

Furthermore, the hostage taker is an abstract enemy, one that is imperceptible until she takes over a space, and one that is gone once that space is returned to the everyday. I am attempting to give this figure a unique materiality with its own architectonics, laws, and climates of growth. In this sense, one should not really look for the subject of the book; the hostage space reveals itself in the tonalities of the atmosphere it produces, the qualities of light and darkness. Through these atmospheric shadows, figures of the hostage taker, the militant, the terrorist, and the resistance-fighter emerge. The matter of ideas therein rests upon particularities of enigmas, irresoluteness, and vibrancies found in terror or in resistance, where personal and global political crisis carry their own meaning. The reader should first allow himself to be carried along the text as the young Albanian immigrant is carried within the entrails of the ship, not as a helpless migrant but as a new being arriving at the shores of western thought.

Finally, it is one thing to talk, another to write, and still another to take hostage. In order to write and inhabit the space of the hostage taker, I had to take hostage of words and ideas themselves, both mine and those of others. In light of the subject matter and its precarious character, and in light of a problematic dance developed with respect to its volatility, I wanted to construct this book as an explosive device. It is up to the reader to defuse it or not to defuse it as she or he pleases.

1

"Being on the Lookout," the Animal

Territory

To occupy, to impose the occupation, to devour space, and oneself with it. To what extent is this statement true of the hostage taker? Hostage taking implies a simultaneous occupation of space (be it inside or outside, private or public, a transportation vehicle or a patch of land) and the inhabitants of that space. The people who are seized receive a new function: they are the fulfillment or failure of a given condition, which means that both the hostage taker and the hostages change their states of being. They change these states together, through imposition. The degrees of their humanity are altered simultaneously through the imposition of fear, threath, stealth, camouflage, etc. This change is possible only because there is, in the first place, an exchange of affects between the hostage taker and the hostages; we could say that the room in which they find themselves trembles. It is this change, this trembling, that affects their very status as humans.

The relationship to a territory and the occupation of a territory is properly animalistic. As a result, the hostage taker only enacts and makes visible the primordial identification of the animal through the specific parameters of space. It is the violence enacted upon the territory that makes the action terroristic. The bodies of the hostages are thus only perceived as territories of the enemy that one can occupy as well. The implicit ontology of the hostage taker lies in his relationship to the space that he occupies and the limited panorama that this occupation provides for his survival. The spatial configuration of the territory he occupies, then, imposes a new definition upon the hostage taker in the same way that he imposes himself on the space and its inhabitants. Namely, the hostage taker is a "being on the lookout."[1] Being on the lookout means being in tension, being intense and without rest, always looking over one's shoulder. This is the same ontology of the animal that is nothing but a constant tension with the world, a high-strung sensuous apprehension of its environment, one that mirrors the animalistic nature of the hostage taker, or better still, the modality within the human which ties him to a certain vector of space. Every animal is, in this sense, properly political because it is tied to a particular territory and its atmospheric conditions.

Being on the lookout means looking after one's properties (bodily and territorial). How then does the hostage taker construct the property of a territory? He imprisons it. The hostage taker deterritorializes himself by occupying a territory and thereby making it hostile against the world—including oneself. In other words, the hostage taker reorganizes a territory's properties (who does this territory belong to?) in the process of seizing everyone present.

Being an animal: being a hostage of one's own affective powers. But from where does this primordial tension with the world come? It comes from the experience of one's body as separate from the rest of the world; it comes with being embodied and with one's feet firmly on the ground, with possessing a ground, and eventually anxiously defending it. Occupying also translates into defending a territory. Here is the first encounter with the notion of the political. Here the occupation of the territory implies a hostility from the outside, the enemy that is (always) to come.

In this location that is an encounter, the meeting point where the bodies collide, the "here" of the hostage space, is where the desire for justice, the resistance to stately power, and the theopolitical vision turn into pure actions. This is where we encounter a hostage taker above all else. First, he belongs to a specific territory (that of the nation-state) and second, he intrudes upon the personal territory of the other and violently overtakes it. The hostage taker overtakes the bodies of others in order to undermine the geopolitics of the other. Thus, the enemy is constructed through the relationship and violation of the relationship to a particular territory. Indeed, if we examine the root of the word "hostage," "host," a range of intertwined meanings opens up. Most importantly, in Latin *hospes* means a guest. So, on the one hand, a host is a person who receives guests (the hospitable aspect of hostaging); on the other, a host is also a person whose immune system has been invaded by a pathogenic organism (the immunological aspect). But other surprises encroach upon the meaning of the word: *hostis* also meant "stranger, or enemy" and in medieval times, an "army"; and, finally, *hostia* meant "victim." A whole conceptual universe unfurls here. The terror of the hostage taker lies precisely in the fact that he overpowers the confines of these words. She is the uninvited guest who turns the host into a victim and herself into an adversary. We also see that at the root (if such a thing exists) of this notion of the stranger lies the simultaneous emergence of the enemy. The hostage taker is therefore an executioner of failed hospitality, which is nothing but the failed attempt to turn the outsider into an insider, to turn the "animal" into a "human," through procedures of capturing and, sometimes, killing.

For these reasons the concept of territory precedes the concept of the political. And further, in this highly political act of the hostage taking, I see two domains that tacitly encompass the concept of the political: animality and territoriality. In general, animality, territoriality, and the political form a complicated trinity which is hard to divest into constituent parts. This is why the figure of the hostage taker is significant, since he brings these foundational molecules of the political to the fore. There are therefore a politics of the animal and of territory that are not necessarily tied to the idea of the state (even though it is hard now to imagine mountains in Bosnia as not being Bosnian, or the Adriatic coast in Albania as not Albanian).

Ideas too are territories. One traverses them, defends them, develops trajectories, borders, gates, passwords, violent implementations, official legitimations, stately and disciplinary powers. One also escapes them, uses them as a rope through which one descends from the cell in the castle of dominant discourses. The hostage taker, in fact, tells us a story of suspension, rather than descent, a suspension that is both a theoretical and physical levitation (negatively manifested in the explosion of the body), therefore never completely resolving the problem of belonging, never completely climbing up or completely going down into the underground.

The hostage taker becomes an animal, literally turning into an animal of prey that uses stealth and surprise to impose terror. But he is already brought to the condition of a powerless or wild animal by humiliation on the part of the dominant state or global economics, which intertwine in their imposition of powers (the so-called neoliberal power that encompasses and expands from the West).[2] "They" are like wild animals; this is the repressed secret of the West. It is secret because it simmers below the surface of democratic humanism, a dirty little secret that constantly leaks out. The hostage taker is thus reduced to the state (if not the shape) of the animal already. Strategically, then, he intensifies this definition toward its most absurd and fatalistic consequences. The man and the woman of irregular war—terrorism—are undoubtedly related to the animal, both in its physical dispositions and its political standing. While naming one an "animal" imprisons him in the cosmology of the other, ascribing oneself to the animal produces opposition to this enslavement—opposition that becomes libratory.

The discussion of belonging to a territory, national or ethnic,[3] thus has to proceed from the discussion on animality. The affair of belonging is of course a profound process of domestication, of a sense of security, protection, and so on. The emergence of empires and states, and their dissipation through contemporary neoliberal networks, must be tied to the process of domestication (evolutionary biology has to be coupled with domesticatory ontology). It is important to note that the supposed "wildness" of the hostage taker is only momentary. Ultimately, this phenomenon can be traced back to a failure of the idea of freedom, since freedom is already tied to another belonging (to one's ethnicity or religious brotherhood, or in light of this essay, to the space of Islamic cosmology). Throughout, I will consistently reiterate this ensuing failure inscribed in the act of hostage taking.

The entire world for humans operates through the interaction of the inside with the outside; the hostage taker maximizes this experience when she overtakes a small particle of space thereby establishing herself as a sovereign of this temporary territory. The hostage taker, in this precise action, expresses her own maltreatment—being treated like a mere animal—by embodying this animality to its extreme, and by using all the technologies and magicalities of warfare, from camouflage to explosive devices to cell phones to religious cries (relating one's body to the architecture of the divine). The animal and the territory are inseparable, just as Bataille famously says that "every animal is in the world like water in water."[4] In other words, the animal exists immanently in the world, without separation from its environment, without the infinite human problem of the inside and the outside (inside the house or outside of it, inside the state or outside of it, inside the law or outside of it, inside one's skin or outside of it). And yet the animal is locked in a permanent impulse to hide and surprise, displaying that its world is immanent but circumscribed by the outline of a territory.

Before proceeding, let us return to a more thoroughgoing treatment of domestication since it is essential for understanding this disruptive practice. On October 23, 2003 Dubrovka Theater in Moscow was seized by 30 to 40 Chechens who were part of the Islamist militant separatist movement in Chechnya.[5] (This event is also known as "Nord-Ost siege" after the name of the musical that was performed in the theater that day, thus giving the entire event of terror a sense of performativity, or of a perverse spectacle with its own "musicality.") After two and a half days, the theater was raided by Russian forces after they released an unknown chemical agent into the ventilation system. This resulted in the death of 170 people (including 39 hostage takers). In the years that followed, there were a number of theater reenactments, the simulation of its intensities, of the

Dubrovka Theater hostage crisis. I mention here only one that went beyond the benign ethical invocations of devastation that this event indisputably produced. In 2008, "La Fura dels Baus," a Catalan theater troupe, aestheticized the events of the Dubrovka Theater through the architecture of the stage, physical attractiveness of actors and costumes, and general excitement that was raised by the slight imposition on the audience to participate in the act.[6] I say "aestheticized" not to belittle the conceptual quality of the performance; every documentary image that emerged from the Dubrovka crisis had a certain aesthetics of horror inscribed in itself. The problem lies elsewhere, in the domestication of the event that occurs in its aftermath: the staging itself puts it into the sphere of something consumable, always safe (despite the minimal provocations by the actors), and in the end educational. The inconsumable aspect of hostage taking stays in the domain of what is unsaid, or in the domain of expectation: that of the lookout. Hostage taking is preceded by the lookout and succeeded by the cry: these are its opening and closing acts. What happens in-between cannot be reenacted nor witnessed. For this reason the ethically problematic proposition is nevertheless accurate: the real siege is the real avant-garde, where the terrorist manifesto is taken on its word, where word and image are not representations but pure experiences.

Another definition that underlies the constellation of this conflict: the hostage taker is one anomalous segment of the figure of the terrorist, which is a segment of the figure of the partisan, which is the segment of the very experience of irregularity. If the body of terrorism, or of what is conceived as the enemy, were that of a starfish, a hostage taker would be one granule of that expansive architecture of plates found on the surface of this animal. One could say that the hostage taker is nothing but a special irregularity, a violent imposition of the irregular. While these notions are primarily political, they can also be approached from the standpoint of pure territoriality. The very idea of the political is of course directly tied to the idea of the territory, and by extension to planetary surfaces and depths (in terms of the economics of oil, for example). This equation is not surprising. But there is another more startling one at work (even though it is basic): politics-territory-animal. This is the equation in which the hostage taker should be situated, as a small actor in the theater of the animo-political—one that disturbs the surface of the state (through abduction of its citizens) while also helping it solidify in unprecedented ways.

In every respect, the hostage taker works through the primacy of the act, through an immediacy that at the same time looks beyond the present moment. Even more, the act itself is aligned with the word; that is the threats are always real, they are never lies, nor are they semi-truths mediated by the political apparatus.

What the hostage taker says he will do, he does. From this perspective, the policy of the state (no negotiations with terrorists) makes no sense, since there is nothing else to do but negotiate if one wants to save the hostages. When it comes to militant acts of hostage taking in the contemporary Muslim landscape, the adherence to the given word (which consists of the threat and the execution of it) is one of the most overlooked instances in the analysis of terrorism. This is also why hostage taking in the domain of the political contains a resemblance to theological values. It is an act tied to the word where the promise (of killing) has divine concreteness. One can trust the hostage taker fully. This is not to support the insensitivities of the popular view of the Muslim terrorist who kills in the name of his God, a claim that shows complete ignorance.[7] But, then again, this ignorance hides the accuracy that should be extracted from it: the accuracy of the immediacy that exists between the act and the word, which finds one of its rare manifestations in the act of hostage taking.

Barayev

Movsar Barayev has been a "being on the lookout" since the first day he can remember. A nephew of the famous Chechen militant clan leader Arbi Barayev (an experienced hostage taker who both executed and freed his hostages in the late 1990s), Movsar became the leader of the Special Purpose Islamic Regiment (spelled in capital letters, just as all other military-legalistic detachments of the state), also known as al-Jihad-Fisi-Sabililah.[8] Regiment that is a rule, of special purpose and meaning. What is implied in this name is the physicality of an act; the regiment has a purpose which propels it into action, into necessary destruction. Becoming a regiment is also already an act of forming a pack or a group with specific goals. An important aspect in this formation of violence that is manifested in militant regiments is the problem of the animal and the hermeneutics of the sovereign, one based on cruelty, provoked by humiliation, and enacted with fatalism. The Special Purpose Islamic Regiment is one of the most notorious hostage-taking groups in recent history. Their operations are of course tied as much to rumors as they are to empirical facts. Here is one of these facts: October 23, 2002, it was Movsar and his 40 militants who occupied Dubrovka Theater in Moscow.[9]

Movsar took his militancy to its final extreme, to death without compromise. For this a special type of ruthlessness is necessary, a capacity for cruelty, but one that comes from where? From the love of one's nation? From one's alliance to

Islamic cosmology? The everyday itself is a threshold, such that even the banal aspects of the everyday are contaminated with the eruptive possibility of militant subjectivity.

The hostage taker complicates this episode of the overtaken theater further, since it is with this act that he creates a bubble inside the homogenous territory of the state, a bubble that will eventually explode; an immanence within immanence constituted by a new law that operates on a small territory (of the kidnapped airplane, or an overtaken village in Bosnia, or a theater building in Moscow). For a brief moment he forms his own microstate of terror inside the dominant space of the nation. This is a bubble that is absolutely enclosed, and not only politically. In this way, hostage taking is an intensification and maximization of the feeling of enclosure imposed both onto the dominant party but also onto oneself. The bubble of the hostage space is so insulated that it feels like another form of earth, with everything outside hostile to its existence. The bubble that becomes a new earth, a situation that signals the geographical aspect of hostage taking and terrorism, is suspended in an antagonistic universe. The event in Dubrovka Theater, the act itself, is nothing but a reaction to an initial indifference of the Russian state toward minorities that turns into hostility (the historical suppression by the Soviet and Russian state of the Chechen minority).[10] It is this indifference turned hostility that gives birth to Movsar Barayev and to the many manifestations of Barayev throughout the contemporary Islamicate world.

Camouflage

Irregular soldier, Islamic militant, hostage taker: each has a new relationship with his own skin. Namely, the way one dresses spans civil clothing, military outfit, and something in between. Camouflage is another way to develop a relationship with the territory, to resemble it, and to become imperceptible, all for the benefit of a more effective attack. Camouflage is perhaps the most obvious characteristic of the animal that any soldier appropriates, for every animal besides the domesticated one relies on the properties of mimicry that lead to some form of camouflage. The history and evolution of uniforms attests to this association, pointing not just to the fact of animality but also to a delirious nonutilitarian history when war was still "bracketed" and not absolute.[11] The armies of the Ottoman Empire certainly did not have the same preoccupation with imperceptibility as the Islamic Regiment of the Special Meaning. Hence, the becoming-animal of the human in war has been well documented but not sufficiently theorized.[12] In war studies and in anthropological accounts of traditional societies, we read about the importance of the animal for the experience of becoming a warrior, but there is very little analysis in terms of what this metamorphosis (even if it is just temporary) entails, what becomings it produces (namely, how it turns the human into an animal or how it questions the static identity of the human).

It is impossible to ignore here the immense contribution of Deleuze and Guattari's concept of the war machine to the question of irregular combat, terrorism, and hostage taking. In this light, the question arises: To what extent is the Islamic militant in general, and the hostage taker in particular, configured through the modalities of the war machine: "an irruption of ephemera and the power of multiplicity"?[13] Only to a certain extent. While the militant inhabits the war machine's functionalism of celerity, secrecy, becoming-animal, and combat against sovereignty, he is still often caught in the political desire for the constitution of the state (for instance, the independence of Kosovo, Chechnya, Bosnia, etc.) as a final goal. Even recent revolutionary movements of global Islam cannot be idealistically seen as the victory of the irregular militant against the totalitarian sovereign since in the eyes of each hostage taker there is a dream of a new state. This is perhaps the greatest failure of the movement itself. Nevertheless, my concerns here are to map out the modalities of the war machine present in contemporary Islamic militancy. This also means inhabiting the exchange of cruelties between the state and the militants.

The emphasis here falls on the powers of metamorphosis that form the mutable essence of the warrior (for the figure of the warrior is one instance in which the traditional conception of the human essence is undermined). The affects of the animal are promptly abandoned by the hostage takers; even the name of the band cited earlier reveals the influence of the State: *Regiment*. The full name of the organization—Special Purpose Islamic Regiment—itself emphasizes the centrality of exercised discipline that is ultimately founded upon the (Islamic) law. This is a foretelling that the religions of the book might gradually lead to the formation of empire or the state (which in turn provokes a suspicion toward such discourses in general, since their prophecies tend to fulfill themselves, sometimes through militant procedures of the animal and sometimes through procedures of international law). Consequently, all of the "primitive" aspects of engagement with the divine are sacrificed for the holiness of the territory (and heaven too is a territory). The modalities of the war machine, and the temporary draping in camouflage, are thus used in the service of the eventual quest for stately independence.

Another example of camouflaging, animality, and theo-sovereignty can be found in Richard Mosse's five-minute terror video shot in Gaza in 2009 with two militants who view themselves as *shahids*, martyr-witnesses.[14] In this video, we see men pointing rifles, posing with their finger of the right hand pointing upwards (a gesture seen in the forests of Chechnya too), embracing each other, reading a statement, and simulating a siege. For our purposes, the most striking feature is the look in their eyes. Mosse inadvertently films the lookout. He stages the event but the men are not acting. The camera is recording the truth of their condition just as it is simultaneously provoking it. They wear uniforms similar to those of American soldiers with additional ski masks across their faces. The only difference is the headband around their heads, which balances out the animality of the uniform—the mutability of forms that modern military outfit initiates—with the inscriptions of the divine world across their foreheads. The divine (the headband with a line from the Qur'an) and the animal (a uniform that makes the human body indistinguishable from the environment) thus impress themselves on the body of the militant, and work in perfect harmony. The divine and the animal are forces which are made concrete in the form of the headband and the uniform; these forces are provoked and inscribed by the militant who wears them, but they are also forces which go beyond any individual militant or soldier. They are impersonal forces that one inhabits but that also overtake the individual. The uniform or the headband are already demarcations of a hostage space (i.e. being circumscribed by certain forces of the state or of the resistance to the state). Are the two men in the video therefore embodiments of divine violence or of divine justice? Their presence, posture, incantations, determinations at least give a tentative answer: there is not one without the other. Or in other words, there is no divine justice (that is to say, supreme justice) that is not also a violent implementation of its will.

Furthermore, even the beards worn by the figures in the video exhibit a type of camouflage, adding to a special sense of invincibility that animal characteristics bestow upon the militant. The beard typically separates the "civilized" westerner from the "savage" Islamist. Even within the Christian Church, a (judgmental) distinction is made between the clergy of the Orthodox Church, the Eastern Church, who, just like the Islamic clerics, wear a long beard that separates them visibly from the stylistics typical of beardless clergy of the western church. Traditionally the beard is also a sign of masculinity and, while it may refer to elegance, as in the dyed beards of the Taliban, it is also beastly, secretive (hiding the face from full view), thus complicating the form of the face. The hair itself evokes a whole range of animalistic qualities too. There is an interesting and unlikely parallel from the field here: one of the hostage takers at the school in Beslan in North Ossetia was a militant with a long ginger beard.[15] Many witnesses saw him. They said he went by the name "Fantomas." He was not caught or killed; he just disappeared. In fact there were three self-identified leaders who shared their *noms de guerre*: Magas, Fantomas, Abdullah; an Ingush, a Russian, and a Chechen respectively. In reading different accounts from the event one finds a recurring description of the hostage takers—that is, the children who were taken hostage repeatedly reported looking up at men with long beards. "One of the girls peered through the cracked door and saw impressive beards . . ." Another child reported that, "A man with a huge beard told me . . ." For the children, it is clear, the beard itself is distinctly demarcated as within the domain of fear; to them, the beard is a masking, a hallucination, a fairytale-nightmare. In every respect, the beard marks, demarcates, and inscribes. It makes one different and at the same time proves one's belonging to a group. As one grows into one's beard one grows into an ideology, or better to say, into a landscape, mountains and rivers of the region. It can be upheld as the first aesthetic-political property of the body that unites and separates.

Exteriority

Hostage taking is only one type of violent expression of the human tendency to reterritorialize. In this respect, militants possess several layers of negative interiority:[16] being encompassed by a dominant state, by ethnic identity, clan, etc. Their ontology is not one of entering or being thrown into the world (a vision of the human being according to dominant strands of western metaphysics) but of exiting, that is, departing from at least one layer of negative interiority. The predominant affect of the Muslim minority in the West: being in the hostile house (where one is a legal citizen of the country but never feels at home). This is the essential experience of an immigrant (or children of immigrants) in twenty-first-century western Europe. Hostage takers in the contested regions are only exploding this pervasive fact, a fact that is also present in the tranquil gardens of the West. Occasionally these gardens burn too: Paris in 2005, London in August 2011.[17] Thus, hostage spaces also refer to the complex interactions between Muslim minorities and European/American majorities in the West.[18]

By exiting the world, or in the militants' vernacular, in martyrdom, the hostage taker creates a space of phantomality. A certain phantom territoriality is constructed as the gift of the being on the lookout, as he exits through ecstatic death. But ecstasy should not be overestimated or idealized; young Movsar Barayev, for example, was found dead on the floor of the Dubrovka Theater with a bottle of unopened cognac next to him. The ecstasy of the banal and of the false has, here at least, the last word after the storming of state forces. The state has to undermine the ecstasy by reducing it to physical causation or to a criminal act. But the community that resists, that voices its political potential, has to be properly ecstatic, or outside of itself.

The transfiguration of one's gaze in hostage taking is enough to turn one into an animal. The gaze of the soldier equally utilizes the technologies of perception that help him metamorphose into a being on the lookout. The constant exchange between the hostage taker, the terrorist, and the state relies heavily on the conditions of visibility. When irregular warfare and hostage taking took its modern shape in the 1960s, being in urban territory, behind civilians, in transportation vehicles, and so on, posed a whole new problem for the state on almost every continent, turning it into a planetary phenomenon— with the highest frequency in the so-called Middle East. Adam Broomberg and Oliver Chanarin have produced a staggering catalogue of photographs taken in an invented model, a false city, a constructed landscape, of the general "Middle East," which addresses this newfound consciousness on the part of the military apparatus of the state concerning the space of impact in new war. Two authors documented the landscape as it is crystallized in American and Israeli imaginations which simulated an Arab town (named Chicago) in order to practice urban warfare: "Located in the Tze'elim base in the Negev desert, this was to become the world's largest mock-up oriental city erected since the filming of 'Ben-Hur.'"[19] The description of the project itself reads: "Everything that happened, happened here first, in rehearsal. The invasion of Beirut, the first and second Intifada, the Gaza withdrawal, the Battle of Falluja; almost every one of Israel's major military tactics in the Middle East over the past three decades was performed in advance here in Chicago, an artificial but realistic Arab town built by the Israeli Defence Force for urban combat training."[20] Mountains, the wailing wall in Jerusalem, the Muslim multitude in prayer, the cutout silhouettes of the terrorists, the forest and the town, burned cars, all is here, arrested in its nonreality. In this way, a phantom territoriality is constructed by the state as a tactical gesture meant to give the state the upper hand over the militant, to take hostage of her space before it even emerges. There is a whole history of terrorism and counterterrorism that testifies to the symbiotic relationship between regular forces of the state and irregular forces of the militant combatants, that is to their animalistic relationship.[21]

The event of 9/11, albeit a tired example, is paramount in the discussion of visibility. From 2001 onwards the states around the world have been "on the lookout" more than ever before. Sovereignty again came close to animality, its archaic principle, in a new way. It is the event of terrorism that allows for these sovereign principles to align themselves with animality, or better to say, beastiality. To be in possession of the sovereign principle is to be independent in determining one's own affairs, and by extension those of others. The sovereign is presumably free, the opposite of a slave, or of an animal. Yet, there is the other principle (embodied in stately offices), which is on a higher alert than any animal could ever be, with its omnipresent eye piercing every corner of the controlled territory. The sovereign is the supreme being on the lookout, an animal par excellence, differing from the militant only in the scope of its gaze. The militant turns to look for danger across his shoulder; the sovereign, embodied in the agents of the state, looks through the entire city, nation, or empire (international political space). The lookout is now performed not only by strolling police in the metro stations but also by inciting citizens to operate as extensions of the sovereign's eye—sovereignty thus being conflated with the notion of freedom (the omnipresent saying coming from every corner of the public space, "see something, say something," first concretized in the New York City subway system). Expressions such as "the land of the free," "the territory of the free," etc., are of course only images of promises that provide security.

The lookout is put into further effect through the constant reconfiguration of technological devices. Primary examples are the ports of entry to the United States: cameras scan the retina of the eye, scanners make digital finger prints (of four fingers), and X-ray hubs cross the entire body. These are all awkward extensions of the customs officers and security personnel at airports that are becoming more and more naturalized, as parts of the extended gaze. All of these technologies are extensions of animal perception, which leads to the following conclusion: in addition to a theological or mystical principle of the law, animal perception—being on the lookout—is likewise central to the very notion of the sovereign.

Abyss

It is impossible to think about or describe hostage taking outside of the darkness which descends upon it from the moment it starts to be viewed as a tactic of liberation. This is precisely where the paradox lies: the thought of liberation that wears the cloak of darkness (the necessity of kidnapping), in the aftermath of which very little remains (in the face of potential death, the destruction of a built environment, and the clearing of power). Yet something remains: the images of terror, the words of condemnation, the grief, but also the alternative engagement with hostage taking that I am attempting to elucidate. Giving away one's life and taking that of another gains poetic singularity in its destruction; not because of the mystical character of death (there is nothing mystical about it) but because of all the thoughts and acts that lead to its construction: the space of phantom territoriality, secrecy, brotherhood and sisterhood in belonging to the politically rejected, and also to the divine sphere of a tradition. Would it be fair to say that Muhammad himself was a hostage taker? In fact, which founder of religion, which great thinker, East or West, North or South, has not been a great hostage taker, overtaking cosmologies no less than physical territories that prostrate themselves to these new cosmologies? All present hostage takers thus try to inhabit the charisma of the prophet-leader, usually a historical figure who attains iconic status.

Hostage taking opens up the abyss between the militants and their hostages, as well as the one between the hostage taker and the state which he resists. Or else, it makes the abyss that was already present for a long time visible in full view. Abyss: a muted cry of the wound. Hostage taking: an animal licking its own wound. A crucial question: is hostage taking an interruption of the regular political flow of the so-called security narratives, of the global processes of circulation of goods, money, power relations, etc.? Or is it only a part of that chaotic semi-regulated circulation? Or, still in other words, to what extent is hostage taking an interruption of the world's well-being, of worlding as such? A wound is certainly an interruption on the body and a wounded individual can even turn into the wound itself, proliferating its loss of form, or normality, through tactics of terror.

By nature of being on the lookout, the hostage taker exists in a permanent state of vulnerability. And so does everyone else. But the difference lies in the fact that the hostage taker does not have the luxury of contemplating the condition of permanent comfort and security under the auspices of the state. The space that is opened up with this sense of vulnerability is the space of pure risk. Every detail of a gesture is calculated and measured through the degrees of risk it entails. By this sheer adherence to risk, the hostage taker always retains aspects of criminality, that is, nondomestication, or deviant comfort.

On a related point, Carl Schmitt offers the following: "Historia in Nuce [History in a Nutshell]: Friend and Enemy."[22] This simple yet immense formula exposes the radical transcendence that is present in the construction of the political world. A binary distinction that marks myself and the other is further bifurcated as "the friend" (part of myself) becomes the opposite (of myself), that is "the enemy." But the enemy himself is still a constituent part of the ways in which I perceive myself. Another formula of a "history in a nutshell" that is more apropos for present calculations: Animal and Hostage Taker. This writing is in fact an attempt to show the collapse of these two distinctions, for herein I argue that they only camouflage the illusion of their oppositions. In reality, hostage taking is in the sphere of war like water in water and oil in oil.

Another complication of terms that lies at the core of this investigation could be expressed through the following gnomic distinction: Mitigate and Militate. There is a strange phonetic and formal similarity between the words that have radically different etymologies: the former means to alleviate (from the Latin *mitis*, mild) and the latter means to impose against or to be "a powerful factor in preventing" (from the Latin *milit*, soldier). These two terms, which are also instantiated as acts in the hostage space (one mitigates through negotiations, or militates through imposition), are separated by an abyss, leaving them incommensurable. But the abyss between the one that mitigates and the one that militates is paradoxically intimate. The hostage taker that militates, makes demands, embodies causes, is tied to the one that mitigates, the one that negotiates on the part of the state.[23] Militation can thus easily turn into mitigation, as negotiations are meant to alleviate the explosive situation. Indeed, the militant mitigates in the only way that is left to him: with militation. One thus crosses from one sphere of experience into the other fairly quickly, just as the friend crosses into the enemy with surprising ease.

The hostage taker is not only related to a specific territory and an accompanying animality, but is himself a territory and region. There is a combatant heritage to which the hostage taker belongs too, but from which he also deviates. The exemplary figures of irregular warfare combatants in the last two centuries are those of the partisan, the terrorist, and the pirate. Schmitt noted an essential characteristic of the partisan figure which defines his very being according to spatial coordinates; namely, the partisan possesses a "telluric-terrestrial character."[24] By this Schmitt means that the partisan emerges from the landscape, from the topography of the region, which in turn means from the forest or from the desert. The partisan is intrinsically tied to these atmospheric conditions of the earth found in the particular locales: the forests of East Europe, the deserts of North Africa, the jungles of South America and Southeast Asia, etc. (It is important to mention, however, that there were partisans in the Adriatic Sea during the Second World War, who fought in converted fishing boats against German fleets, which implies that partisan warfare was not exclusively telluric.) Indeed, partisans fought for territories, for the land, but those among them who emerged from maritime cultures (such as those in the Adriatic) had no problem in skillfully using the smoothness of the sea to their benefit. But in general theorization of this principle, the terrestrial aspect of the partisan and the ways in which this determines his engagement with the regular armies still stands.

This spatial concern, moreover, changed the very nature of war: "He forces his enemy into another space, in other words, he displaces the space of regular, conventional theaters of war, to a different darker dimension—a dimension of abyss, in which the proudly worn uniform [of the conventional soldier] becomes deadly target."[25] A strange use of the word "abyss" (which Schmitt actually reads and takes from another source) here demarcates the precision of darkness. The hostage taker takes her entire experience further into the abyss, where the question of the uniform becomes interiorized, as the enemy of the hostage taker becomes a civilian. In fact, civility itself is targeted—the civility that has turned the hostage taker into a beast from what preceded the very beginning of their engagement. The hostages thus wear the uniform of their state on the inside and are treated as the representatives of that state by the mere fact of participating and being under protection of its laws. Hostage taking is a form of battle with the law and its embodiments, with the military force of the state as well as its embodiment in citizens.

But the hostage taker goes further than the partisan toward the abyss. Hence the idea: phantom territoriality. Being on the lookout intensifies the place it occupies which can be any place. He has no determining spatial characteristic except for phantomality. In other words, a regular, everyday location is suddenly turned into a hallucination, or, better yet, it is revealed as a hallucination, a deadly chimera. Hostage taking is a fascinating and terrible predicament, for it is a liberation and imprisonment at the same time; just like any irregular combatant, the hostage taker seeks some type of new regularity, which is the demand of new legal recognition (e.g. recognition of Chechnya, or Kosovo, or Bosnia as independent states), while also stranding the world in a profoundly exilic moment, one of extended displacement and disorientation.

There is a crossing of the limit, then, in hostage taking. The limit of what? A number of things, as illustrated in the hostage taker's trespass against conventional concepts of humanism and humanity. Most importantly, though, the hostage taker pushes to its limit the very notion of the law, or what is legally allowed, or the acceptable ways in which people can be treated morally and legally. More clearly, the hostage taker pushes the idea of the law to its unacceptable proportions. Consequently, one should not view hostage taking as the transgression of the law but as a maximization of the law under which the hostage taker is bound to live—a maximization that necessarily leads to rupture and death.

The aforementioned young man Barayev, a Muslim granule in the body of post-Soviet politics, is now more like a starfish itself, pulling a whole body-politic from the intertidal surface of everyday hostage taking into the abyssal depths of identitarian territories ("my free Chechnya," as Chechen militants cry out). In many ways I prefer to write about the starfish than about the hostage taker but as I proceed I see that they are not so different: much like the militant cell, there is an asexual reproduction among some of the starfish that comprise its politics of survival. Fishermen sometimes cut them into pieces and throw them back into the sea thinking they are dead. But the starfish regenerates from the fragment, producing a whole new individual organism. They reproduce by fragmentation. The sovereign powers of the western world showed an immense ignorance of this process with the recent capture and execution of Osama bin-Laden, followed by self-congratulatory pats on the back. But surely Barack Obama did not believe in his own speech when he elevated the killing of bin-Laden to the event of the year.[26] What does it mean to a starfish to have one of her rays chopped off? And in the end, is not every animal "militant"?

So, the desperate political act is tied to the primary act of the animal. What does this tell us? It tells us that the confines of the political discourses revolving around the war on terror are stale and unhelpful. The resolution of the conflict lies not in the resolution of the crisis but in the new way of treatment of animality— including and especially one's own animality—as a threefold dependency on territory: physical (the gravitational pull of the earth), ontological (either being thrown into this world or else being strangled and looking for an exit, as the sovereign of the outside), and esoteric (belonging to the divine). Only then will one also be able to resist constantly being on the lookout—the insecurity of an outcast, as well as the false comforts of political subjectivities.

Enemy

It is easy to see how the figure of the partisan transmutes into that of the terrorist. Yet there are essential differences between them as well. Here I address only the telluric determinism of the partisan which the terrorist and the hostage taker do not have. There is a more specific reason for this: the transmutation (as another domain of the animal) occurs at the level of the relationship to the territory. The hostage taker is himself a territory, as I mentioned, in a sense of being both a representation of it and an immediate implementation. For instance, a Chechen hostage taker is like an island, a little patch of Chechen land introduced unnaturally into Russian territory. In the same way, the hostage taker is a heterotopic space incarnate whose body is perceived as a battlefield, where the conflict itself occurs, and as such has to be annihilated.[27] In this respect, the most important announcement in Schmitt's text on the partisan occurs in the last six pages of his book, where he analyzes and laments the transfiguration of the real enemy into an absolute enemy (or, following the original German wording, the enemy turns into the foe).

The consequences of this turn are profound. The enemy is no longer a legitimate opponent, a familial form that challenges me and confirms me, but a foe that must be destroyed.[28] Schmitt locates this transfiguration at the beginning of the twentieth century, more specifically with Lenin and other professional revolutionaries. With the loss of the "bracketed war" the enemy could be denigrated, disposed of, and destroyed. We can leave aside to what extent the bracketing of war was more or less humane in western and eastern histories in order to assert that this change in the perception of the enemy solidified present global politics to the extent that we now barely remember any other way of waging war. Namely, the terrorist is presently a figuration of an absolute enemy, a representation of evil, yielding a new binary that allows the so-called good side to do as it pleases: bomb, interrogate, use or devastate the natural resources of the enemy, etc. The smooth machinery (i.e. the spectral apparatus of globalization) necessitates this kind of crude binary distinction of moral fronts. The enemy, the hostage taker, or the terrorist, is not only an animal, but the animal maximized— that is, a monster. Faisal Devji says as much about this exchange of natures: "So it is only natural if today Islam seems to confront the liberal State with its own founding myth, having become the Frankenstein's monster of its history."[29] However, the monster now takes a life of its own, independent of the origins of its emergence. The terrorist is not only a reactionary subject but a teratological agent with his own creative and destructive potentials.

At the same time, the hostage taker is by his very nature an absolute enemy since he has no autochthonous relationship to the territory but rather an allochthonous one. What ties him to violence is the injustice performed against his humanity (to use Devji's terminology), as well as against the theological modalities of Islamic expression. It is the earth of Islamic law and sociality that interests him, not the geological sediments of the particular terrain, even though this fixation with the abstract concept of space later necessitates a precise knowledge of the area's geography (i.e. mastery of underground channels, cave networks, desert dunes, etc.). More interestingly, the hostage taker is in a way a counterterrorist since he is already born as a hostage of the sovereign state that rules over him. The rule of the capitalist West is one such hostage-taking sovereignty that necessarily generates absolute enemies.

Daniel Heller-Roazen has contributed to this discussion of the involutions of the irregular fighter by writing about the pirate as the "enemy of all."[30] And even though he is aware of Schmitt's distinction between the partisan and the pirate, Heller-Roazen seems to collapse it by emphasizing the fact that new terrorists, such as the members of the Palestinian Liberation Front PLF) who kidnapped an Italian ship in 1985, traverse the liquid surfaces of the earth as well, turning terrorists into non-telluric partisans. But this suggestion is inaccurate since the PLF fighters were absolutely tellurian, fighting awkwardly at sea for their own piece of earth, Palestine (i.e. for the release of political prisoners in Israel).[31] They were deterritorialized geographically but not conceptually. They fought at sea for the land and were apprehended after a few days in Sicily. The militants were clearly not pirates, as Heller-Roazen states as well; but neither were they "partisans at sea" since the sea did not form the modalities of their combat, nor the smoothness of their bodies, nor their perception of the horizon. In other words, they had no relationship to the sea which would determine who they were as combatants, or even more, as individual beings. They nevertheless remain partisans, not only politically but also in their geo-sensual formations: having the sense of the urban landscape (alleyways and rooftops), as well as the sense of the mountains. It is in the modes of combat that these sensualities, these bodily tremors (we could also called them terrors), come to the fore. To develop this further, we need to extract pure movement from each local or regional geo-sensuality and understand its particularities. Hanah Arendt intuited this power tied to pure movement when she said: "Terror is the realization of the law of movement."[32]

While the pirate also uses hostage taking as a modus operandi, there is a distinction that makes him different from the Islamic militant. The militant desires liberation, a new law, justice, and respect of Islamic values, which are the values of the book. The pirate cares merely for day-to-day survival and is permeated by an excess of non-belonging where the image of the skull provides values of dead sovereignty, values of the dead god. For the present purposes, we could say that the causes and effects of these two forms of hostage taking are radically different: one is theopolitical (that of the militant), the other is ethically and theologically indifferent (indifference being a value in itself in the cosmology of the pirate).[33]

However, the relationship of law and territory that piracy ruptures is worth emphasizing: "In either case, the place proper to piracy thereby undergoes a fundamental change. The region in which 'enemies of all' commit their violent acts is consequently unbound from any single segment of the globe."[34] The pirate, or the transfigured absolute enemy (hostage taker, militant, terrorist . . .) thus becomes a territory himself. The contemporary iterations of international law always contain a double bind according to which it functions: on the one hand, the law crisscrosses the entire globe, making the earth itself into a subject, including the control of all the planet's materialities, be it natural resources such as oil (as in Chechnya), or mythical materialities of regions themselves (as in Kosovo, a place without lucrative natural resources except for the legends and contested histories); on the other hand, it creates exceptions that allow some states to be excluded from it (the supreme sovereign then is not one that gives the law but one that legally evades it).

All of this leaves us with an imposing question: Is there power in hostage taking and, if so (since the question already announces the answer), of what kind is it? Without idealizing it, I proceed into this terrain of the brief yet fundamental raising of powers that occurs in the act of overtaking a space (and turning subjugation on its head), albeit through self-destruction.

2

Biopotentiality and the Enemy

Immunity

The biopotential of *jihad*. What is the biopotential of a "struggle" but also that of war? *Jihad* is nothing but the manifestation of a capacity for the future. (The genealogy and evolution of this term in its political, theological, and existential meanings still needs to be divested, since at present, in the West, it operates as a word which solely demarcates the enemy.)[1] I am not concerned here with the question of whether *jihad* is essential for Islam or not, but rather with its propensities and temporalities, with a natural science of *jihad* (its chemistry and physics) and by extension those of war itself. Let me be clear: the implementation of this capacity is done through immense cruelties. But they too have their architectures, sciences, and sorcery, for no one is immune to one's enemy.

Again, the history of the world could be defined by these two modalities and their interaction: Health and War. The hostage taker is a loud pronouncer of this equation. He struggles for life that is overtaken by the forces which stifle it. Hostage spaces, then, are locations of exhaustion of political discourse whose final breath is an explosive one. A space of final measure, where there is nothing else to do, supposedly, but to intensify all the forces against oneself. Desperation turned into determination.

There is nothing more disturbing than the hostage space. Its disturbance lies not only in the disbelief of what is going on, but also because the space of hostage taking suddenly acquires intense power (let us call it an abrupt power of destruction) that transforms the very air, the faces, and the thoughts of those inside of it. Namely, it becomes a space of pure enmity and a hidden battlefield that discloses itself instantaneously. This is the nature of the hostage space which changes the nature of space itself, that is the atmospheric conditions found on the inside.

The study of *jihad*'s biopotential should thus be one that corresponds to an aggressive therapeutics, a type of therapeutics produced by the antagonism between health and war. Or, more specifically, the diagnostics of *jihad*, within these aggressive therapeutics, is generated by three distinct procedures: (a) that of contagion, or being affected by contact with specific words and images, or by a charismatic individual who operates as a word and an image; (b) that of anti-poisonings, incited by direct attacks on individuals as mediators of the western state; and (c) by the regulation of one's death, or theopolitical sacrifice.

The hostage space is thus a site comprised of numerous intensities (rather than symptoms): that of trauma (of course, predictably), political collapse, theological implementations, celebration of violence, and most of all of exhaustion; and it is here, in this multi-dimensional space, where biopotentiality, one's potential for life, one's capacity for becoming something other than what one is, self-destructs. A hostage space is but a miniature demonstration of the earth's geopolitical gravity whose invisible pull prevents one's capacities to be put into effect in a creative manner. In other words, hostage taking is the negative creativity of biopotential—the supplication of aggressiveness as a value. And there are good reasons for this predicament. How else are the Kosovar, or the Chechen, or the Bosnian to reply to the physics of humiliation that have been amassing its negative electrons for decades? In light of this, Peter Sloterdijk has provided an important reading of rage through its energetic dimension. Rage is, in this context, primarily an "intensive form of energy that is ready to explode or be transferred."[2] These energetic components of rage make the person who is possessed by them into a "donor" of rage, a giver of furor. It is not difficult to see the emergence of the militant figure here. Rage, in these confines, is both a resistance to the immunization of the state (conformity to its oppressive laws) and an injection of sorts, one that energizes and pushes one to action.

To this end, Jason Bahbak Mohaghegh unveils the secret: "It is a long-held Eastern saying that if a scorpion is surrounded by a ring of fire, realizing it has no escape route, it will eventually sting itself, and it is no overstatement that rage follows this paradigm of interloping and eloping actors."[3] It is clear that rage already overrides one's subjectivity before it overcomes the body. It is primarily a physical force since it gives kinetic powers to the body (it moves, it produces blows). One is consumed by it, which means that rage extends into a space beyond one's body. Rather than take the image of the scorpion as a metaphor of the enclosed hostage taker, one should focus on the aspect of animality found in the image of the scorpion. The animal, even an arthropod, uses rage for its being-in-the-world. In fact, being-on-the-lookout is a zero degree of rage, we could say, since animals are not immunized against their own affects by the societies in which they live. They live in accordance with their affects (however limited these might be in numbers). More interestingly, to follow the saying further, the scorpion destroys its capacity for life on its own. It takes the right to self-destruct. I say takes the right, because the political subject usually has no right to destroy herself; suicide is in religious spheres deemed a deadly sin, and secular societies have often attempted prevention by criminalizing it as officially illegal. To an extent that is apparent in the saying, the scorpion becomes a political subject by subversion, by "stealing" a right to give itself to death from the forces that surround it. A question then arises: Does the scorpion contain something of that primordial divine rage without knowing it? And is it by coincidence that all sorts of paramilitary units bear names such as that of the scorpion, identifying with the animal in order to evoke no less than to produce speed, fatalism, lack of hesitation, etc.?[4]

Before it finds itself in the sphere of politics and ethics, the question of animal (self)destruction is one of eschatological biology—one of mortal immanence where life is organized according to the consumption of the other, where one animal eats the other, and so on toward infinity. This is the first instance of cruelty, if by cruelty we mean "tearing," coming from the Latin *crudelis*, the tearing of the flesh primarily, but also just the act of ripping apart. Cruelty is therefore a physical act first and foremost. This physical aspect, the initial corporeal movement, then occupies ethical, political, or creative domains. It must be so that those who execute cruel acts see them as simple physical gestures before these turn into ethics. To tear something is indeed the very first image of destruction. But destruction is not in and of itself ethical. Louise Bourgeois demonstrated this more precisely than anyone else. When asked if sculpting is a violent procedure, she took a sheet of paper and twisted it; "this is sculpture," she said. "And of course it is violent."[5] The act of twisting already implies violence; by extension, tearing implies that intensified dimension of violence which we call cruelty. In other words, the intensification, or maximization, of an act of violence leads to cruelty, to destruction of the thing (or being) in one's hands. Violence can thus be subtle but cruelty cannot.

The hostage taker, by subsuming the bodies of others, "twists" not only the political dimension of everyday space but also the form of the state. She is a sculptor in an inverse sense, destroying in order to create, or to regain her independence, or else the independence of her people. This creation, however, is too focused on the particular task for it to be pure expression in itself. It ends as a pure expression of terror.

To what extent is rage a matter of ethics then? Normally, the soldier enraged is better than the one that is indifferent (e.g. one without cause or without hatred). But then again, indifference has been used for more atrocities, more executions, more rational and institutionalized procedures of extermination than any impassioned battle has ever done. Indifference is a matter of training; one is trained and cultivated (by nationalism, love of the same, and so on) to be indifferent toward the other. So it is with indifference that Bosnian Muslims were killed in Srebrenica in July 1995. The indifference of the procedure of killing is visible in the vast amount of planning that went into this massacre as well as in the methodical executions which occurred in the span of a few days.[6] Almost all the terror videos from Bosnia, Kosovo, and Chechnya proliferating on the internet attest to the fact that such cruelty aligns itself with indifference. In this sense, indifference is a passion of the zero degree.

Is this precisely not the difference between the revolutionary type of war and that of the imperialist? "Revolutionary" and "rage" seem to be synonymous, for there is no revolution without the implementation of rage. Indeed, revolution occurs when masses, or the multitude of people, turn toward rage. Nevertheless, for rage to turn revolutionary it has to be part of a certain heritage. Despite states' and empires' attempts to immunize against rage and, ultimately, revolution, as ancient sacred texts attest to, even foundational human institutions such as the family are not free from contagion. For instance, according to the Qur'an and other sacred scriptures, Cain, the son of Adam, was born an "evil one." His very inception ruptures the health of the family; he is the mythical originator of this aberrant heritage of the countercurrent in human societies. He ruptures the belonging to his own bloodline and thus creates the platform for the very idea of the inevitable enemy; from Cain onwards, we see that the enemy is not only my friend, he is my brother. Through this relationship of enmity, he constructs his becoming, suffering, and wandering. He is therefore a sign, a warning, and remembrance. Cain becomes a mark of ontological experience—being a killer— which has an effect of permanent exile, that is constantly being outside and moving without an aim. This then is the first instance of deterritorialization, albeit a forced one. Later Islamic sources, however, resolved this meandering by bringing Cain to Yemen, therefore turning the onto-geography of drifting into a localized geopolitics.[7]

Revolutionary rage is the manifestation of explosive thinking turned into action. Sloterdijk, however, makes a distinction between personal acts of revenge and carefully cultivated rage: "Vengeful acts of expression mean nothing more than a narcissistic expenditure of energy. The professional revolutionary, who is working as an employee of a bank of rage, does not express individual tensions, he follows a plan."[8] It is the planning and harnessing of rage that makes one into a successful revolutionary (Fidel Castro said, in the same vein, that the Cuban revolution succeeded only because all of the conditions were ripe for it).[9] But revolution is not always only a strategic confinement of rage; it is an expression of immediacy, irrationality, and one's own capacity for pleasure in destruction. Cain is narcissistic; he does not accept the ways in which relationships in the institution of the family are set up. So he destroys them. The whole heritage of revolutionary action relies precisely upon this unacceptability of the social relations in which one finds oneself (from peasant uprisings to antislavery movements to communism to global Islam), without necessarily having a plan for global reformation. It is in this light that we can position the hostage taker as both revolutionary and narcissistic.

Hostage taking should, therefore, be a study in the explosiveness of the body, of the temperament on the edge; for the hostage taker suspends the entire form of the state (represented by the hostages) and molds it accordingly. The whole world becomes mute as he makes his point. But this muteness only lasts for a moment. He forms the hostage space as an alternative institution, one that is outside of modern sensibilities yet equally submergent; in other words, terrorist sensibilities are carefully constructed as physiological and theological forms. They represent a new type of formalism that sweeps away both the aesthetics and politics of sense, that is, all of the aesthetical and political forms that preceded it.

Moreover, there is no dialogue in the hostage space, only negotiations in the most narrow sense of the word: as an imposition of new regulations (regiments). Roberto Esposito writes: ". . . no politics exists other than that *of* the bodies, conducted *on* the bodies, *through* bodies."[10] The hostage taker therefore constructs a politics of naked bodies, exhausted bodies, tortured bodies, and, in some instances, headless bodies. There is a clear logic of immunity here that runs opposite to the immunization project of the state institutions. Esposito has gone farther than anyone else, via Nietzsche and Foucault, in explicating this immunological project in modern western thought: in order to provide security and peace among the individuals, the state creates institutions that shape, restrain, and secure its citizens. The state thus injects a type of rationality which precludes every thought of war and conflict as being affirmative. But it goes so far in this immunization that it destroys any creative engagement that emerges out of conflict (first of all, in the struggle that occurs within oneself).

We can already see how different *jihad* is in its immunological paradigm, in its valorization of resistance, including its positive, tolerant, and participatory expressions. For example, the "intellectual *jihad*" proposed by Tariq Ramadan who naively sees it as a revolutionary reform that accepts and immerses itself in the multiplicity of the world:

> We must make a similar effort to educate ourselves in order to bring together the search for meaning and for God and respect for the principles of justice, freedom and human fraternity. Against the temptation to close ourselves off, to see reality in black and white, we need an "intellectual *jihad*." We need to resist (*jihad* means, literally, effort and resistance), to strive for the universality of a message that transcends the particular and allows us to understand the common universal values that make up our horizon.[11]

I suggest that this argument is composed naively because it posits notions such as "justice," "freedom," "human fraternity" (and what about sisterhood?), on a universalist plane, as if they are, or could be, universal values. This type of humanism as a search for meaning still does not know how to deal with multiplicities and singularities which emerge in radically different cultures or positions. It is not the "common universal values" that we need in order to navigate through our horizon. Rather, we need to step into the particular and constantly shift our horizon so that in the end we have a multiplicity of perceptions, a multiplicity of horizons, none of them the same, all of them singular. The problem is not to enforce (or in milder terms, persuade) universal values on everyone; the difficulty lies in entering into an exchange with the other, with that which is different, and forming a becoming which will change both myself and the other. In short, one needs to define what kind of justice, what kind of freedom, and what kind of values we are to accept in this "intellectual *jihad*" in order to see the type of relations that can be developed. In the old version of the state, the sovereign (who is always tied to the priest) is like a doctor who administers the right prescriptions for social ailments (which are physical implementations of punishments such as imprisonment, torture, and execution). Through these prescriptions, he imposes domination over others. Resistance is only a counterpoint to these recipes. It is not inaccurate to speak here of a poisoning that occurs through ideas and concepts: one is molded (in Foucault's terms) or encoded (in Deleuze's terms) by the words and actions one performs (by what one sees, reads, interiorizes), by the comforts to which one chooses to submit oneself.[12] But one is only able to submit oneself through the negation of one's temperamental dispositions. Hence, we read our favorite authors for pleasure or as an interpretive exercise, rather than as a writing of the accomplice; as a member of the same phantom (delusional or schizophrenic) society. The hostage taker reads her favorite texts precisely in this second experiential manner; her hermeneutics are those of fanaticism, or, put more positively, of non-compromise.

Another axiom of the physics of *jihad*: hostage spaces are not spaces of self-preservation but of the expansion of force on the part of the militant; for while there is always a reason behind the hostage taking, be it territorial (e.g. the liberation of the Bosnian territories), religious (e.g. the imposition of Islamic laws), or humanitarian (e.g. stopping the disgrace of the Palestinians), there is also the underlying sense of the physics of radical force relations. There is a secret life of the radical force which trembles like a tightrope walker on a string that separates life and death. In this way, the force of the radical arrives through four different definitions: as the fundamental change of one's nature; as a root that precedes the causes of actions; as a member of the political party or brotherhood, and; as an uncharged molecule that is still highly reactive and short-lived. (In the physics of militancy, if one is willing to stretch the definitions beyond their realistic bounds, "molecule" means the smallest fundamental unit that brings together particles of radical politics. Just as we use the word cell for secret militant groups, the small units in a network, so I take the analysis of the nucleus of this radical political activity to be molecular.) All of these things together produce the movement of the force inside the hostage space.

The ancient art of immunization primarily involves the production of forms of power and the setting up of hierarchies among them (the form of the majority being a higher form than that of a minority). The gift of the state is one of form; the citizen constantly feels in debt, with presumed responsibility toward the security that the state provides for her. The state implements forms and distributes them accordingly (the form of family, of dress code, of proper faces, of the official language, etc.). The form of the state is a crystallized cycle of particular habits (Christian, secular, of ethnic particularities, etc.), the point being that the state does not tolerate diffused forms of difference. When the Russian state, for example, does not recognize the Chechen citizen as an independent form constructed through Islamic beliefs, her own aesthetic of being, and her personal tendencies, it turns her into a lower denominator, a deformed being, only partially delineated. The same principles were present in Kosovo under Serbia and for Bosnian Muslims when it came to all former Yugoslav countries. In the 1990s, this hostility intensified and Bosnian Muslims were in fact seen by their neighbors as nothing but a "Turkish root," a historically adversarial form, and one that should accordingly be destroyed (uprooted from the soil, and from the national territory itself). This by extension is the situation of the Muslim minority in western Europe and the United States today. The whole problem of multiculturalism is posed precisely on the notion of tolerance of those that use different forms of praying, dressing, eating, dying, etc. However, this is an extremely vulnerable process since it is still bound to the respect of forms rather than to the valorization of the amorphous, the formless, the unformed, etc. It is part of stately thinking (thinking alongside the state, or in the spirit of the state) that difference leads to diffusion and formlessness. A little theoretical cipher written as a dictionary entry for *Documents* by Georges Bataille (dis)entangles the problem of the form in the following way:

> A dictionary begins when it no longer gives the meaning of words, but their tasks. Thus formlesss is not only an adjective having a given meaning, but a term that serves to bring things down in the world, generally requiring that each thing have its form. What it designates has no rights in any sense and gets itself squashed everywhere, like a spider or an earthworm. In fact, for academic men to be happy, the universe would have to take shape. All of philosophy has no other goal—it is a matter of giving a frock coat to what is, a mathematical frock coat. On the other hand, affirming that the universe resembles nothing and is only *formless*, amounts to saying that the universe is something like a spider or a spit.[13]

The mischievous definition of formlessness above nevertheless proves useful in its intuition. Simply put, the academic impulse is one that necessitates the creation of shapes; it is the same impulse that belongs to the state as it encompasses all official discourses. It therefore follows that all acts of resistance to the state introduce the thought of formlessness. To be formless is not to belong to the state (i.e. the thinking produced by the state). In short, political and epistemic immunization is providing immunity against formlessness. These notions, of course, apply to the world of the political in the contemporary Islamic landscapes as much as they do to poetry, music, and architecture that is yet to come, that is yet to be built.

The militant, the hostage taker, reacts to immunization by the state with her own love for the root, for preserving her belonging. As can be seen above, the construction of the hostage space constantly wavers between the preservation of one's root (ancestral lines) and the cosmological belonging to the earth, or even to the universe itself inasmuch as it is seen as the formation of God's will.

Fear

Esposito continues: "Certainly, other authors—from Hobbes to Tocqueville—recognized the onset of immunization first in the fear of violent death and then in the demand for protection with respect to the danger of individual passions that are highly combustible."[14] We already see how the hostage taker stands in opposition to this modernist frequency. The whole western apparatus of thinking and governing is set up in a way to prevent fear from creeping into the citizens' homes. This of course makes sense: fear is one of the least attractive affects since it is tied to the dissolution of forms. It changes qualities of space, intensifies the whole environment, and turns one into a being-on-the-lookout (one is either hunter or hunted, pursuing or running away). Then there is the inevitable fear of violent death, or the horror of thinking (or is it a confrontation with the impossibility to think?) of oneself without form. This is not to psychologize the political but rather to underscore the importance of affective powers in contemporary conflicts. In light of this, Ramadan speaks about a "global ideology of fear" that is omnipresent in the world separated into West and South.[15] It is this fear that distorts the reality and the relationships with others, like binoculars that are out of focus, preventing one from seeing the entire open horizon. Fear separates spaces and individuals into those that protect (and serve) and those that threaten.

But this position needs to be justly complicated. Fear is not a purely irrational emotional response. Indeed, the contrary of fear is not reason. Nevertheless, reason cannot resolve the problem of the separation between self and other. Reason, in fact, attempts to order and organize the emotions, structuring and tunneling degrees of their appropriateness. Fear is the heightening of the environment, which means the acceleration of the affective qualities of space. (One trembles by stepping into a room where the interrogator waits. The source of fear, an interrogator, is experienced as the source of increased excitement.) Next to this spatial quality, fear is a rush of blood in one's body, and thus a type of bodily reasoning. We forget the extent to which fear played an unparalleled role in the development of western civilization. In fact, all monotheistic cultures were built on an essential and primordial fear, that is the fear of God (which is also love). "To frighten" has the same root as "to revere." Thus, it is not the understanding of the other that turns him into a "friend," as Ramadan contends,[16] but rather the sharing of one's fear with the other that prevents him from becoming an enemy. Societies form because they do not want to live in fear anymore, and in order for them to rise to certain levels of power they need to be united either by vision or by fear (and sometimes by both at the same time).

Fear is the opening of one's vulnerability. In order to understand the other, one can proceed either with arguments or with tolerance, as both lead to a degree of understanding. And yet another way of understanding the other is to share one's vulnerability, that is, one's fear. Or else, to share vulnerability is to enter into the fear of the other. Once I have experienced (even conceptually) what it means, for example, to be on the receiving end of military intervention by the West, I can understand the fear of the other. Since fear is an affective and atmospheric condition, one steps into it, into its bounds, and loses oneself (as the borders of one's subjectivity loosen). Or put in a different image, I can try to understand what it is like for an illegal immigrant to travel in the entrails of a ship from Albania to Italy, but it is only through a sense of fear (and resistance to it) that I actually share the affectual powers of that ship and the position that he occupies. The overwhelming space of fear is a new dwelling place for the one that travels illegally.

It is also true that fear is used for all sorts of security procedures that immunize western nations (and Israel) from the threat posed by Islamic militancy. Since the threat is constantly emphasized, the sense of fear becomes intensified. Fear is then paradoxically combatted by the implementation of more fear (leading to the preemptive war). In the post-9/11 world this tactic is famously exemplified by the saying "If you see something, say something." The threat is everywhere, or it could be everywhere, and the alterness desired from the western citizen is essentially tied to fear. Even the courage that is celebrated in nationalistic narratives is only a degree of fear.

In this sense, fear operates as a form of addiction. Soldiers often speak about the rush and thrill they attain while in the field, even during the most traumatic instances. This small degree of fear is even evinced in military video games (simulations). But, most importantly, fear is tied to the sense of exploration, childhood, and storytelling (which includes all kinds of monstrosities). The hostage taker takes fear at face value; he steps right into it. Fear is his blanket of comfort. He is not merely fearless, since fear overwhelms him too (as it overwhelms a soldier in a battle, no matter how trained he might be), but rather, he is intrepidly fearful.

Along the line of fear, Arjun Appadurai has characterized global geography in terms of passions or affects, primarily that of anger. One of his arguments is that terrorists want "to install violence as the central regulative principle of everyday life."[17] Violence is the essence of militant ontology; it is its very reason for being. But the terrorist does not actually operate for the pure pleasure of destruction, nor for the reign of violence. On the contrary, she seeks a world based on law, just a different type of law. It is a matter of degrees of violence and not its absence in democracy or the West in contradistinction to its presence in terrorism. In other words, terrorism is formed by the enactment of a particular type of violence, with its own degrees of force, just as western democracy has its own embodiments of violence in what it calls practices of security.

This is why it is important to investigate, what could be called—the physics of terror. The normalization of so-called peace is just an immunization principle that subordinates all potentials for alternative life—all the strife one might have within oneself that leads to the experience of life outside of the security zones. Peace is actually not "the natural marker of the social order,"[18] as has been repeatedly demonstrated in many traditional societies throughout the world prior to being subsumed into an empire or into a state. Warfare was in fact a celebratory activity in many societies (but only in its bracketed version, never in terms of the complete annihilation of the enemy). This aspect of the celebration of warfare is part of the meaning found in the habits of the war machine, a force that emerges outside of the state, within nomadic and seminomadic tribes that resisted the formation of the state.[19] In other words, there is conflict which is not of the same order as political and religious violence. This is the same conflict that Schmitt had in mind when he defined the necessity of the enemy as a category without which there cannot be the category of the friend either. This is a form of enslavement which is both conceptual and existential. But what is enacted by liberal democracies today is even worse in a sense that the western political citizen defines himself through abstraction of the enemy (in contemporary language, this is the Muslim terrorist, who can be anyone with an Islamic cultural or religious background), or else through abstract tolerance of the other (as long as it does not imply change). In each case, self-definition is tied to the removal of the other, of her presumed insubstantiality, where her embodiment is perceived only as a carrier of fear. In this light, Paul Virilio asks a disruptive question: "Who invented peace?"[20] A troubling and inappropriate question that nevertheless elicits a smile on one's face.

The contemporary hostage taker being explored here, or the terrorist that I am pursuing, taps into this force of the war machine, and even enters into a certain type of nomadism (*mujahideen*s that travel through a dozen countries in order to fight or elude international law), but his desires belong to the dream of unification (not dispersion). Is the dream, if we could call a certain vision a dream, of the militant not supposedly the same as that of the prophet himself? If I could condense the dream, in all its scholarly inaccuracy, it would be: to unite all tribes, to restore the law. The terrorist, therefore, provides another version of globalization, a prophetic version of it, one not based on the market economy but one stemming from a specific theological economy that necessitates sacrifices of the body, or at least its humiliation, folding in prayer, and sometimes, in some forms of worship, the lashings of chains on one's back. What else can one offer to the divine but the highest offering, one's own body or that of the other? While prayer is not the same as hostage taking, similar effects are desired from both offerings. In fact, the terrorist act usually concludes with an invocation of prayer and could thus even be seen as an extreme form of it.

Violence

In the sphere of biopolitics, curing the illness of violence only produces larger manifestations of it. This is the paradox in which the western logic of immunization finds itself entrenched. The entire medico-political approach has been flawed from the very beginning, producing binary distinctions (us vs them, good vs evil) and antibodies that will happily destroy themselves. What is necessary is not only an alternative theory of terrorism but also a new theory of violence that is not merely a critique of it. The excess of violence that we see today in the world, including the violence within hostage spaces, only reaffirms distinctions between what is "horrible" and what is "normal." The onslaught of violent images in the media does not encourage us to think about violence—to think violence itself—but rather it simultaneously heightens our fears of the other while desensitizing us to the pain endured by victims of violence. This only leads to a desire for revenge and finally to extermination. Nietzsche's diagnosis explains how this procedure works on a molecular level of thought as well: "Whenever man has thought, even there, he has also inoculated the bacillus of revenge in things."[21]

The modern western subject thus imagines herself immune of radicality and fanaticism, even though it is within modernity itself that radicality can grow, like an underground root, as a barely visible flower of evil. A radical individual is part of the landscape of fear, one that we want to avoid treading on. But radicality still emerges even in the most benign of places; and once it emerges and is perceived, it is quickly proclaimed an aberration unnatural to modern democratic principles. This is apparent in the case of Anders Breivik, the Norwegian man who in July 2011 killed 71 and injured 151 others in Oslo and on the island of Utoeya where a youth camp of Norway's Labor Party was hosting a meeting. Breivik stated that what he had done was horrible but necessary in order to protect Europe from a

"Muslim invasion." He was recently pronounced insane, diagnosed as suffering from paranoid schizophrenia (what else?), and, instead of going to trial for the crimes he committed, he will be sentenced to compulsory hospitalization—a legitimate form of medical immunization.[22] In the media parade that followed the aftermath of his killing spree generated by extreme xenophobia toward Muslims (he also called for the support of Serbia in their fight against Kosovo Muslims), Norwegian state officials and citizens alike distanced themselves from Breivik as one would from a monster, someone who has lost all appreciation of good form (of what it means to be a human). But, most importantly, everyone was in disbelief that an event such as this could occur in one of the most "tolerant" countries in the world (perhaps the most tolerant indeed). In this context, one of absolute separation of the monstrous act from the climate of political tolerance, it necessarily follows that Breivik must be insane—a "logical" conclusion formally affirmed by a panel of psychiatrists. In fact, their diagnosis reads: "He lived in his own delusional universe where all his thoughts and acts are guided by his delusions."[23] Delusions equal insanity. In Norway, as in most other nation-states, paranoia and schizophrenia go hand-in-hand and have nothing to do with society; they are purely individual phenomena. This proves that we still live in a world where the health of the nation is determined by a panel of expert psychiatrists who cannot fathom the causal relationship between mental disorders and political economy (let alone see reality itself as an illusion).[24] But paranoia and schizophrenia are not conditions that can be contained behind the hospital walls since they are predicaments of planetary economics, not to mention religious and secular dispositions. The physiological reactions of paranoia and schizophrenia (which are in themselves two different manifestations of disorder and should not be combined with such diagnostic ease) are always tied to the social conditions in which they emerge.[25] Hostage takers and terrorists are, in this sense, only signals, a collection of "trigonometric signs" (to use Benjamin's image of the destructive character),[26] which point to the forces of the extreme that are either bubbling under the surface or else already overflowing.

It is the right time to ask: Who is immune to radicality? According to popular discourse, almost everyone besides the insane.

Humiliation

In botany, the "radical" denotes that which arises from or goes toward the root of a plant, springing directly from the root or the stem. Similar permutations occur today in what is called radical politics. The need of the radical (individual, group) is as follows: to protect the root that is threatened by the outside force, to reject the historical humiliation which goes beyond history—namely, humiliation that is always present. The Kosovar feels the ancestral hurt from the Serb as if it were performed this very minute. The root (e.g. one's ethnic origin) has to be protected. There are thus two forms of hostage spaces: (a) one of hyper-nationalism, that is local, and (b) one of planetary intensification, that is global. Nationalism and radicality, nationalism or internationalism on the fringe, are here disparate arts of gardening which produce strange flowers of destruction.

Let me return to the earlier point: that the hostage taker is the extreme, a figure at the periphery of Islamic discourse, thought, and practice. This extremity of the fringe is a scream of the unspeakable (of the bomb, of the gun, of the knife), and it needs to be engaged as such rather than as a sensational media image. The hostage taker, one of the builders of the hostage space (the state and its institutions are another), creates a space that simultaneously opens (with the desire for a better future of the community) and closes (with the method of bodily sacrifice). The power of being on the fringe lies in the fact that through this position the hostage taker steals his way into the mainstream, cuts into it and creates a crack, an opening, an abyss. And this is not a matter of insignificant conceptual interruption. We are talking about "breaking news" (a complete destruction of the Twin Towers). Hostage taking is a tactic with multiple essences: military in nature, economic in gain (as concerns the exchange of prisoners, money, or sovereignty), theological in affect, sometimes humanistic in goals (despite the approach) though often inviting the inhuman (as will be shown).

Peter Sloterdijk is correct in his assessment of humiliation as a fuel for rage, the ancestral hurt on which civilizations were built and broken down. Consequently, politics have always been a kind of therapy. And the micropolitics of humiliation are at the core of hostage taking; they configure the epicenter, the hearth, of the hostage space. There is no rage in this sphere (which also includes divine rage) that is not tied to a violent process of humbling. Are not all God's punishments, in stories that permeate the Qur'an as well, based on humanity's lack of humility? Is not the contemporary reading of *jihad* itself fueled by the arrogance of the West? Is not the prayer, the folding of one's body five times a day, a literal physical expression of one's humility and thus ability to defuse divine rage? More curiously: Do hostage takers not spare those that (humbly) convert—which means, those that change their form? This is not to categorically say that Islam is a religion based solely on humility, nor that hostage taking, suicide bombing, and militancy are purely related to the divine. But this investigation must also not ignore the molecules of humility and humiliation alike that are paradoxically tied to the most radical fringe of Islamicate thought.

In this respect, humiliation reigns in the phantom territories of the sovereign space: taking hostages is an act of absolute mortification, where the hostage loses his face, or is debased. The humiliation can be so profound and physical that in some instances one loses the entire form of one's body through decapitation. Decapitation is, in this sense, only the last mark, an exclamation point that closes up the meaning of the word. The head flies off and with it the beliefs, the ideas, and the memories that this head once held are forfeit.

To capture is to humiliate. I recall the video of one such radical loss of form. In the Summer of 1993, a unit of Bosnian Muslims (*Bošnjaka*) captured a half dozen Serbian soldiers, out of which at least one was beheaded, with the entire act (the overture of interrogation and joking, and the closure of a scream and the fallen head) caught in a digital format.[27] The man who performed the final act spoke Bosnian with an accent, a foreigner, a combatant within the so-called *mujahideen* (*mudžahedin* in Bosnian) unit. The *mujahideen* were masters of hostage spacing and phantom territoriality; it is still not clear how many volunteers there were in Bosnia (several hundred or several thousand). Examples of *mujahideen* from Bosnia who gained legendary status are Abdelkader Mokhtari, Fateh Kamel, and Karim Said Atmani, all of North African origin—a jet-setting cadre of the *mujahideen*'s culture—who visited dozens of countries and cities in the mid-1990s. All three exemplify a "being-on-the-lookout" on a daily basis, as well as phantomality, the negative movement of the war machine, and theological identitarianism.

Devji has written about the influence that these types of videos from Bosnia had on a number of martyrs and kidnappers in the years that followed the conflict in former Yugoslavia.[28] He ties this inspiration to the consumption of mass media through which *jihad* in fact assumes its universality. It is indeed correct to state, as Devji does, that the *mujahideen* did not have an interest in local politics as such (the creation of an independent state, Bosnia, for example), but rather in consolidating a phantom space of Islamic force through which other operations could be performed. However, his dislocation of local versus global does not diminish the affective powers that underlie the experience of humiliation. Even if we do not want to give it mystical origins, humiliation is certainly part of theological storytelling (being created from dust, prone to sin, tied to the divine law, the endless trials of the chosen, etc.), of the participation in the unconscious transmission of legends, as well as in the images of global mass media. It is ultimately a matter of charisma (and the intrepid fearfulness that accompanies it) which is transmitted in such videos, just as it would be in songs and oral storytelling. Fundamentalism is built upon the metaphysics of charisma, on the spirit of the leader. It is, therefore, not enough to say that the causes for Islamic militancy are based on pure abstractions of individual duty.

Radicality

So where does radicality come from? I mentioned the physics of humiliation as one source and temperamental intensifications as another. But ancestral hurt is not only part of the tribal justice to which only "primitive" mountain men of the Caucasus and the Balkans adhere. Rage underlies the very foundation of western criminal law as well. In his analysis of suicide bombing, Talal Asad draws our attention in this direction when he says, "Durkheim's famous thesis on criminal law, it may be recalled, was that all legal punishment is based on a sense of popular outrage and is therefore motivated by passionate vengeance."[29] Civilized law is not that far from the spirit of the mountains. Besides, as Agamben has already pointed out, law is primarily preoccupied with punishment rather than with justice.[30] The hostage taker, on the other hand, exists outside of the law and thus brings justice (his own) and punishment all prepared in one homemade explosive package. This justice of the explosive is of course part of a divine justice which consists of heavenly regulations (though now made to fit neatly in the materiality of an incendiary device).

Radicality is also tied to the love of the new, where the consciousness of the future (the absence of humiliation, the new rules that are yet to come) is present in the immediacy of the act. We thus speak of the futurism of the act: "Fanaticism, whether congenitally founded or purely political in origin, is a kind of neophilia."[31] A further paradox of the hostage taker rests in his apparent traditionalism, the hatred of the new; but this is only partially true. Since the militant takes inspiration from different times and eras, all conjoining into a single temporality of the unfulfilled present, he is actually still waiting for the new regulations that should govern the earth to come. That is why the military terminology of the avant-garde (originally, in Middle English and French, denoting the vanguard of an army, those that occupy the frontlines) still applies for the contemporary hostage taker. The mainstream terminology of radicality is imposed on the militant. But, for him, radicality is normal, it is not radical; it is part of his desire. And did not the avant-garde movements also want to set up little societies that would have their radicality as a norm, as some kind of elitist mainstream?

There is a whole tradition of "terrorist" philosophy in the West too (a philosophy of antimodernity). Hostage taking is a misapplication, so to speak, of antimodernist (in a sense of the avant-gardist rather than conservative) values. Here, one wants life but opts for death. The manifestos of contemporary terrorists deserve today the same attention that the manifestos of the early European avant-garde received at the beginning of the twentieth century. But when would Mohammad 'Abdus Salam Faraj's "Jihad, The Absent Obligation," for example, appear on the cover page of the *New York Times* as The Futurist Manifesto did on the cover of *Le Figaro* in 1909? Terrorist manifestos, or even avant-garde manifestos, are now only published in the aftermath of a catastrophe, as a warning and an evidence of insanity. Manifestos are significant only in art history, as objects of interpretation, not of inspiration. But hostage takers still operate under early avant-garde rules of engagement. Hence, the twenty-first century is basically a testing ground of terrorist manifestos. The fear of radical ideas is precisely the fear of their actuality, of their actionism (which, coincidentally, is a name of a late-twentieth-century Austrian avant-garde group).

Although I mostly speak about the hostage taker in the singular, he is never truly alone; he is always a network, a cell, a secret group bound by shifting ideas or the desire for justice, independence, etc. It is a group bound by desire. Roger Caillois, thinking about religious orders and political parties, writes:

> Of course, these communities were aggressive by nature. But one should note that this reflects their structure's extreme density and unitary form, as if, to create an order, it were first necessary to constitute an order in the concrete sense of the term, as when referring to a monastic or military organization. Hence, it is as if order and health tended to propagate themselves, gaining ground from one thing to another, like rot and decay, through a process of contagion.[32]

Here we may recall the Special Purpose Islamic Regiment who, with divine immunization, issued rules and regulations for its members. The rules of the "order," or party, should not be overlooked here. In contrast, Devji has argued that al-Qaeda's uniqueness lies in the fact that it not only wants to destroy the form of the state but also that of the party. This is what makes it different from other radical movements of the twentieth century such as communism and fascism. But is not al-Qaeda already a society, albeit of cells, but also of friends, brothers, and sisters, an order of sorts? Even though there is not a party around which a totalitarian regime could entrench itself, there is still a society that wants to implement regulations of divine order.[33] Still, one might conjecture the next stratum, the next morphology, where such authoritarian inclinations of belief would cave in, leaving only relentlessness and fever of the deed.

If we take hostage taking as a problem of politics, and a form of radicality, we must also see it in light of health procedures; that is, a healing of the wound, be it ancestral or recent, through the production of an even larger wound. Since suicide is the ultimate domain of sovereignty over one's body, the production of death that emerges from this act has to be also seen as a form of biopotentiality.

The kidnappings themselves are a way to force a suicidal friendship; they reveal the type of intimacy or friendship that is shared between two groups, namely that of death. In this respect, death is the intimacy of absence. Friendship is the building of bridges over the abyss. This politics of forced intimacy is explicit in the blowing up of bridges and, in the final extreme, of oneself with the bridge. What stays is the abyss that is monumentalized, with new disorienting coordinates of sovereignty. Enmity reveals itself as the friendship of death.

The Head

If biopotentiality is a potential of life that constitutes the capacities for change within every human being, one whose implementation turns one into a revolutionary, then the hostage taker taps into this potential and at the same time betrays it, becoming one's own enemy. There is an obvious fatalism in hostage taking and militancy in exposing oneself to the risk of death globally, by flying from country to country in search of conflicts (as certain *mujahideen* do), observing the landscapes of the world only as intensified diagrams of conflict. A fatalism of the giver of rage, one that comes to ring up the check of humiliation, one that cannot be measured. All temporality becomes indistinct for him: the mythical past to which he corresponds, the present of injustice, the future of heaven, all of this becomes copresent in a new space-time, that of phantom territoriality. This indistinguishable space-time is not a matter of mystical individuality. The force of contemporary capitalism infinitely reduces the experience of space-time through a particular tactic: "Fear, as a product of spatio-temporal contraction, has paradoxically become cosmic. It was already cosmic at the time of the balance of terror. Now it has become cosmic in the sense of space-time."[34] Fear, the affect that underlies the procedures of security in the contemporary nation-states, becomes a measure of time and space, both of the hostage taker and of the western citizen. The hostage taker, however, inhabits this sphere of fear, until he turns into it himself. Fear incarnate.

The hostage taker does not bracket war, and shows no respect for the coupling of friend and enemy; he does not just struggle, he wages the war of annihilation, turning oneself against the western hemisphere but also against one's own body. These are his negative therapeutics.

The enemy is beheaded. And in beheading: the absolute loss of form. In other words, the human being loses his head, the source of his "humanness," and the source of whatever amount of sovereignty he possesses. But also loss of life. It is a terrible predicament in which we live, where the head is still valued as the central standard of sovereignty by both majorities and minorities, and whose loss can only be equated to death. The real radicality would be to find a way in which to lose the head and preserve life (to destroy sovereignty in order to proliferate free life), or else, to create a sovereignty of the unformed. For this a new counter-poison is necessary, a veritable uprooting of oneself. And while some hostage takers may be doing exactly this, they are still doing it under the umbrella of the original healer, the ruler of all that exists. Hostage taking and beheading makes one larger, it increases one's phantomal character. And the capacity to destroy form makes one shudder, for it is a characteristic reserved for God (the only absolutely unrepresentable form).

And yet the hostage space remains, even in the absence of the hostage taker and the hostages. It is still tied to the mythology of mountains in the Caucasus, in Kosovo and northern Macedonia, but also in the squares of the Middle Eastern megalopolises, and on television sets and computer screens. We could therefore say that the architectonics of phantomality are rising proportionally to the ways in which sovereignties are waning.

3

Architectonics of the Hostage Space

Enfolding

The celerity of terror. The uniqueness of the hostage space lies in the fact that it turns the everyday space into the space of exception in a matter of minutes. It is constructed in secret, by the secret, which then explodes into the public. Furthermore, every space (whatever its constitution) has a potential to become a hostage space through the reordering of its physical and affective architecture: from an airplane to an elementary school. Turning toward "hostage-like" qualities is therefore a matter of potential. The extraction and manipulation of this potential is only possible because every space is a constructed space, that is, with different energetic or physical properties. Even a void, a presumed empty space, is still an atmospheric condition filled with the potential for transformation. More precisely, architectonics suggests a composition of a specific type of space; it suggests that a hostage taker is an architect of sorts: a chief builder of terrorist (affective) space.

Thus, the role of the hostage taker is manifested in two ways. First, she is a builder because she transforms the space, any space, into a previously unrecognizable intensity, captivating each site in her hands and overtaking it. In other words, she has no respect, so to speak, for the space of the building, or that of the airplane, or of the train as previously construed. Before humiliating the hostages or the state, the hostage taker first humiliates the space under siege. It is through her imposition of temporary sovereignty that she reconfigures the space. The citizens under the law of the state, on the other hand, respect and take the space at face value as it is given to them; they divide it into private and public spheres and move accordingly. We are thus confronted with an anomalous situation. There is an immensity of space on the globe, endless in every direction, which is divided by the stately (borders) walls, and yet there are only two categories of division in operation: public/private. (And then also domestic/wild, but more in the imagination than in the law since even the so-called wild space is domesticated, being as it is always under the supervision of the state.) The hostage space, by contrast, destroys the division between private and public; that is the space where the hostage taker enters simply becomes hers, or that of her collective.

Second, she is a builder because she implements a cosmological architecture of the law (*shariʾah*) of the omnipresent master builder. According to one conservative view, *shariʾah* is the "governance according to Allah's Law in reforming both the ruler and his flock."[1] The law is again related to the sovereignty of the state and the hostage space epitomizes the first implementation of that state both in terms of territory and in terms of existential conditions. The very first architectonics of the sovereign space thus always corresponds to the act of hostaging. The state builds by devouring a territory, by expanding the borders. Moreover, to capture is to take possession of someone or something; there is a latent aspect of hostage taking in every territorial extension, conquest, or manipulation of space. The entire history of western imperialism itself is nothing but an exercise in hostage taking (taking possession of space and all biopotentiality, all life, that finds itself within that space). A bold but accurate statement would be this: the history of the world is an endless application of hostage spaces. The history of colonialism and slavery is only the highest degree of this application (we see this action still unfolding today at the checkpoints in Israel and elsewhere). The historical here corresponds to the movement of the cosmological. The universe unfurls itself into creation, expanding indefinitely (an astrophysical argument), just as the world is created by the gesture of some divinity and given to humans to govern it accordingly. The expansion (a theological argument) occurs only because there is the idea of governance. But everyone is affected by this gesture of expansion that arrives from the cosmological unfurling. And the concept of the political is simply the sensitivity to territorial determinism (being tied to the territory and needing to rule over it).

In this sense, the devastating hostage taking that occurred in Beslan in 2004, for example, is just one small moment in this long genealogy of hostage taking (both its political and cosmological application). When it comes to the architectonics of the Beslan hostage space, rumor converges with empirical reality to create exorbitant images: the composition of fatigue, drugs (heroin found in the blood of the hostage takers which allowed them to continue fighting even after they were badly hurt), wires across the gymnasium of the school, the endless crying of children, and the music of the German band Rammstein which hostage takers played for themselves. All of these instances together compose the ethnographic surrealism of the event of hostage taking. The concrete situation in Beslan shows the cosmological aspect of reality that is tied to the banal procedures of the everyday. Hostage taking is an act that unites the cosmological impulses that lie behind the obedience to the law, the desire for overtaking territory, the political injustice of humiliation that some ethnic groups withstand, and the ordinariness of the act itself. To analyze the event of hostage taking only through one of its aspects would therefore prove reductive. In order to enter into the event, one needs a certain theopolitics of the banal.

What happens in the image of the school in Beslan, in its ordinary extraordinariness? The inside of the public space that is, by its nature, transparent and open (though not always, since there are restrictions in the democratic principle of the public space) becomes obfuscated by the militant's imposition; it becomes enclosed by demands, maskings, and threats. The images of the photographer Yuri Kozyrev taken during the storming of the school in Beslan reveal this exceptionality without the spectacular.[2] The spectacular is undermined by the despair that visibly emerges through each photo, as the presence of the catastrophe that is not immanent but rather immediate. There is nothing beyond this very moment captured in the photos of the father carrying a dead child, or of the immense fragmentation of the space of the school, no less than that of the bodies.

Through effects of the staged destruction (the siege, the storming, and the actual killing), hostage taking becomes a form of spectacle. Through its affective architecture of terror, the hostage taker extracts the spectacular from the banal through techniques of pure violence. Of course, there is an ancient link between the spectacle and the violence of war. In this respect, Paul Virilio borrows an expression from Clausewitz in order to describe the situation of a rookie soldier "who, before facing the battlefield for the first time, looks at it from afar in astonishment and 'for a moment still thinks he is at a show.'"[3] Even though technologies of perception have changed (from satellite mapping to night goggles to video simulations of the battle), the astonishment experienced still remains the same. But the spectacular aspect of conflict has most notably changed because of the change in spatial dimension of the encounter with the enemy. Namely, the terror now happens on the inside (inside the Beslan school or inside the Iraqi homes during nightly US raids of Baghdad); the physical inside of a building, an airplane, a train, etc. Hostage spacing is thus an enfolding of the conflict into its own lap, into the body's most intimate position. Or, to speak in the language of the architectural, the public space is turned into a space of intimate horror. We see here that the construction of the private (the implosion of the public space in hostage taking) corresponds to the sphere of the cosmological. Namely, one is embraced by "the message" and participates in its universality (whether one likes it or not). Everything becomes private and also cosmological. But this transition from secure public space to abrasive private space can only be accompanied by delirium and hallucinatory perceptions. Hostage takers are perceived as fanatical, which is usually taken to mean ardent, compulsive, obsessive, fervent, and, informally, crazy and wild. Fanaticism is therefore typically conceived as a type of psycho-political disorder.

With a slight digression, I would like to consider another disorder here, that of schizophrenia, for it is an important paradigm in the discussion of the architectonics of space, not anymore as a diagnosis of the particular hostage taker but as a radical transfiguration of space through new affective perceptions. It is therein that Roger Caillois writes: ". . . schizophrenics invariably reply, *I know where I am, but I don't feel that I am where I am*. For dispossessed minds such as these, space seems to constitute a will to devour. Space chases, entraps, and digests them in a huge process of phagocytosis."[4] The experience of schizophrenia leads us to stop perceiving the boundary of our own skin, as we do not differentiate anymore between the outlines of our own body and that of the outside surroundings; or, to be consistent with the preceding formulations, one could say that the schizophrenic loses the perception of his own form—in fact, all forms, the entire environment, change and transfigure. Caillois continues, "He feels that he is turning into space himself—*dark space into which things cannot be put*," so that finally, "he dreams up spaces that 'spasmodically possess' him."[5] The space itself takes hostage of the schizophrenic, paradoxically healing him from the ruptures that define his condition, but then again turning the world around by taking him outside of his senses and into an undifferentiated existence. The collapse of the private and the public is therefore properly schizophrenic: the intimacy of the absolute inside, a space of dissolution of all forms.

Sometimes, however, this type of schizophrenia is called pantheism or mysticism (which, depending on the historical conditions, is either proclaimed a heresy or a legitimate religious experience). Caillois thus writes about Flaubert's writing on Saint Anthony, a Christian icon who throws himself into material space so as to be devoured in its fullness. The (pantheist) desire of Saint Anthony is therefore oriented as follows: "to penetrate each atom, to descend into the heart of the matter—*to be* matter."[6] If it might be too far-fetched to think of the architectonics of the hostage space in terms of a dissolution of all forms (and thus inducing a terrorist version of pantheist schizophrenia), this idea becomes more concrete when we define certain militant Islamic movements as a form of political pantheism: the desire to fold the entire cosmos into the lap of Islam, through its laws first, that is through the form, and then through God's dispositions (the affective components of mercy and judgment, and everything that arrives in the aftermath of these two modes), which is to say, through the absence of form. In short, the globality of such strains of militant Islam is moved by the tension that emerges between form (of the law) and the unformed (God). Schizophrenia is hence as good a term as any to describe this political rupturing occurring on a planetary level.[7] The breaking-down of the public zone into a cosmological space of indistinction (as mentioned earlier) can also be seen as a pantheist fold of privacy (of the Islamic message) into which the entire world collapses.

Niqab

There is another detail in the Islamic everyday that speaks to such patterns of cosmological hostage taking: the *hijab*. In Arabic, while literally meaning a "curtain" or a "cover," *hijab* is a way of enveiling the body through garments that many Muslim women use as a dress code. More accurately, then, it is a spatial curtain that divides the private from the public, an enfolding that separates the sphere of the everyday from the sphere of the cosmological. The private sphere is just a tiny fold within the cosmological. The privacy is never from God, but, on the contrary, it is through the veil that the women are with God. This dress-code is of course tied to Islamic legal principles and enduring theological concerns, most of which refer to the affective principle of modesty (we return to the force of humility here). The body, and the body of the woman in particular, has to be enfolded into humility. But the garment is also a tender yet impenetrable wall that separates the private space (of the body) from the public space of interaction (the outside).

This form of cloaking is also a form of becoming-hostage (voluntarily for some women) through the participation of one's desire.[8] I am addressing here only the spatial aspect of veiling, since it primarily designates the architectural affects of space (the division of space that leads to the passions which give rise to morality and immorality). We have read about the recent controversies in France, England, and Turkey, about the practices and consequences of wearing the *hijab* and *niqab* in the public western space. These controversies emerge primarily out of a poor understanding of the problems tied to the concepts of public and private. The materiality of the veil thus concerns the political, spatial, and theological problems not only of the Islamic world but also that of all other geo-ideological coordinates.

One theological explanation: *hijab* refers to "the veil which separates man or the world from God."[9] Why is it that women have to wear this separation and men do not (even though there are instances such as the Tuareg people where men wear face coverings)? Is it because men are presumed to be in closer proximity to the absolute? Or is it the women who are in fact closer to the deified plane because they are closed off to the public already, and therefore participate in the cosmological more intimately? This intimation of the woman's body with the divine is further complicated by the menaces that some Islamist militants (like the Mahdi army in Basra, Iraq, which in 2007 killed dozens of women) exert on women who refuse to wear the face covering (*niqab*); namely, these men threaten with the destruction of the face (in the strategy of throwing acid, for example), as if the woman's face were a face of the enemy, or, more fearfully, as if the face itself were a forbidden representational image of God that must ensuingly be defaced. Hence the *niqab* is recast: the mask or face-veil that stands as the final protection from the ordinariness of the public space. The *niqab*, in its semi-circular flares and triangular under-scarfs, is the maximal intensification of the veiling process. In this way, the politics of the *niqab* are profoundly aligned with the architectonics of the hostage space. (In the former Yugoslavia they were banned by the communist government; in the postcommunist era, they are allowed yet again.)

There is a strange discontent in that small piece of the veil that folds so precisely around the woman's face; the discontent of secular politics no less than that of metaphysical dogmatism. Moreover, it determines one's acceptance as a citizen, as a friend, or else as an enemy. There is a proper esotericism of the veil too: the face is enfolded, and what remains is a fold that operates as a pantheistic space of concealment (behind the veil, everything is private).

Ground Zero

The image of Ground Zero renders a different portrayal of potency both in terms of the space itself and of the event that gave us the concept—"Ground Zero," the absolute unveiling. Its poetic-technical nomenclature does not actually signify an event with no intensity (zero intensity). 9/11 is quite the opposite, with Ground Zero referring to its architectural grounding: the architectonics of the building (and by extension of the city and of the whole nation) having been brought to the ground. There is also another way of seeing this name, as a catastrophe before which, when one is physically present in front of it, one remains mute. The crater of the fallen towers is the abyss that connects the actual image with the imagination of what an abyss might look like. It is assumed that being in front of it requires stillness, prayer, meditation. While these are streamed toward the victims, the stillness itself is initiated by the sudden vulnerability and disappearance of the immense verticality of the architectural objects. The towers have been "humbled," they have folded up, in a prayer of death. The enormity of this particular event rests in the fact that not only the airplanes have been hijacked but so have the towers themselves. In fact, barely anyone addresses the planes and the people in them. Towers are the most visible manifestation of the hostage space, but also of a phantom territoriality that emerges in its aftermath.

Ground Zero, the product or the result of the terrorist avant-garde, is a new form of spectacle, one of zero intensity whose impact nevertheless vibrates throughout the globe. The spectacle of images that followed the catastrophe was still part of the old society of the spectacle that Guy Debord wrote about, while the event itself went further, ushering a new formation of the social, more apparitional and imperceptible than the flashing images of twentieth-century capitalism. Debord wrote that "the spectacle is implicitly in its totality—*the communication of the incommunicable*."[10] Is there a better definition for what we call Ground Zero? A ground that communicates the incommunicable. But because of the inappropriateness of calling the event of 9/11 a spectacle, which sounds too banal, the site was immediately turned into a monument. The most amazing apparitional monument was the very first one, only a few weeks after the actual transpiring of the event, formed by two large light-beams that streamed their rays upward until they were lost in the darkness of outer space, until the border of the beams became undecipherable (a schizophrenic light). This was persistent proof that the state could not allow for the site to be divested of all architectonics.

The monumentalization of the site continues today with the new towers emerging through the master-plan of Daniel Libeskind.[11] Libeskind himself sees Ground Zero as a "sacred site" and so upon the original drawings we see the utmost importance of the "memory foundations." He thus introduces theological dimensions into the architecture of the site, which by now grow diluted through more corporate concerns, but which still remain imprinted in the otherwise purely economic purpose of the towers. In fact, the entire site is imagined by Libeskind as a memory for the victims, a chronic and interminable memory of the catastrophe. In contrast to this invocation of sacred memory found in the original diagrams, the actual models of the future buildings look just like any other structure of corporate functionality found in global metropolises. There is a disparity between the diagram (in its radicality) and its physical manifestation in the model (in its functionality). The architectonics of muteness are suppressed in favor of a victorious architecture wrought large and vertical. However, there is a consciousness of the abyss in the architect's mind that comes through in the imagined 70-foot-deep openings that reveal the foundations of the original towers. A memorial to the victims that also, secretly, reveals the knowledge of what has occurred in hostage taking: the very reorganization of the architectural politics of space. It is this secret which is inscribed in the continual process of memorization (and memorialization), accompanied with an always necessary dose of hopefulness that is inseparable from the ethics of every monument. In this sense, Ground Zero is a microcosm of the world composed by the architectures of witnessing; it is here that we see the conflation of health and war again, the health of the state that is generated by its reactions to the hostage taking, and revealed through specific manifestations of economic power (inscribed in the actual offices in the towers), and sacredness inscribed in the memories and the physical memorial of the abyss.

Even before the catastrophe the towers were already maximized, turned into a zero gravity by another "hostage taker": Philippe Petit reduced the monumentality of the architectural to a zero degree. In 1968, when he first saw the sketch of the towers yet to be built in the French newspapers, he drew a line that connected the two towers. After this line was drawn, he spent several years in preparation for the endeavor of walking between the buildings on a tightrope. This he accomplished in 1974, with the use of a 450-pound cable and a custom-made 26-foot long, 55-pound balancing pole. The event was so mesmerizing for the viewers on the street level that they spoke of it in terms of a mystical experience. It is true that Petit exploded the scale of the buildings and that of his body. He was simply out of scale, the body in immeasurable distance, turning into immeasurable body. More significantly, he spoke of constantly walking on the edge (a certain type of radicality) as a life principle, which he concretized literally on the tightrope. And not only did he walk on it, he danced. This was the first hostage taker that the architectonics of the Ground Zero site drew upon themselves.[12]

These instances are just a few in a long line of constructing hostage spaces in the history of the globe. Let me go back to the pre-Islamic world, for a moment, in order to prove this point—Mesopotamia 700 BC. The Assyro-Babylonian kings commanded the abduction of images and monuments as one of the most important strategies of war. Zainab Bahrani writes about this practice in the following fashion: "At times, wars were fought specifically for images, to acquire royal monuments and the cult state of a god, or to recover a divine statue that had been carried off by an enemy in an earlier battle."[13] The statues of Assyrian, Elamite, and Babylonian kings and gods were treated as actual bodies. The imitation of reality was enough to change the very nature of the object, turning it into reality itself, into a subject with all the senses. Hence the statues could be tortured as well by piercing their lips, cutting off their tongues, chopping off their limbs, and so on. The proliferation of images of torture (such as impaling, flaying, and abducting) was itself a narrative of the spectacle meant to encourage the victorious side and to frighten the enemy. These narrative images were public and, more than that, they were considered official representations of war, directly conflating aesthetics with violent sovereignty.

There is an undeniable resemblance of such procedures in the taking of images of the prisoners in Abu-Ghraib—in this case, photographs—which occurs incidentally in the same territory of former Mesopotamia now called Iraq. In fact there is only one difference: the images from Abu-Ghraib were not meant to be public; they were part of private archives of the aesthetical practices of today's war, with the same intensity of cruelty but enclosed in the veil of semi-secrecy. The magicality of the images, however, and what they do to the reality of the war, stays the same. More precisely, the images capture the event and enlarge the charisma of the participant-torturer and of all those associated with him. Torture fragments the body of the victim but enlarges the body of the torturer: this is the poetics of its terror.

These contemporary acts implement the machinery of torture which has already been established by the Assyrian kings; that is there is a little bit of the sovereign tyrant in every soldier who participated in the Abu-Ghraib interrogations. That is, the architecture of the hostage space changes degrees of severity, ages and geographies of its appearance, but not its essences.

Furthermore, the movement of monuments, cult statues, and images in ancient Mesopotamia created a certain phantom territoriality which was a result of the "strategy of deportation and banishment."[14] This was one of the first instances of exile and a proto-form of ethnic cleansing, even though the populations that were deported were displaced but integrated into a new location. What Mesopotamian civilizations also show is that representations of gods were not considered mere representations of the divine but rather as gods incarnate. The god was always inside the statue, as the interiority of the material used to forge the statue and was made alive through ritual. Hence, through the abduction of the cult statues, god himself became a hostage and by extension so did the entire city to which he belonged and which he protected.

Almost three millennia later, in sectors of the contemporary Islamic landscape, with a completely new form of representational thinking—namely, the other pole of the cult statue, the forbidden representationality of God, but without the absence of aesthetics—we still have a similar tactic of hostage taking. The ten hijackers (in two airplanes) who brought down the twin towers took hostage not only the passengers but also the towers themselves, no less than the entire megalopolis of New York City, and by extension the nation-state itself. The towers themselves could also be seen as cult statues, this time not as gods but certainly as representative of the absolute sovereign power, that of the US empire. The ancient strategy of war thus returns in a new light, albeit with different formal techniques and new "magical" technologies (those of the cell phone and flight navigation) but with the same principle behind it (the reconfiguration of space and destruction of the enemy's sovereign power). There is also the magicality of the terror, of the affective powers of fear that envelop the bodies of the citizens, of terror as an affect with its own sovereign power (as the sayings "the holy terror" and "the reign of terror" attest). This is the fear and trembling that occurs already in children's stories and which enters a completely new dimension in the war stories of the state.

The architectonics of the hostage space are still what they have always been: an architectural dislocation. By this I mean the dislocation of buildings, statues, monuments, but also of populations, media images, and even of the divine powers of the state. The war itself emerges as a result of these dislocations. In this sense, the irregularity of the combat, the bracketing of war, has always been a dormant possibility in the conflicts engaged by different empires throughout history; or, put simply, the act of terrorism is not a postmodern strategy of warfare but one that has been practiced for millennia. The theory of the partisan that Schmitt so skillfully developed, and to which all discussion of irregular warfare recoils, has to be augmented with the energetic dimension of terror that passes through the ages; not conceived in a linear fashion but as a transmutation of forms that bubble up in different moments of time and space as unpredictably as the eruptions of a dormant volcano. Terror is thus an affective state that creates medico-political dispositions (fear, hatred, grief, lamentation), dislocations (geographical migrations), and somatic disorders (traumas, physical and mental injuries, mutilations). But these are also productive/constitutive aspects of a terrorist architectonics. For the reordering of space, even of this kind, "creates a new space and a new world order that allows new social contracts and state formations."[15] It is this potential for a new spatiality that needs to be investigated in the aftermath, in the Ground Zero, of humanist thought.

Message

In this analysis of ancient contemporaneity, there is another relevant detail for present concerns in the architecture of the temporal. The demarcation BC, or "before Christ" (coupled with AD, *Anno Domini*, "in the year of the Lord"), for entire eras already testifies to the hostage spacing of Christian metaphysics and its worldview. The temporality of the globe is designated by (an approximate) historical birth, or incarnation, of the cosmic Christ-figure. The entire globe folds itself to this event through the careful and violent implementation of hostage spaces produced by Christianity. The hostage space thus emerges through the charisma of the founder, of the prophet. He (in most cases, "he") is the initiator of the storm, of the movement, the winds that carry the ships (today the airplanes and satellites), that carry the message of salvation, which is primarily that of the law, the law of submission, the law that asks for everyone to become a voluntary hostage of the message.

The message is the push that forms the movement, it is its gravitational core. The founding force of the movement, of any political party or religious brotherhood, moves through time and space with different qualitative and quantitative frequencies, but it always moves. Ayman al-Zawahiri, another voice from the so-called extremist fringe, provides the following definition (the importance, or lack thereof, of such a voice I leave to the reader to determine): "All movements go through a cycle of erosion and renewal, but it is the ultimate result that determines the fate of a movement: Either extinction or growth."[16] Movement is here addressed through its physical properties, through its fluctuation but also with its consistency that is permanent. The life of the movement (political and embodied) is seen as cyclical, always returning.

The message, the constant: "When we take this broad meaning of the word 'defense,' we understand the true character of Islam, and that is a universal proclamation of the sovereignty of God and His Lordship throughout the world, the end of man's arrogance and selfishness, and the implementation of the rule of Divine [*shari'ah*] in human affairs."[17] It is all here: the divine sovereign and his law (still that of the father), but also the revolutionary character of universal liberation, a desire for the world without enslavement and as result a world that would have to be without forces of the political, and ultimately without sovereignty (i.e. without the slightest sense of domination, or hostaging, even on a molecular level). I do not lose sight of this tension at the core of such strands of Islamic thought but I do not aim for its resolution either. Rather, one should try to inhabit the chambers that constitute the tension and unfold its principles, its numerous building blocks, and its fatal diagrams. There is one intuition that I am pursuing—the intuition that fatality contains a molecule of liberatory principle, the concept of freedom that is at present still tied to a theopolitical paradigm. Let us continue with the analysis of the architectonics of this molecule (or, in older terminology, of the chamber), the molecule of the message.

The message is what is continuous and what remains, both as a force of the contemporaneity of Islamicate thought (the simultaneous enjoining of diverse historical events) and as a phantom territoriality which occurs after the storm of the actual hostage taking (the abyss of explosion, the ground zero of experience, the disembodiment of the message). The message remains because it is essentially both a remainder and a reminder: a memory of the future. This is the very paradoxical core of the hostage space: the infliction of the message, or in other words, the enjoining of the cosmic with the everyday. The hostage takers are all already voluntary hostages who want to create a world of hostages. The crucial difference is that they reject the hostaging of the western secular state (still operating according to BC/AD temporality and through Christ-like sensibilities) and its accompanying laws in favor of the law of another prophetic vision.

There is a consistency in the experience of temporality in the wake of the hostage taker who sees all eras as copresent, especially in relation to the message of God which must remain atemporal. In light of this, we can isolate a close tie between the diverse hostage-taking situations mentioned above: Beslan, Mesopotamia, the emergence of the prophets (both Christ and Muhammad), and all others that are yet to come in the future. The great machine of hostage spacing has in fact been set up from the very beginning of life-formation on the planet, as it is visible in the collectivities of the molecular world, in cells and molecules. The contemporary language of biochemistry and cell biology returns us to the concept of political immunology. Namely, scientists today still speak about viruses in terms of "enemies" who attack healthy cells of the human organism. In fact, viruses "hijack" the cells.[18] I leave the whole paradigm of war vocabulary, which is quite problematic, for some other discussion and concentrate only on the procedure of hijacking here. This hijacking of cells' pathways that lead to the nucleus is part of the biochemical investigation of what are called "viral entryways." In this territorial battle of the molecular, cells internalize molecules through endocytic machinery (a complex of vesicles and proteins) and viruses find ways to kidnap this "machinery" in order to occupy the territory of the cell and reorganize its architectonics. The organisms fight, now with the help of scientists too, to protect these entryways.

One of the most common images in the history of the political and anthropological theory of the state is that of the state as a human body (with the sovereign as the head) and that of the enemy as the sickness attacking the body of the state. Nazi Germany went the farthest in this philosophy of the biological but we can still see the same images of thought occurring in present-day western democracies in different forms of xenophobia. What is important to emphasize here, then, is the actual process of hijacking (and the specific use of the word) that occurs already in the sphere of the molecular. And if one is reluctant to speak of the society of cells and molecules, no one can dismiss the cellular character of social networks, and thus also recognize a certain type of interactive sociality in viruses, cells, and molecules. We therefore speak of terrorist collectivities as "cells" because the molecular character of the perception of the world permeates our vision. Brotherhoods, sisterhoods, secret societies, become networks and cells, in that they change their form without losing their essence.

Lowintensity

Besides the spectacular destructions of buildings and monuments in recent decades, there is also another form of hostage space, one developed through so-called lowintensity war, perfected by the Israeli Defense Forces (IDF). Eyal Weizman has shown how this specific stage in the evolution of war emerged (and is still in the process of surfacing) from the military-scientific "laboratory" of urban warfare constructed in the West Bank and Gaza.[19] In fact, it is the knowledge of architecture and urban planning that is crucial in this evolution of war strategies, one that is also referred to as "inverse geometry." This particular concept made its appearance when the IDF, chasing Palestinian guerrilla fighters, developed a new technique of pursuit, as Weizman describes:

> . . . they used none of the city streets, roads, alleys or courtyards, or any of the external doors, internal stairwells or windows, but moved horizontally through walls and vertically through ceilings and floors. This form of movement, described by the military as "infestation," sought to redefine inside as outside, and domestic interiors as thoroughfares. The IDF's strategy of "walking through walls" involved a conception of the city as not just the

site but also the very *medium* of warfare—a flexible, almost liquid medium that is forever contingent and in flux.[20]

The IDF, the state army, appropriated techniques of the guerrilla war machine that is outside of it, namely those of the Palestinian insurgency, and added to it forms of destruction that only a sovereign power can afford. Namely, newly enlightened IDF soldiers blow up the walls of private homes and run through the living rooms as if these were the training grounds for their cadets (also another way of destroying the dichotomy of the private and the public). Palestinian territories are of course already permanent hostage spaces, quintessentially fabricated (with all the checkpoints, walls, regulations of movement, affective modalities of fear and humiliation, etc.).

Also interesting is the use of the word "infestation," as if the consciousness of cell biology somehow seeped into the mind of the military personnel. Not only does the state fight against the enemy that it perceives as a virus but it becomes one as well. The goal of the state is not, as it used to be, to preserve the absolute health of its body, of its territory, but, as Weizman points out, to generate permanent "lowintensity" illness which actually allows it to experiment with new weapons on the fringes of its body and also benefit from the development of a cutting-edge military-scientific complex. The IDF is a leader in experimental political endocytosis, finding viral entryways and overtaking natural resources of its (Palestinian) hosts more effectively than any other virus ever could.

In this respect, in the irregular, nonlinear conflict, one creates holes in the space and the surrounding architecture (e.g. by walking through walls). The IDF officers speak of being like "worms" eating their way through the barriers. Animals that puncture the surfaces of the earth. Now the ground, or the underground, has been raised above the surface where warrior and civilian, animal and human, mingle and remain on constant lookout. In fact, there is no more underground as an image of the revolutionary resistance; the animal of the irregular hostage space is that of the serpent rather than the molehill.[21] The hostage space opens regions up, turns them into gaping voids; what was familiar now turns terroristic, where one's body is in need of permanent recovery (recovery from the walls that provide constant humiliation).

The Islamic militant answers directly to this strategy of "walking through walls." She flies through them (the Twin Towers), thereby intensifying the movement through the walls to the n-th degree. Even the walls are the enemy now. And further still, the city itself is the enemy, hence the (selective) destructions of Grozny, New York, Jenin, Bethlehem, and Priština. If this postmodern war-waging shows us anything, it is precisely the fact that the borrowings between the state and the war machine of the militant, insurgent, or guerrilla, have not stopped in the least. Instead, they mutated according to the shift in the terrain of the battle (from the open spaces of steppes and forests to the urban spaces of cities to the troposphere and the stratosphere where satellites abide). And we see how the composition of punctured space benefits the state army. But the militants themselves are only temporarily irregular. Hamid Dabashi says the same in the context of Shi'ism: ". . . as a religion of protest, Shi'ism is successful and legitimate only when it is combative and in a warring posture, and it loses that legitimacy the instant it comes to power."[22] The problem is thus not only how to develop the theory of the hostage taker but also how to define resistance (the insurgency), since both are tied to the definition of and the relative relationship they have with the state. (What would the state of constant conceptual uprising look like, and would it need a divine inspiration?)

To molecularize the architectonics of the hostage space further: it is actually the message that we have to view not only in textual, theological, and anthropological terms but also architectonically—as the very first building-block of a community, the first inhabitation of a space; the message as a tent, a protection from the hostile elements, a sentence, sometimes an incantation, that extends spatially, conquering the world, waging wars, consoling and blowing up. Thus the message is a sentence (a set of words) that sentences (provides judgment and punishment). As I have shown, one becomes the hostage of the message voluntarily or by force, as the charismatic magnetism of the message, the inside and the outside of the prophet, gives a feeling of being in an indestructible fort. That is the sole reason why the hostage taker, who is at the same time the hostage of the message, feels invincible. The message enjoins the body of the individual with the sentence, or the law (a sentence exploded into multiple prescribed meanings), protecting her from a twofold danger: the precariousness of the environment and the rage/love of God. The hostage taker thus inhabits the fringe of the discourse because she walks across the message, a line, as if it were a tightrope, and which becomes both her lifeline and her deathline. (She looks at her own hand to see the line that runs across her palm in order to see where it ends.)

One can inhabit the microsphere of the message, just as one can inhabit the medals that one receives as an award. In other words, there is a microspherology (to use Sloterdijk's term) of a space constructed through intimacy. A space is here defined as a certain location, or intensification, in which one finds oneself, without it necessarily constructing a physical space: microspheres of a message, of a medal, of a monument. For example, a former US marine, Jon Turner, recently ripped his medals from his chest and threw them from a stage on which he was speaking about the everyday operations he conducted in Iraq. He, in a way, lived inside these medals—they were his home, the dwelling that marks his belonging and service to the state, the pacification of his destructive character, the cheap therapeutics for the trauma of killing. He ceremoniously divested himself from them and, as a consequence, from the image of the hero they embodied. The intimacy of the medal is the same as the intimacy of the memorial. In fact, the medal is a personalized memorial, a reminder of the past event through a very particular reading of it ("this, what you did, was a great thing in the end . . ."). It is also a form of medication, or more precisely, a sedative. It is significant, furthermore, that the medals do not look like "medals." They too have changed their aesthetic coordinates. Now they are small abstract squares of monochrome colors (like miniature Kandinsky paintings), strange forms of aesthetical avant-garde with a precise functionality (in the sense of creating hierarchies). Jon Turner rejected the fate of living inside a medal, being a hostage of the medal and of the reward, thereby denying the state the opportunity to inscribe its own monumentality onto his body.

Peace

The architectonics of peace rely primarily upon the impossibility of its completion, as if the construction of peace itself necessitates terror and all the building blocks that form it: torture, interrogation, beating, hostaging, killing, etc. The radical actors on the contemporary Islamic stage agree, as is evidenced by the manual of al-Qaëda:

> The confrontation that we are calling for with the apostate regimes does not know Socratic debates . . . Platonic ideals . . . [n]or Aristotelian diplomacy. But it knows the dialogue of bullets, the ideals of assassination, bombing, destruction, and the diplomacy of the cannon and machine gun.
>
> . . . Islamic governments have never and will never be established through peaceful solutions and cooperative councils. They are established as they [always] have been:
>
> by pen and gun;
>
> by word and bullet; and
>
> by tongue and teeth[23]

The writer of the manual invokes Greek philosophers as the foundation of western social and political thought that is rendered impotent amidst present forms of political negotiation. Peace is as obsolete as the ancient Greek foundations; what counts instead is war, but also the physicality of words and of the body (tongue and teeth). As early as 1932, Schmitt ends his essay "The Concept of the Political" with similar predictions: namely, he confirms that the state and the political cannot be eliminated from the social life of human beings. He also states that the omnipresence of war will not be diminished with the rise of global economic forces as some theorists had hoped. This is of course what we witness in the twenty-first century as the new "means of annihilation" are being invented with the help of science and technology research teams. What does this mean for the development, or better yet, construction of peace? Schmitt continues:

> For the application of such means, a new and essentially pacifist vocabulary has been created. War is condemned but executions, sanctions, punitive expeditions, pacifications, protection of treaties, international police, and measures to assure peace remain. The adversary is thus no longer called an enemy but a disturber of peace and is thereby designated to be an outlaw of humanity. A war waged to protect or expand economic power must, with the aid of propaganda, turn into a crusade and into the last war of humanity.[24]

Both texts, that of al-Qaёda and of Schmitt, retain a prophetic character. The first speaks with desire for violence in the construction of Islamic governance; the second predicts the same propensity for violence (though without the explicit desire for it) at the core of economics in liberal ideology. Two different architectures of peace are visible therein: (a) explicit-terrorist, based on war and conflict; and (b) implicit-liberal, based on the imperative quest for peace which subjugates with new weapons of destruction. This is not to say that they are equal in force or in the degree of radicality. But it is important to note that dichotomies which are set up, starting from that of the friend/enemy, do not stand at present, and, if we happen to believe in the prophecies, never will. Peace is not a metaphysical reality in itself that needs protection against its adversary; it is rather a supplement or a by-product of the conflict. The enemy is always the same; in abstract terms, it is the one that dislocates forms (of peace), or else, the architecture of the state (buildings of the megalopolis)—a stirrer, disturber, fanatic, interrupter; al-Qaёda is in a sense more optimistic than Schmitt. It speaks in terms of future terrorist activity, the construction of Islamic governments yet to come. Schmitt, on the other hand, invokes the "last war of humanity." Perhaps this is because he did not have the concept of the inhuman, a new form of relationship with the world, neither properly human nor properly animal, one that emerges out of the hostage space as neither a hostage taker nor a victim.

Now we can ask: What is the role of the peacemaker? Is it a humanitarian intervention, a prophecy, a healing of the trauma through reconciliation? Didier Fassin and Mariella Pandolfi accurately diagnose the health of power that underlies humanitarian action: "Even dressed up in the cloak of humanitarian morality, intervention is always a military action—in other words, war."[25] Historically, then, the peacemaker is always at the same time the warrior. Is this not also a definition that encapsulates the force of the prophet Muhammad (and that of Christ as well)? Hostage takers side with the war but, then again, is not war sometimes the most "humanitarian" thing one can do? Mujahedins in Bosnia went further still: they cut off the heads of those who wore uniforms which initiated the ethnic cleansing of Bosnian Muslims. The problem with intervention is not the act of intervening but the definition of it: peace-full. The very designation that carries the name of peace means that someone is implementing something: a set of rules, buildings, new divisions of public and private space. To this end, the most spectacular architectural building presently emerging in the western Balkans is the Open Parliament of Albania, a castle-like silver structure with a massive transparent dome. The amazing aspect of this project is the way in which architectural practice takes the political concepts of the state literally, demonstrating the way in which the architectonics of the two go hand-in-hand:

> The design incorporates fundamental democratic values such as openness, transparency and public co-determination. The simultaneity of competing political concepts within a democratic society is translated into the design concept: Different building elements are not opposed, but coexist in one building ensemble with a contemporary aesthetic that allows visualizing new functions and meanings.[26]

A transparent dome created by an Austrian architectural cooperative Coop Himmelb(l)au is a polar opposite of the architectonics of Enver Hoxha, the authoritarian Albanian leader of Marxist-Leninist persuasion who presided over Albania until his death in 1985. One of his architectural contributions to the landscape is a complex of 750,000 concrete bunkers (in a country of 3 million inhabitants) which acted as lookouts and gun emplacements equipped with chemical weapons. Being on the lookout is a definition of the animal, as well as of the inhabitant of the hostage space. Albania in particular was itself constructed like a bunker from the Second World War until the fall of communism.

And all things hostage are far from resolved there. Just beyond its northern border, operating as its fringe, is one of the most volatile regions of Europe: Kosovo. This is a region that is fighting for its own transparent dome, its own sovereignty, using both the peacekeeper (found in the UN, NATO, NGOs) and the militant (found in the KLA—Kosovo Liberation Army—or Ushtria Çlirimtare e Kosovës in Albanian). The tactic is straightforward and twofold: first, abductions and decapitations; then, the building of the parliament. The transition of these spatial reorganizations and architectural politics is punctuated by a curious act: the mutilation of the icons and burning of the frescos with holy images in Serbian Orthodox Churches. In one act of defacement, we see the image is the face of Christ (a cult image) looking into the void as it was scratched out by the passing army. All this in 1999 AD.[27]

These transitions, permutations of a subterranean sovereignty, are also embodied in certain individuals: for instance, Hashim Thaçi, a prime minister of the Republic of Kosovo and the leader of the Democratic Party of Kosovo. A man with a BA degree in philosophy and history from the University of Priština and an MA degree in International Relations from the University of Zurich. Also, a former leader of the Kosovo Liberation Army, with the *nom de guerre* "Gjarpëri" (the Snake): an animal that sheds its skin, emerges anew from the interior space of its own conflict—an animal of the underground chambers and holes, rising up. A figure both ancient and new: a warrior-democrat.

4

The Movement of the Black Stone

Balkan pragmatics

A marginal religious tradition, a heretical one, appeared in Bosnia with the founding of the Bosnian church in the thirteenth century. The traces of it are visible primarily on tombstones scattered around the nation's landscape. These tombstones are monuments to the early fusion of Christian and Islamic teachings; but they also point to a specific experience of the stone, its potential as a theopolitical space and poetic liberation.

This thinking through the marginal, cryptic amalgamation is a distinctively Balkan approach to the stone. Bosnian poet Mehmedalija "Mak" Dizdar is famous for his writings influenced by medieval tombstones with esoteric inscriptions and drawings. He extracts the power of their esoteric lines and brings them into the contemporary political space (that of former communist Yugoslavia, but also now into neoliberal Bosnia). More importantly, he extracts the poetry from the stone. Not every stone is the same, and such so-called *stećci* (the medieval tombstones) are already imbued with the vitality of their own. Dizdar excavates this vitality (poetry is merely the means) from the inanimate, where the stone becomes an event at the crossroads of the historical (with precise dates of their erection), the heretical (with the effects of their original purpose), and the eternal (with the goal that surpasses their context). In Bosnia, one is captured by the prevalence of stone. Houses, bridges, tombs were all erected out of local stones. The stone is the first principle, the foundation, of the house and, by extension, of the city; it provides form to the built environment and to the collectivity of thought that conceives it.

Hence, there is a "pragmatism of Balkan Islam"[1] that is imbued with the properties of the stone (esoteric and banal): the heaviness, the durability, the hardness, the impenetrability, where thought and action fall like a rock, quickly and heavy-handed. Dizdar is the master carver, a "scholar-poet"[2] who elevates the stones so as to reveal what lies beneath them (often a figure with a raised hand). He is thus an utterly Bosnian thinker but also universally heretical; or better yet, his interest lies in, what was considered centuries ago, the radical, the fanatical strands of poetic imaginary carved into the stones around him. (There is a sensitivity here for radicality that is relevant for the project of hostage taking.) In other words, he provides a minor (as opposed to major) understanding of the powers of the stone. In unraveling and engaging with the cryptic lines captured on the tombstones, he both clarifies them and makes them more perplexing, more stone-like:

But now in the stone's heart these tired hands are living on alone.[3]

In the stone's heart, the living fleshness of the stone, the hands find their way of living, their energy and survival. There is a dismemberment of the body and an implementation of force to singular parts (the solitary hands).

The stone is a "radical" fragment of the message of God, a surface on which the messages are inscribed. (The hostage taker is a "stone" in the same vein, a fragment of radicality, a carrier of the message.) The message in turn has its own geological intention, so to speak, and the stone makes the message material. With this Balkan sensibility, and Dizdar's take on these objects, I approach the stone of all stones: the black stone in Mecca. I approach it with the tactical naivete of a "scholar-poet" in order to address its materiality and its configuration as a hostage space—this time not to see what or who sleeps under it but rather what veils it.

Circling thoughts

The power of the object could be measured by a series of powers: its capacity to move things (people, animals, ideas, beliefs, philosophies, etc.), the power it contains to initiate (ritual) practices and everyday habits, the power it contains to motivate the body, and the power it contains to do all this without even moving an inch. The Ka'ba and the black stone within it have exactly this power. And more than this: the prayer exits the mouths of the believers and moves toward Mecca. Thus the Ka'ba is like a large mouth that swallows millions of prayers, absorbs them and therefore affirms them. We should say from the start that the stone does not create desire for prayer, or that it is a source of the prayer. Rather, it provides prayer's directionality. More prosaically: it is said that prayers are directed toward the same destination in order to confirm the unity and oneness of God (all lines are streamed into one place).

The black stone of the Ka'ba is the gravitational core of the prophet's message. The message, that operates and congeals itself as an object, draws a pilgrim— one who traverses foreign territories and hence constitutes the very first figure of a foreigner. In this event, we can see clearly the threefold movement of phantom territoriality: pilgrim—hostage space—Ka'ba. In light of this, the greatest gravitational force in the solar system for Muslims is not the sun but the black stone. The stone, the center of the world, dark yet illuminating like a midnight sun.

The Ka'ba: the ancient stone building toward which the body folds in prayer. The black stone: a stone that presumably fell to earth during the time of Adam and Eve, at the dawn of humanity, a stone that works as a catalyzer of sins on earth.[4] The stone absorbs the sins and turns its original whiteness into black discoloration. A planet of its own, the black sun, around which multitudes of men and women swirl in endless rounds, getting closer and closer to it.[5]

The Ka'ba itself looks like a massive box wrapped in a glorious cloth. The cloth is always there (even though it is carefully replaced yearly). In other words, the Ka'ba is never unwrapped, it is never naked. It operates as a veiled body. The aspect of never being fully revealed is one of the most important characteristics of the object itself and of the experience it generates for believers.

The politics of this gravitation are well known: one first belongs to the family and then, through concentric circles, to the tribe (e.g. the Quraysh tribe that was in charge of the Ka'ba until Mecca fell into Muhammad's hands, who himself is part of the Banu Hashim clan which belonged to the Quraysh), to the ethnic group, to the nation. It is this circularity of belonging that permeates every religious and political conflict. The territoriality of belonging starts with these genealogies, but the stone then coalesces these affiliations and superimposes itself as an all-encompassing chamber. (That is why the orphan, the deserter, the vagabond, and the nomad always remain figures of contestation positioned on the fringe of society, since their bond with the major gravitational source is hard to determine, but are endowed special focus in Islamic narratives given the compensatory power of the black stone to include all visitors.)

For the militant to emerge, the hostage space of the Ka'ba only needs to be intensified in order to maximize the sense of one's belonging; this alone is enough for political injustice to be seen as redeemable only by the act of hostage taking. From the perspective of this kind of militant, hostage taking is a theo-medical act that is meant to alleviate the social and political aspects of sin (the insulting of the law).

In the same respect, everything related to hostage spaces has to do with gravity. A crystallized definition of hostage space is this: the gravity of the theopolitical. Taking hostage is the implementation of a gravitational pull on the other; the hostage cannot "leave" the space, he has to remain in the orbit of the hostage taker. This is also a miniature model of the gravitational aspect present in all theological formations. Every icon, every statue, every image, every incantation, contains its own degree of a gravitational pull, a different degree of theological physics. The black stone was itself abducted in the tenth century and then given back, thrown into the Friday Mosque of Kufa, wrapped in a sack. It has been a source of abductions throughout history, just as it is itself an object that abducts.[6]

The Ka'ba operates according to a single rule—the law of God—the logic of an enclosed world in which human beings (and indeed the entirety of creation) move in the direction of a being-toward-hostage. This is its ontological function. But on the other hand, the Ka'ba is an object, an object-ontology, that is open to the infinity of worlds—namely, to all races, classes, nationalities, languages, ethnicities, and genders. That is its cosmological function.[7] From all of these "worlds" though, the one relying on gender is the most complicated, since the construction of the Ka'ba itself relates to the narrative of the initial relationship between Eve and Adam. It is in fact questionable if the power of the object, of the Ka'ba as the force of attraction, would even exist if it were not for the Eve/Adam narrative, and by extension for the problematic dimension of gender relations.

The formation of an orbit. We see this in a literal sense during the hajj pilgrimage when believers, mostly men, circle around the static object in the middle, the aforementioned black sun. The square of the Sacred Mosque exceeds its function of the public space and turns into a galaxy, with different vectors of movement corresponding to each body. More precisely, the orbit of the Ka'ba corresponds to the question of human nature, that is to its goodness (acting in accordance with the law) and evil (acting in discordance with the law). The entire gravitational pull of the Ka'ba is there to attract the negative aspects of human actions. This conception of the human being, from the perspective of circumambulation, will be "decisive for the presupposition of every further political consideration, the answer to the question of whether man is a dangerous being or not, a risky or harmless creature."[8] The Ka'ba, in fact, already answers this anthropological question and sides with the essentially dangerous nature that the being-toward-hostage inhabits, hence its role as the cosmic catalyzer of all the dangerous acts inflicted by the human.

The Ka'ba encapsulates a cosmology of the object whose force imposes a restraint on one's passions (those that would lead to sin) by ecstatically engaging the Ka'ba itself in a circumambulatory frenzy which necessitates that the passion be given as a gift to the stone which absorbs it. The Kaʻba is a force of extreme proximity, body to body; a force of immanence and fragmentation at the same time. All distancing is precluded here. In other words, the participant is not allowed to create a gulf between herself and her acts, herself and others, herself and the sacred. And while there is certainly a major difference between being close to the other in one's own community (as in pilgrimage) and forcibly being enclosed with strangers (as in hostage taking), both are situations that deal with the issue of the negation of distance (the former by voluntary engagement with the other, the latter by enforced proximity). In this light, the hostage taking itself can be seen as a form of deadly pilgrimage.

The Kaʻba is the epicenter. It means that the force of the black stone cancels the geographical demarcations of the West and the East, of the South and the North. There are no lines of separation in its orbit, just as there are no geographical points in a spiral. The Kaʻba is, in this sense, properly cosmological and one of the few material manifestations of the cosmo-political (this time without any ties to a megalopolis); the black stone speaks to the cosmo-political aspect of the geological world, for even geology is impregnated with the theological. But if we say that the black stone is a geopolitical epicenter—that is, a geographical point that exerts precise political influence—then we can also say that the stone is the epicenter of power. The black stone forms its own biopolitical frequency, the implementation of power that both liberates and subjugates, and in which the hostage space is nourished.

The Kaʻba cancels out all animosity, at least within its immediate sphere of swirling bodies, because it cancels out all otherness. Such is the movement of the black stone. And if there is an inherent danger in the process that leads to unification of the bodies through the implementation of the principle of One (one valorized point in a geographical location, one law, one God, etc.), there is at the same time a magnificent cancellation of the catastrophic history of humankind (one based on the friend/enemy distinction).

Carl Schmitt reads Hegel without the consciousness of the Kaʻba but his reading proves a crucial point: "The enemy is a negated otherness. But this negation is mutual and this mutuality of negations has its own concrete existence, as a relation between enemies; this relation of two nothingnesses on both sides bears the danger of war." In contrast to this, the Kaʻba is absolute positivity, not only in the sense of the proliferation of friendship (no one is "other" within the swirling orbit) but of bodily proximity that necessarily leads to ecstasy (by circling the Kaʻba seven times no matter what the body feels), which in turn leads to the exigencies of the inhuman (going beyond the form of the human).

What occurs here is a cancellation of the negation. This relates to the fact that sin could be perceived as an act of negation, from the negation of freedom to the negation of otherness.

The Ka'ba is a cube, the essential geometrical form of a dwelling-space, the cube that is the most sacred destination in the contemporary Islamic landscape, a cosmological and thus atemporal site despite its long history. The site of unification, not only of all Muslims but of all humans, for the origins of the Ka'ba are the origins of the human being herself. The doors of the Ka'ba are made of pure gold weighing 300 kilograms and they rarely open to permit a view of the inside.[9] For millions, there is only the outside of the veil and the encapsulated, partially visible fragment of the black stone. There is only the outside, that of the massive movement of bodies, which is in a way the extension of the stone and the Ka'ba itself, such that all the pilgrims are further veilings of the stone. And what is behind the stone? Nothing. Only direction and cosmic climatology. A compass to God.

This is why it is correct to say that pilgrims do not worship the stone (evading idolatry); they enter its climate (the climate of the divine, of which the climate of the earth is only a small fragment). The entire genius of veiling is in fact corresponding to this fact of climatology, playing both into the physical atmospherics of the desert, the heat, the degrees of temperature, and to the energetics of the cosmic climate; at one and the same time, the veil is a protection and intensification. Protection against the elements (winds, rain, sun) and protection from the affective powers of the erotic (in the case of veiled women), pridefulness, lack of humility, etc.[10] The creation is therefore: a whirlwind, concentric circles, void filled with spiraling. In speculating on creation, one could say that this fullness of the void corresponds to affects of love, hatred, despair, honor, sinfulness, and so on. These also correspond to the divine law that becomes the very manifestation of the concept of the political.

The environment surrounding the Ka'ba is thus a type of intertidal system, with ebbs and flows of individuals moving to and fro. How does this extend to the movement of the law? The half-moon adorns each mosque, each scripture, each word, and therefore, in a way, speaks of the law. It is through the luminosity of the crescent moon (whose surface is made of dark stone) that Islamic law comes to light.

Its four corners correspond to the cardinal points of a compass. In fact, the Ka'ba is the theological compass of Islam toward which all the bodies of believers point, like needles inside a regular compass. The cube thus fulfills the only acceptable directionality of the profession of faith, of the words uttered in prayer, which would otherwise be lost in the winds of idle chatter of the world. Even the folding of the body could be seen as a projection, giving speed to the words, the precision of their movement, in order to reach their destination intact. The destination: the cube (which beckons toward the concept of divinity). But there should be no mistake. Saudi Arabia of the twenty-first-century CE is not the Mesopotamia of the seventh-century BCE. Namely, there is one crucial difference: that of representational thinking. The objects and images of today are representations of God, not embodiments. The Ka'ba is thus only an object that points toward the mystery.

But what does it mean for an object to only point toward an absolute mystery (without embodying it)? In Dizdar's approach to tombstones, in the poetics of his engagement with the stones, the objects, images, and landscapes are anthropomorphized. This is not to take away from the physical properties of the image or of the site nor from their sacred character. Rather, this is to introduce an element of literalism (i.e. being strict, simple, exact) as opposed to that of the symbolic or metaphorical interpretation. This is a Dizdarian gesture of Balkan pragmatics. And the goal for this is simple: to transform experiences into intensities and reorient the discussion to the intensive plane rather than the purely interpretative (or textual) one.[11]

Outside of the discussion of textualism, the life (vitalism, experience, intensity) of the black stone can be addressed in seven analytical manifestations: Historical (arrival, treatment throughout the ages, what it has "seen," for example the faces and events); Geological (the geological properties of its materiality, mineral history, and esoteric climatology); Secretive (the concealment of its powers, its origins, and its destiny); Theological (its functionality as the absorber of sins and the catalyst of human nature, as well as that of the corrupt state of the world); Political (the violence and mercy it elicits); Aesthetic (the beauty of its concealment and that of the orbit of movement/dance it elicits); and Physical (the gravitational aspects of its immobile being).

Adam

According to the tradition, the Ka'ba is the first mosque in the world built by Abraham in 2150 BCE. Another story says that it was actually only reconstructed by Abraham, while it was initially built by Adam himself. It is therefore a first house, a first mark of dwelling, the introduction of human-built interior architecture. A house that introduces consciousness that the outside world is dangerous, the first sacred site (outside of the garden, but also its theopolitical instantiation) that allows for some continued communication with God. The Ka'ba: first mosque—first house—first sacred dwelling room. This dwelling, then, is in many ways not only formed by the first humans but also generates the formation of the human form itself (the clear distinction between Adam's body and the rest of the world), and other forms and distinctions that followed, including those of animal and plant, domestic and wild, family and stranger, etc. Adam in his nakedness (only the mad or the savage roam around naked) and the lack of differentiations that ruled before the fall (of what is good and evil, for example) is certainly more schizophrenic than the form of the human that arrives after him, a form that needs to be veiled.

It is impossible to ignore the presumed temporality of the stone, which has a veiled origin but is eternal, as represented by the figures of Adam and Eve since they are the only temporal (and mythical) demarcations of its arrival. The relationship of Adam and Eve further initiates the appearance of another atemporal affect, that of sin, an act that violates a rule. It is an act that puts one into the sphere of evil and illegality, an act that performs the forbidden. Let us consider one understanding of sin that sees it as tied to the act performed rather than one's state of being; against this backdrop, it is acting-in-the-world that creates sin, acting which does not conform to the commands of God.

Adam and Eve, on whose bodies sin first makes its appearance, were the very first hostages (of God), that is to say, of the law. Being-hostage is thus at the core of being-human. It is in fact at the core of biopotential, at the core of everything that contains potential for life, since one exists as a being-on-the-lookout. One is on the lookout because being-hostage is at the heart of human experience. And to respond to the law is to respond to the call of hostaging. This indeed is the very first instance of biopolitics, or the administration of the law, of what is "good" for one's body and what is "poisonous" for one's social being. It is also the first rebellion against it (eating the poison, that which will destroy the divine health of the human condition). The scene in paradise is thus the very first invocation of illness where the poison of the fruit (or wheat, camphor, etc.) reflects the interiorization of sin. Illness, or sin, becomes an existential mode through the act of ingesting the fruit. Here the law elicits its own breaking, enjoying the deception of its own immutability.

Adam's relationship to the world, to creation as such, is thus determined by his alignment to the law and to the breaking of that alignment. It is the sense of belonging that turns him into a moral being, deserving of divine mercy. Consequently, rejection of that alignment is what makes him an outlaw or a sinner. Is it by coincidence that the material object that is used to "repair" this relationship to the law (alleviate the sins) is the stone itself (hard, durable, immoveable in its substance)?

The role of Eve (or of a woman) is more complicated and devastating. Eve provokes the act of sinning, the act of deviation from the law and, as a result, has the capacity to induce a break with the original alignment, and in turn can diminish the gravitational pull that law produces.

The practice of veiling women can be related to this supposed socio-sexual propensity of the woman (Eve) to induce deviation from the law, a desire that unleashes movement contrary to the scales of judgment. It is in this sense that women's bodies are concealed so as to restrain men from sinning. This is at least one aspect of the veiling (the aspect of "humility," submission of desire). Of course, veiling also anticipates unveiling, unfolding, unwrapping, which is related to the experience of the erotic, or a sense of surprise that elicits attraction. The veil is nothing but the permanent promise of the surprise. The backstory of Eve is therefore primarily one of veiling; to be in the world after the fall is to be veiled, not because of sin but because of modesty and, potentially, necessary separation from the divine.

The black stone is, in this narrative, a great helper of humanity since it absorbs the sins of the world, it absorbs all the wrongdoings one has committed. It absorbs on behalf of humankind, and thus serves as a gift of the inanimate that collects passions without being affected by them (except for the discoloration). It turns black so that the hearts of humankind do not have to turn black. It is a concentration of passions that becomes a void, a zero-degree of sin. In order for the absorption to occur, a whirlwind is needed; hence the intensive spiraling of the crowd, perfect circumambulations where the individual loses himself, becomes part of the intensive gravitational pull and yet at the same time faces toward the stone and is irresistibly attracted by it. The desire intrinsic to this movement is uni-directional: to touch, to kiss the indented opening of the Ka'ba where the stone protrudes with a frame made of silver.

Relic

If the gate of the word is just a dream a fairytale
Still I will not leave this door
Here I want to live once more
This supreme
Dream.[12]

To live inside of an image, or a word, as if it were a house, with a particular gate, is the enigma posed by the presence of the Ka'ba. The word lingers and remains, having a life of its own. It becomes a gate, a fairytale, a dream (not of a distanced imaginary beyond, but of an invoked dwelling).

The Ka'ba as a relic. It is a site/building/house that remains. It is a remainder that extends itself to the future, a form of consolation and alleviation of present suffering, a medico-theological device that "heals" nations and races from the negative application of their nature, from their sin (a psycho-theological syndrome).

The relic, even as a dream, has an intimate relationship to the state since it is always under its institutional protection. The Saudi state, for example, protects the Ka'ba as one would the body of a divine citizen. The relic has its rights, which it also surpasses since it is the embodiment of the law and participates directly in the mystery that is behind the law. The relic is a proof that all can be submitted to the mercy/rage/love of God, that the perfect believer is always a hostage of the law (even if that is the law of mercy and peace). And still, it is only the refusal to surrender that is ever experienced as a subjective crisis, as the burden of an unfulfilled freedom.

Karl Marx had a similar intuition when he said that religion is the opium of the masses. Nevertheless, he put this dependency on submission to the divine law purely in negative terms, turning believers into an ignorant formation. In any case, the gravitational effects are not only economic or ideological but also physical and affective; effects that are not only tied to an objective epistemology of the secular state but also to the ways in which this epistemology is tied to the esoteric influence of daily practices and mythical narratives.

The relic should be viewed as a body; in fact, it is a special type of body-thing which, by its very nature, participates in spheres of both the human and the divine. Moreover, it is a fragment of the divine-human body. For this reason, the actual body parts of saints throughout history are revered as relics. It is by the law of contagion (the rule of being touched) that the relic assumes its power. As such, the piece of clothing that touched the body of the saint or of the prophet has to be considered sacred as well. When touching the black stone, one also touches the divine energy contained within it.

The relic is further fragmented into an amulet, a miniaturized form of the relic. A name of a person is also a relic in this sense; for example, the name of a prophet, or a martyr, or a loved one. (The names of those that have passed away, for example, evoke a range of feelings, those of love and hatred, loyalty or enmity. The names of historical martyrs are thus brought into the present with full force simply by invoking their names.) The relic contains a certain necro-vitality that makes the object alive. The amulet or talisman works in a similar way but with a more specific purpose. First of all, it protects. Consequently, it is another form of "veiling," creating a wall against the evil that can be inflicted upon the individual.

Furthermore, Islamic amulets (which can be rings, tablets, cloths, blades, scrolls) have their surfaces inscribed with scriptures. Besides the names of God, sayings of Muhammad, and Qur'anic verses, a common apotropaic sign is that of the prophet Solomon's seal, that is a hexagram (a six-pointed star). Apotropaic magic is used to deflect or turn away the harm that is sent toward the victim. Sometimes just the inscription is enough. (E.g. in an account of a counterinsurgency missions in 2009 in and around Mosul, Iraq, we see the image of apotropaic magic at work among the US soldiers: on the windshield of a Humvee, a verse from the book of Job is inscribed in order to protect the vehicle from the grenades of the insurgents.)[13] The inscription also operates as a house of sorts that protects the object or a relic or a person. A house within a house, protection within protection.

The Ka'ba is rejuvenated daily by the millions of prayers streamed its way (the metaphysical aspect of rejuvenation), and then once a year by the changing of its garment, or of the veil, that is the cloth (the physical rejuvenation), and then by the movement of the bodies and the touching of its surface during hajj (its amorous rejuvenation). But if the Ka'ba is indeed a relic, it is a climatological one, as much as it is properly Islamic or religious. In other words, it sets up the atmosphere of submission, unification, joy, ecstasy, and movement of the bodies that resembles the movement of the whirlwind, as the bodies surrounding the Ka'ba create a vortex of air. In this sense, the black stone is still in its meteoric passage. If one looks at the swirl of the pilgrims from above, it looks as if the entire Ka'ba is moving, as if the black stone is still pushing through space. It is the pilgrims that give immobile movement (static in its presence, moving in the effects it produces in the pilgrims) to the stone, just as the stone gives them energy to move (to arrive from all the corners of the earth). The black stone is thus initiating constant departures (the essential experience of "exiting" by the hostage taker mentioned in the preceding chapter), operating as a vortex of forces, bringing one closer to the will and affects of God.

From this perspective, the Ka'ba is a site of peace precisely because of its inclusivity (of course, only if one belongs to the Muslim cosmology, but this cosmology is open to all to submit themselves). And even though it benefits from being in a geographical location that is safe and affirmative of its presence, one could still argue that the stone by its very nature (emerging in the sphere of Adam and Eve) cancels out violence. It is only when it is appropriated by nation-states, turned into an image of the crescent on the flags, that it assumes an antagonistic character. It is not by coincidence that the most potent images of the crescent in the history of Islam emerge alongside the most powerful empires: the Ottomans and the Mughals. It is also significant that the black stone is superior to any image of the crescent; that is to say, the unformed (the unclear form and the concealed shape) of the black stone is closer to the perception of the sacred than any geometric shape such as the crescent.

Dizdar writes of the moon:

> Carve his sign in the soft white of limestone
> So you may absorb as faithfully as can be
> The image of your infinite pain and hope.[14]

The moon has to be inscribed onto the stone, as an expression of affects that run through the poet. Without this image, the sense of pain and hope would remain enclosed, invisible, and perhaps nonexistent. From the sky, the atmospherics of the moon transpire and settle into the stone, remaining there forever.

The primordial character of the stone and its formlessness also speak to its importance as an intensity of the enduring and eternal form, not tied to the symbolics of any particular state. This is also why the Ka'ba and the black stone should be viewed as relics which are radically different intensifications of the theopolitical than any other symbol or representation.

Reza Negarestani invokes a study on relics (probably a fictional account) in his "Notes on Reliquology" in order to say that "the charm of the relics as 'outsiders' precisely originates from their autochthonic characteristics, the oscillation between the domestic and the foreign packed into one object."[15] The black stone, however, is the absolute outsider; it is the most allochthonous of all materials since it is extra-planetary, arriving as a composition of another celestial body. It is a relic that becomes a charm because of its original deterritorialization (being, presumably, a fragment of a meteorite). But in order to become a relic, it has to reterritorialize, and the absolute outsider then turns into a machine of territorialization: bringing tribes, ethnicities, and races together into its gravitational field, healing the otherness of the others. That is its paradox, one that follows all instances of reterritorialization. Through a great process of domestication, which consists in turning the historical and social climates to its favor, eliciting the affective powers of the people, and setting a precise and immoveable geopolitical coordinate of its "home" (consisting of the layers or veils manifested in the protective nation, the Sacred Mosque, the Ka'ba), the black stone becomes a relic and a site of sacred affinities.

At the same time, and in this Negarestani is correct, the relic retains its "foreignness"; a foreignness that makes it a stranger to the earth but not to the cosmic laws of God. Being from elsewhere, the relic conveys to the believers their own distance, estrangement, and foreignness with respect to the actual divine plane. In this way, it reminds the onlookers that they are from the wrong place, that the earth itself is a displacement. In other words, the black stone is dislocated from the present world of politics just enough to remain an object which can never be rendered banal (it can never be just a stone). In a similar fashion, while it is precisely positioned in terms of geographic location (coordinates 21°25′21.15″N 39°49′34.1″E), it is also an extra-geographic site, focused on the movement it necessitates from the people, ultimately being positioned on the ethereal geography of sin, the geography of Adam and Eve, the geography of origins, rather than that of the Arabian peninsula. Through its particular intimations of the foreign, it attracts in order to envelop, expiate, and protect. (Even things can attract through their charm, that is, their seductiveness, appeal, magnetism, and charisma.) The drawing power of the relic is therefore its semi-open secrecy which fascinates those who face the object-secret, the black stone, in prayer.

Veiling

Gods reveal themselves in objects, in the speech of the prophets, which means that they have initially been veiled from the everyday or from humanity. This is the case in both pre-Islamic thought and in contemporary Bosnian Islam. God is pointed toward, gestured at, and it is the veil that stands as the testament of "his" occluded power. At the core of believing, there is the issue of the veil.

The black stone itself is veiled. Even the body of the relic has to be veiled, as if any relationship with the cosmic sphere has to have a proper separation. A veil, however, is not an ordinary wall; a veil can unveil as quickly as it can cover up. That is its superiority and its elementary magic: it closes and discloses, in rapid fluctuations. The role of concealment (this includes the veiling of a woman too, which makes her into a sacred relic) is a straightforward one: to disclose the body is to be vulnerable, to be too open to the world that is permeated by temptation (from sexual desire to the desire for domination). Veiling is therefore a form of immunological protection.

There is more. The Ka'ba covers the stone, and the Kiswah veils the Ka'ba. The Kiswah: a type of pall, a cloth or a drape also used to cover caskets, made out of black silk with golden threads used for the embroidery of Qur'anic verses. It is kept for a year, after which it is removed from the Ka'ba, cut into pieces and distributed to pilgrims. As is usual with veiling, there are layers through which one passes in order to reach the core, which in this case is the black stone. But what is the core of the black stone? We should recall here the famous formula of Elias Cannetti: at the core of power lies secrecy.[16] The geological merges with the immateriality of secrecy (that which is unknown but constantly leaks). In a way, the stone is an absolute manifestation of the secret, of its concreteness, without losing its magicality, or of its esoteric powers that are at the heart of the theopolitical. Whatever is at the core, it is concealed. The Kiswah itself is the skin of the secret and, quite possibly, the only content that secret contains (i.e. the secret is without content except for its surface, its skin). For this reason, veiling is an interplay of surfaces.

Heidegger advances this conversation by way of the following excerpt: "The uncovering of anything new is never done on the basis of having something completely hidden, but it takes its departure rather from uncoveredness in the mode of semblance. Entities look as if . . . That is, they have, in a certain way, been uncovered already, and yet they are still disguised."[17] The secret is never absolutely closed; it is, rather, always partially cracked. The Kiswah is there to magnify the opening corner where the black stone protrudes from the cube. For, even when uncovered, the black stone is still under the mark of concealment, always on the border between uncoveredness and concealment.

In light of this, how horrible and indecent would it be to display the stone "nakedly," in its bare unformedness, as if in a museum? This would turn it into an art object instead of a relic that brims with vitality. There is a "semblance," not in the sense of guise or pretense but as an actual façade of the secret. The Kiswah is that which covers the secret and it is only a façade, a protection of decency (the ethics of secrecy) that prevents its defacement (full disclosure) that would ruin its potency. The veil is the façade through which the secret communicates with the world. It is also a site through which the secret welcomes the other, the outsider. In fact, only by learning how to navigate within the phenomenon of veiling can one be a part of Islamic inclusivity, or umma (i.e. community, derived from *umm*, "mother").

A passage from Heidegger stands out again: "Truth (uncoveredness) is something that must always first be wrested from entities. Entities get snatched out of their hiddenness. The factical uncoveredness of anything is always, as it were, a kind of robbery."[18] The extrication of truth from a secret is a form of "robbery," a forced hostaging, something that must be violently divested. The factical coveredness, one could say, of the Ka'ba testifies to the effectiveness of the object-site (an "entity" in Heidegger's terminology), because the pilgrim, believer, and sometimes a militant too, does not divest but touches and kisses, respecting the surface of the secret and its frequencies of the gravitational pull. The concern of the poet such as Dizdar, however, is not that of the truth or untruth but rather of health and sickness, where the tombstones of Bosnia, just as the relic, operate as a form of theopolitical pharmacology.

The Charm

Furthermore, the words that are offered to the black stone assume magical powers, becoming incantations of reality (which corresponds to a form of healing by the process of submitting oneself to the word) through which existence itself becomes an incantation. This is how the entire world is conjured, for the origin of all charms is the incantation. The murmur of the spiraling crowd around the Ka'ba both reveals and conceals, for it is the murmur that unites not anymore in prayer but in that which is unsaid (the unformedness of the murmur) in the black stone.

The charms of the prophets, their charisma, stem from the same process of becoming a relic, by simultaneously deterritorializing and territorializing themselves into an intimate sphere of the other. This is also the negative charm of the hostage taker who imposes all of these characteristics upon the hostages (he can in fact be without charm, for he wins over the other by the threat of the explosive or of the knife).

Negarestani continues: "If the Outsider is manifested in the persistence of its exteriority and invasiveness, then its advent should not be anticipated from the outside as that which is external to the boundaries, but from the inside, as that which has already invaded the system and now resides within the boundary."[19] The aspect of the outsider which draws in or, in a way, is already positioned inside the boundaries that separate the inside and the outside is crucial here. The black stone, just as a hostage space is the phenomenon that exists on the boundary between the inside and the outside. Demarcations such as friend/enemy, domestic/wild, patriotic/traitorous, sacred/profane, earthly/outlandish are all related to the general problem of the inside and the outside. In fact, the black stone defines the boundaries, sets up geographies of belonging, and determines who is the insider and who is the outsider through conductions of passage and recitation. The closer one gets to its physical being (by pointing with the arm, by gazing, by touching, and finally by kissing it), the more one enters into its folds, both earthly and cosmic. Every Muslim is encouraged to perform the great pilgrimage of hajj at least once in her life. This is the process of healing (alleviation of sin) that is required and which makes the believer inhabit the boundary of the relic and thus intensify her own charm, her own powers of attraction.

Touching

The greatest moment marking the gradual movement toward the black stone, from any corner of the earth, is the moment of touching it, something few get to do (only those that are able to swim out from the whirlpool of the swirling multitude). Why is touching the stone important? First, touch is a form of sensuous communication. Second, it is a transformative event which can affect one's very nature. The old theory of sympathetic magic developed by James Frazer is still relevant here. Frazer argues that there are two laws which govern sympathetic magic, or the law of sympathy: (a) the law of similarity, where "like produces like" and (b) the law of contact or contagion. The former means that by imitating we become the very thing we imitate; the latter means that by contact we become contaminated by the touched substance which continues to have effect even when we are separated from it.[20] The black stone thus exerts the sympathy of the divine (its care and affinity) through contamination, or else by taking upon itself the contamination of sin that comes from the person who touches it. Through touching the stone, one's aura is increased as it would be when one comes closer to the core of the secret; the body of the pilgrim expands, as the black stone increases its sphere of influence by enlarging one's own territory.

The smoothness of the surface. The black stone is a celestial body. It exerts a desire on behalf of the believers to touch it by its extraordinary origins (a stone from Heaven) and by its extra-terrestrial arrival (outsider, outlandish, and yet unifying). It is both physical, with its own crevices and imperfections, and metaphysical, with its own theoretical concepts. But more importantly, it is delineated, it has physical boundaries and size (12 inches in diameter) which allows it to be touched; in other words, it is not closed in on itself. Rather, it opens up its influence and initiates the movement of other bodies. Its primary relation, or influence, is thus with the outside.

The stone breathes affects into the bodies of the pilgrims that overcome them; by being touched, it implements joy, ardor, fortitude, the powers that animate the pilgrim and also surpass his "carnal envelope" (as Jean-Pierre Vernant would say).[21] But the body of the black stone does not shine or exhibit any splendor besides the silver frame which keeps it secure. It affects the bodies through its discoloration, through its atemporality, and through its gravitational pull that asks for a gesture of friendship, an individual touch. It is the body of the veil that is not closed up, and is hence the opposite of the state, a body that has no borders. Once again, this is the paradoxical nature of the black stone and its effectiveness in taking hostage, or overcoming, the bodies that willfully submit themselves to it.

The ritual of circumambulation (seven times) has its intensified ending, then: to touch the black stone with one's hand or with one's lips. The movement of the stone is therefore sensuous as much as it is ideological or theological. In the end, it is the touch that heals, just as it is the celestial body that overtakes the earthly one. The entire problem of the hostage space (overtaking of the space/territory of the other) is ultimately a problem of touching.

To be touched by someone or something is to have one's feelings aroused; it is to exhibit gratitude or rage; to touch is to move, to create a movement of humiliation or of encouragement. The prophets, those exemplary humans in the theopolitical landscape, first of all "touch," either with their message or with their hands. In fact, their message is their hands and vice-versa. They work and, in a way, they think with their hands. They let their hands speak. They are "blind," in a sense, like fanatics, touching their way through the space. Dizdar invokes the presence of hands thusly:

> I bore these hands like two banners
>   through fields of living stone.[22]

The way to "see" the inscriptions on the tombstones is with one's hands, with fingers following the enigmatic lines of letters and figures. Similarly, when striving toward the Ka'ba, one moves through the crowd with one's hands, not with one's eyes.

Touching is either a communication (which is already an intimation) or in more impactful fashion, an association, a stronger bond of loyalty, faith, ideology, or thought (one has to be touched, in a way, to become a radical). All rituals, as forms of contamination, necessitate touching, the laying of the hands. The black stone does not touch, it summons to be touched instead. That is its movement without moving. The hostage space par excellence. It invites the murmur and the touch through its veils.

Touch is also a primary sensation having little to do with the intellect (unless we see it as enfolding the intellect), and all sentient beings react to touch with either sympathy or animosity. One befriends the other (animal or human) if touch is accepted.[23] The black stone, as well as the Bosnian tombstone, is an aesthetic and theological entity filled with the capacity to interact (absorb histories/destinies), and hence reacts to touch in a twofold way: by consuming affects and by transforming the one who touches.

In this respect, the black stone is the opposite of the desire that runs through the state. The space around the Ka'ba is neither public nor private but cosmic and so it abnegates the idea of the enemy. In the whirlpool of bodies, where every body is in contact with someone, who can emerge as an outsider? All this is just to say the following: the black stone dissolves the dichotomies, even those that exist within an individual (good and evil acts). It purifies and pacifies; but also moves one further, into the very delirium of air.

Delirium of Air

Theopolitical pharmacy

Besides its ecological significance, the air has medico-political qualities as well. In this respect, political systems could be judged by the quality of breathing that they generate. For example, how can one breathe fully in totalitarianism? The law of the air is not the same as the air of the law. The former is tied to the rules of atmosphere used in breathing and photosynthesis; the latter is tied to the set of environmental or affectual proclivities of the practices of subjugation. Atmospherically speaking, air is composed of layers of gases that change temperature depending on the impact of solar radiation. We are thus already enveloped in a set of transparent veils that protect us from the influence of the sun. We are all thus already in the sphere of political solarity: of veils and protection.

To be precise, I am discussing here specific types of of "air," that is environmental conditions of the theopolitical, that a figure of the militant produces and inside of which she exists. The air of the militant's law. Ideas and individuals alike create and embody a certain aeriality which follows them and in fact composes them (one can perceive the militant as a set of affective and environmental conditions). The confrontation of ideologies therefore occurs first at the level of air. But ideology is not the right word here. Especially since the militant (and in the western imagination, every Muslim) carries a certain geography, a being that is a region already. And since the militant is a region, the battle is thus enacted wherever his body is.[1]

The becoming-region of the militant/terrorist is also a further step in the evolution of the irregular combatant. The telluric partisan was tied to the earth (the forest, the desert, etc.); she did not carry it with her. The terrorist that is a region, on the other hand, carries his regionality with him, not only as the embodiment of an idea but as a set of proclivities which can be prostrated anywhere, even in the air (in the airplane). To be a region, a landscape, makes one more susceptible to delirious perceptions or mirages: hallucinations, apparitions, visions, and the simultaneous absences and presences.

In light of the discussion on militancy, delirium should not be viewed only as a clinical syndrome corresponding to the problems of mentation. Delirium is also a critical state of intensified perceptions, a new form of lucidity based on ecstasy. Etymologically, delirium means "to be deranged," but this is a lexical prejudice that entered scientific and popular vocabulary alike. Further still, and more interestingly, delirium in Latin relates to the term "lira," which means furrow. To be delirious is thus to be outside of the furrow, outside of the dominant trench, rut, or channel. Or in other words, it is to produce another kind of furrow, another kind of inscription of oneself on the surface of the earth, another arrangement and clearing of the garden. This is not to idealize the psychological condition of trembling and derangement that comes with delirium. Rather, the point I am trying to make is that there is a need for a redefinition of the experience of delirium that is not tied to the western psychiatric modeling. This process of redefining necessarily requires extraction of other characteristics of the experience that do not reduce it to a mere psychological symptom. In line with the preceding arguments one could thus say that delirium is in fact a theopolitical syndrome, a form of affliction or illness that liberates as much as it constrains. The trembling of the mystic's religious body and the terrorist's political body, trembling that is a rupture of one's regionality or belonging, is only one manifestation of this intense rearrangement.

Moreover, the entire earth works as a theopolitical pharmacy where the medicine (rules) is administered either by the state institutions or taken (deliriously) on one's own. If all the conflicts emerge from a certain humiliation (and the accompanying rage), then how can we not say that politics is primarily about the health of the people? Politics as an affective appeasement or as provocation of a delirium. Air raids are primarily affective, in that they create physical and mental traumas. Freedom and breathing. Air is therefore a central source of the theopolitical pharmacology. Political and theological confrontation occurs first on the level of the air since the freedom to think, believe, or express oneself depends on breathing without restrictions. When in hiding, when operating in secrecy, one breathes slowly, out of concern for not being discovered. On the other hand, in the affective space of fear one asphyxiates. In terrorism, likewise, when considered as an atmospheric condition, even the air is suffocating. In the war on terror, the psychosomatic disorders that occur on the ground by those that withstand them, in addition to or as part of post-traumatic stress disorders, should be related to this lack of oxygen generated by military occupation. The villages in Bosnia and Kosovo that have been razed to the ground by the passing armies and paramilitaries become identified by the smoke that rises from the burning houses and haystacks in the process of occupation and its aftermath. The smoke is the announcement that the administration of death is in the process of establishing its supremacy. Death is manifested in painting the air black. Similarly, the tear gas thrown by the Israeli army on the Palestinian resistance changes the properties of the air, turns it dense, with miniature lethal clouds that make the state of Israel visible. These small gestures of the transmutation of air correspond to the will of the state, and the very fact that these transmutations arise, that they can arise, speaks to the medico-political properties of both air and the state.

Invisibility

To be both visible and invisible is the nature of the phantom; the interplay of revealing and concealing is the way in which the phantom territory is constructed (whether by a phantom or by the process itself is a cipher for another discussion). The illness of the militant is therefore that of a phantom territoriality; in other words, it is not psychological but regional or spatial.

There are many ways to approach the delirium of air (both delirium and air, and their coupling). In light of this, let us "inhale" the analysis from the perspective of the female-mystic and the male-militant, and their relationship which exhales the problem of Islamic militancy with new transparency. Dealing with this nexus, the Belgian filmmaker Bruno Dumont created an exemplary product of ficto-criticism.[2] In his film *Hadewijch* there are two main characters: a young girl named Hadewijch and a young man named Nassir. Despite the apparent limitation of being characters in a movie, they are also theopolitical figures representative of Christian mysticism and Islamic militancy. Moreover, the story is both contextual and cosmic since Hadewijch (of Brabant) was originally the name of the thirteenth-century Flemish mystic about whom little is known outside of her scattered writings and poetry (this is known: she was not a nun and she was rich). But most importantly, in the film, her affective micro-politics find their way into twenty-first-century Paris. The young girl carries the same air of the medieval mystic (we could call it—the Hadewijchian air) which becomes entangled with the air of the terrorist. But there is no good and evil in this story, only the air of Nassir and Hadewijch against the dominant air of the world, that is the western air. It is in their "economic" engagement with life, with pure intensity established on a few gestures, a few words, yet with capacity to encompass the world, that they encounter each other's humility.

Dumont shows this life of minor suffocations of the everyday with clear precision: a girl from a convent converts to Islam. How? The passageways of the divine are also banal. The meetings of the Islamic study group occur in the backroom of a cheap restaurant in an immigrant neighborhood, in one of the urban projects of Paris. The neighborhood is itself already a form of phantom territoriality for most Parisians of French descent, and thus operates as a hostage space in which are embedded multiple other hostage spaces. The local religious leader, a young and charismatic man (Nassir), teaches a specific lesson of the day: a Sura from the Qur'an that addresses the invisibility of God, his simultaneous presence and absence. It is an enviably eloquent, lapidary, and philosophical exposition. In reading and hearing Sura 72, verses 26 to 27, we actually see the instantiation and intimation of the very first phantom territoriality, which is the concurrent disclosure and hiddenness of God. It is God himself who is a phantom (invisible) and a territory (of love and the law). Nassir takes language in the direction of a deconstructive turn (and perhaps proves that the hermeneutics of deconstruction are always theological) when he says, "God is present in his absence; he is most manifest when he withdraws . . ." The important aspect of this divine invisibility, then, is its intertidal movement, arrival and withdrawal, the to and fro of the divine will. Or, in other words, the hostage space overtakes in order to liberate. It is important to note that the hostage space of course is not only tied to the political acts of hostage taking (and the war on terror) but also to the essential experiences of the divine (absolute sovereignty), the political (the secular law), and the architectural (the inside/outside).

The theological and political contexts of different centuries have changed but the humility of fanaticism, also its ecstasy and love, remains the same, as it is a part of both the individual and social desire. The coupling of, on the one hand, incredible humility and, on the other, extreme regimentality and discipline found in religious orders and in militant affects needs to be further analyzed. (If politics are about temperament, one cannot have a clear picture of what liberal democracy is, or will be, without the analysis of the so-called extremes that formed affective communities, religious and secular, throughout the centuries in both the East and the West.) Hence, Hadewijch in Paris is ravished as she suffers and exalts the invisibility of God and sides with the act that will bring her closer to him: extreme violence, or, in political terminology—terrorism.

The problem of terrorism and the construction of the hostage space is not one of delusion (e.g. being manipulated or tricked by the fascination with violence). Hadewijch, Nassir, and the Islamic militants all have a clear vision of the world that is actually not as mystical as it might seem in the beginning, for such mysticism is always precluded by the concurrent maxim of social justice: we as people are humiliated. Coincidently, this humiliation comes from the air through two major experiences: first, the xenophobic air of Paris toward Muslims and, second, the bombings of the western inflection throughout the Middle East. Hence, the decision of Hadewijch to participate in a Paris subway bombing in Dumont's story comes after Nassir drives her through an undisclosed Middle Eastern neighborhood in the aftermath of an air raid. It is this humiliation from the air that turns her into an armed militant. And is there a greater kind of delirium than that of the rain of bombs falling from the sky? The air raid is not only a political confrontation after negotiations have failed. It is a tool in the theopolitical pharmacy of the West. It produces clinical, existential, economic, and theological effects that necessitate specific procedures of repair. And, in contemporary times, the West has a range of repairs already set in conjunction with the raids; these are called humanitarian actions, from the rebuilding of destroyed cities to the psychiatric treatment of victims.[3] The delirium is produced and then subdued. And those that reject this coupling of violence with humanism run the risk of being viewed as terrorists.

It would be too simplistic to quickly equate a metaphysical militarism with the terrorism on the ground. One is chosen to be a militant, so to speak, when one is ravished, seized and carried off: that is, taken hostage by the lover or by the assassin, turning into a being-captive. In order to further define such theopolitical hostaging, I paraphrase Hadewijch in light of her encounter with Nassir: to be ravished is to be enraptured by love but also to submit to a forceful intercourse, and always to be taken against one's will. In the confusion between these two kinds of takings, militancy emerges. The Hadewijchian approach to the problem of air is to respond to the suffering of the world with the suffering of and through one's own body. Or in more humble terms, to respond to the suffering of the region where one finds oneself is to suffer in one's body (which is also nothing but a region).

This brings me back to the geographical aspect of the theopolitical. First, there is a conversational landscape that opens between Nassir and Hadewijch that also involves the region of the body; second, there is a prayer that they now perform together, the conversation with God that occurs in a small apartment in the projects. As I tried to demonstrate earlier, prayer has a geographical proclivity (orientation toward Mecca and the black stone), but there is also a topology that accompanies it, the surface on which the folding of the body (often, not always) and the incantation of the theopolitical occur: the prayer rugs (*sajajid*). The rugs on which Nassir, Hadewijch, and Yassin (Nassir's brother) pray are themselves small isolated territories on which prayer is intensified. They are teleportational surfaces. The rug is a diagram of a garden, which in the final analysis is the garden of God, a specific arrangement of abstract hills, steppes, deserts, and oases. And the garden is strictly a representation of order or the implementation of certain laws in the presumed chaos of nature.

Furthermore, it is not only nationality that is invoked by the rug but more specifically a regionality (the names rugs bear are often of the provinces or villages in which they were made, as for example, the famous Shindand or Adraskan from Afghanistan). It is the order of the garden that provides the capacity to pray and to become closer to God. What is in the West called "ideology" is in fact a form of becoming-closer-to-God. Or alternatively even: ideology = becoming-God. This was the case in twentieth-century communism as well where every citizen was expected to first become an idea (of brotherhood, sisterhood, and unity) that was in fact equally transcendent as the idea of a god. This is also why it was natural for religious sentiments to take root in the hearts of the people as soon as communism fell apart. In all postcommunist spaces (especially those such as Kosovo, Chechnya, and Bosnia), the garden of Islamic thought bloomed because the abstract notions of communism lost their genuine intensities and were replaced by a new order, at once emergent and yet also the oldest region, that of God. It is this cosmic geography of the divine garden that is laid out on the surface of the rug. A patch of oasis in the projects. And more: the rug as the cosmic map of a divine region in the middle of terrorist affectivity.

In the film *Hadewijch,* we see one possible encounter between Christianity and Islam that occurs underground—that is, in the secluded spaces of the megalopolis or outside gardens of a convent (still secluded). This is where the interfaith encounter takes place, in the projects and the phantom territoriality of the convent (again, she carries the territory of the convent, he carries the territory of militant Islam). Where exactly lies their ecumenical, in a sense of the universal, or better to say latitudinarian, encounter? It is in their individual atmospheres, in the joining of fervor and heat, where they become delirious in unity. The meeting of the regions: the desert of North Africa encountering the tepid Flemish flatlands in a zero-degree of intensity, the lucid delirium of theopolitical love (or just love). In their individual latitudes, they let each other breathe. And the degrees of their regional difference intersect on the celestial equator (God) rather than diverge (as they normally would). Their temperatures equalize, giving them the opportunity to expand the range of their freedom to act. In light of this, it is no wonder that Hadewijch enters the hostage space of terrorism. For one enters the interfaith latitude through the delirium of submission that comes from the convergence of temperamental regions rather than from philosophies or civilizations or ideologies (in any case, how could one expect to bring "civilizations" together?). They conjoin because they suffer, endure, and undergo the withdrawal of the divine in a world that humiliates and puts to test. It is the air of invisibility that brings them together into the same garden.

Needless to say, this type of meeting or fusion is something that no official religious authority would desire since Nassir and Hadewijch are deemed "fanatical"—Hadewijch by the superior nuns in the convent, Nassir by the non-Muslims (and some Muslims) around him. In the end, they are the hostages of the invisible (the interchanging forces of the garden, law, love). The difference between the delirium of interfaith relations between Nassir and Hadewijch and that of the official religious experts of Islam and Christianity is that, for the couple, it is not only an earthly intersection, in terms of universal tolerance, but one that actually occurs at the level of their corporeality (praying together, planting explosives together) and at the level of the invisible (in sharing one's affects amidst the absence/presence of the divine). The theopolitical pharmacy works here in two opposing directions: one the one hand, by injecting humanitarian or spiritual pacification and tolerance and, on the other, by projecting delirious latitudes of the ecumenical encounter. One produces institutions (convents, Islamic schools), the other terrorist love (being outside the furrow). It is indeed the "land within" Hadewijch and Nassir that has been possessed by God; it is that land from within that unfolds into the world and into the everyday of the Paris neighborhoods.[4]

The romantic character of mystical politics: Hadewijch suffers the absence of her lover (Christ) in the most delirious fashion. But it is also this delirium that turns her into a theopolitical subject through the ethics of the extreme. Similarly, Nassir the militant philosopher acts out the delirium of justice that he sees, or hallucinates, in the endless demand that the invisibility of God poses. He thereby leaves the furrow of French normality where his minority community is gazed at with a dose of political and social suspicion. As a result, Nassir and Hadewijch are less abstract than the liberal democracy in which they live, for they bring God to the zero-degree. Or else, God manifests himself in his withdrawal, which is to say, in the violence that needs to be performed in his name (the name of the law and justice). He is present only in the primacy of the act and the act needs to be violent (how else does one respond to humiliation and air raids inflicted by the western world?).

Delirium is always social, connecting or dividing individuals with their community, with God, etc. In brief, the theopolitical domain of delirium is intricately bound to the politics of health (to respond to the suffering), and one must see figures such as Nassir and Hadewijch in this light. It is in their delirium, being out of the furrow, that they are free; yet this freedom is only achieved by the hostage space of the divine in which they have to give themselves as a gift, as an explosive sacrifice. Delirium is thus a cosmic exhaustion where the corporeal enters into the sphere of the theopolitical. The question now stands: how does one repair this exhaustion, with what humanitarianism? For now one confronts the peculiar contours of a Hadewijchian exhaustion, one that arrives from the perception of a world that is capable of inflicting immense suffering. If one therefore asks what motivates the terrorists, one should also ask what motivates the endless movements of God.

How could we not be able to see the indicted war criminals from the former Yugoslavia in light of this same predicament (of the delirium of air)? One of them, Radovan Karadjic, leader of Bosnian Serbs, was a practicing psychiatrist in Sarajevo and published poet prior to the war in Bosnia and Herzegovina in the 1990s. The war was in fact just the continuation of his psychiatric practice, a new manifestation of "health" through the implementation of ethnic cleansing and the poetics of grenades falling on Sarajevo. And is it a coincidence that he was visited on the battlefield, in admiration, by a number of Russian writers? What seems an obviously political and legal question, namely that of justice (the struggle for one's ethnic group), reveals itself as a question of psychiatric cosmology (i.e. what makes the territory of Bosnia more "healthy" for a specific ethnic group). The practice and the poetics of ethnic cleansing are precisely this concern with the health of one's people, a very specific type of health which gravitates to one's own gravitational core, or the purity of one's language, religion, and ethnicity.

Injury

First, the obvious question: to what extent are narratives of hostage taking narratives of trauma? There is an irksome moral expectation in mainstream politics (we could also call them western, liberal, modern, enlightened), such that, in the aftermath of the attacks on the Twin Towers, everyone in New York City and, furthermore, in the entire nation, should feel traumatized. In fact, there was a simultaneous reaction of the mass media, psychiatric services, and city government that coincided with this view of the instantaneous omnipresence of injury in which symptoms crystallize into the experience of trauma. Didier Fassin and Richard Rechtman diagnosed this predicament by saying that "the idea of trauma is thus becoming established as a commonplace of the contemporary world, a shared truth."[5] Put simply, it is through trauma that one coalesces various bases for solidarity, no less than support for military intervention. It is indeed naïve not to see how the entire discourse of trauma (which includes professional psychiatrists, literary critics, and public officials) goes hand-in-hand with the war on terror, the construction of the enemy, and other traumatic productions. Since the war on terror is in part a medical solution to the trauma of attack (through arguments of the prevention of future attacks and the uprooting of "harmful" systems of the theopolitical body, that is those of militant Islam), so is the humanitarian mission that accompanies it the psychological solution to its negative aftereffects. In this respect, the surprise that psychotraumatologists exhibited at the fact that African Americans and Latinos in New York City used mental health services in considerably smaller numbers than white Americans only reveals ignorance.[6] There is nothing surprising about this scientific evidence. Living in certain parts of Brooklyn or the Bronx means living with the air of terror: on the one hand, of the gangs and, on the other, of the police. Similarly, the West sees the militant Muslim as irrational and fanatical without taking note of the sphere of injury inside of which the militant blossoms.

Trauma is a physical or psychological (emotional) injury. Or, more exactly, in light of this project, it is an affective injury. However, I find the word, the concept itself, to be gravely overused and too all-encompassing. Even though it is not inaccurate to diagnose individuals, and indeed entire nations, with post-traumatic stress disorders, an alternative corporeal experience that underlies it (that of injury) necessitates further exploration. Right from the beginning, one should deterritorialize injury from the medical sphere and place it into that of the theopolitical. At its very core, the term is already denoting "a wrong" (*injuria* in Latin = in + *juria*, "right"), which makes it part of the legal-ethical apparatus that separates right from wrong. Injury thus belongs first to the theopolitical territory, and we have seen the ways in which this is manifested on the molecular level of humiliation of the other (through subtle racist, ethnic, and orientalist subjugations, even in the democratic territory of the West), as well as in the crude political confrontations that find their language in the glory of explosives (from air raids of the state to car bombs of the insurgents). This is not to say that all injury is the same (nothing is "the same" in the sphere of the theopolitical); there are of course different degrees of injury that make them essentially different (the injury from a thrown stone is not the same as the injury from a bullet or a tear gas canister).

Following the same logic of conceptual and experiential displacement, one should also see sin not as a moral or theological category but as a medical one, as the illness of the body, both of its interior and its exterior. Sin: the corruption of the atmosphere of health (the productive relationships between people and the world), sustaining the emergence of "evil" (the destructive governing of the world through violence).

In light of this, is not the very first story, that of Adam and Eve, already one of overtaking (as I implied above)? The figures of Adam and Eve become territories as their bodies are inscribed with a divine geography that is then botched by the enactment of their desire to step out of the transcendent furrow (the moral law of God, the freedom constrained by a prohibition). Their desire leads them into the delirium of sin but also into the delirium of creation. The human being in the sphere of the theopolitical is therefore a being-in-injury from the very beginning; or, put in worse terms, a being-in-trauma. The biopotentiality of the human, the life of desire, is then precisely the resistance to this being-towards-injury. Let me provide an illustration. In Dumont's film, a younger brother of Nassir, Yassin, breaks and steals the scooter of a businessman that stares at him and Hadewijch as they embrace. The gaze itself was enough to provoke rage. The specificity of the gaze turns it into a theopolitical occasion, wresting it toward the sphere where affects of entitlement and humiliation exert rules of engagement. In other words, not every look is the same; some are imbued with affects that operate as projectiles/weapons.

The delinquency of young men of North African descent in the capitals of western Europe today is a reaction to the consciousness of not being a victim, exhibited in the implementation of their own violence against property that runs counter to the expectation of what a young man or a young woman should be. Hadewijch is traumatized by the hostage space in which she lives, the space of God which makes her maximally sensitive to the suffering of the world (a process that is devastating), just as Nassir is "injured" by the fact of air raids that rain bombs on civilian neighborhoods in the Middle East. Or, stated otherwise still, it is not only trauma that is veiled and can jump out from the depths of the individual psyche but also resistances to this very trauma, all kinds of becomings, in vitalist terms, that connect the "victim" of violence with the delirium of the theopolitical (the collision between God's law and the desire to resist it, between ecstatic ruptures and passive submissions, etc.).[7]

And so, a second, less obvious question arises: can there be trauma without a narrative? Trauma is viewed primarily as the trace of a violent event that a victim underwent in the recent or distant past. In the process of retelling one becomes conscious of trauma. It is thus true to say of trauma that it is a particular kind of storytelling. But the importance lies not only in what is said, or in what happened, but in how it is expressed, in what ways the fabulation of the event takes place. Different ways of storytelling have different medicinal properties. The Albanian visual artist Anri Sala says as much: "It's the camera, the movements of the camera, that makes me cry. It's not the story."[8] It is not by coincidence that narratives of Muslim folklore and philosophy were forbidden during the days of communism in the Soviet Union and the former Yugoslavia. Indeed, communism was a system that annihilated stories altogether. In line with this thematic focus of the delirium of air, Vaclav Havel pointed out that totalitarian systems anesthetize the entire society and in this way prevent stories from surfacing; or, in other words, communist societies lived in the state of perpetual "asthma," a story no one wanted to hear since every real story has and needs a direct relationship with death, not just a bothersome illness (hence all top journalistic stories gain importance by the number of deaths they are reporting).[9] And the greater number of deaths in the story also means a greater injury in the collective mind of the community (or the nation).

One could also say that the immense ethnic conflicts that emerged in Chechnya, Bosnia, and Kosovo were in part results of the sudden explosion of stories, both of ethnicity and of poetic resistance (this is most certainly the case in Kosovo, a territory tied to the primordial stories of origins for Serbs and Kosovo Albanians alike, such as the one of the Battle of Kosovo that occurred in 1389). The point, then, is that storytelling is a form of breathing (be it asthmatically, through censorships, through liberal market logics, or through other constraints) which manifests itself in the delirium of words or sighs. If the discourse of trauma is constructed by western psychiatric practitioners and victims (no matter how plausible the circumstances might be), the storytelling precedes all of these constructs. And it is in the very mode of the theopolitical to be simultaneously traumatic and liberating, as in the story of Adam and Eve. The world begins with an injury that the human being performs upon himself. After that, history piles up multitudes of injuries, separating the conflicts into West and East, to the extent that now, in the world today, Yassin senses these injuries in the very gaze of the rich French businessman, just as Hadewijch sensed it in the land, or region, within herself. As a result, they break things and cry out. In short, the delirium of the Islamic militant is less some process of irrational blindness than one of remarkable suffocation: the hallucination or lucidity that occurs when one lacks air. And the air by itself is both gentle and wrathful.

Dumont extracts the figure of the terrorist from the French everyday, just as he extracts the figure of the medieval Flemish mystic from its same interstices. It is the explosiveness of the air that ties these figures to one another and then ties them to the exigencies of the everyday.

Through a similar explosiveness, it was gas bottles that were most commonly used in the 1995 bombings in Paris (e.g. Saint-Michel station in July and a number of others in October) by the Armed Islamic Group (GIA). The gas bottle is an everyday object (in aesthetic terminology, a "found object") used in this case for theopolitical purposes (or more contextually as a weapon for expansion of the Algerian Civil War into French territory). The gas bottle: a bottle of compressed and stored gaseous substances, a delirium of air. The bottle is sometimes constructed with an inner and outer shell separated by a vacuum (a so-called Dewar flask which provides thermal insulation) so that low temperatures can be maintained by evaporative cooling (the cooling through evaporation of the water). The bottle built with veils of the inner and the outer, with the void and the evaporation of the air—an object that receives a new purpose.

The mismanagement of this type of delirious air has its own antiheros. Khaled Kelkal, a twenty-four-year-old Algerian entered the void of the bottled gas as one of the participants of the 1995 bombings in France. His fingerprints were found on one of the unexploded bottles, and he was then chased down and shot in the forest of Malval outside of Lyon, in a place called "La Maison Blanche" (White House). Also recall that Russian Spetsnaz forces pumped an "unknown" chemical substance into the ventilation system of Dubrovka Theater in Moscow when it was occupied by Chechen militants. The control of air has in fact entered into the field of terrorism at the beginning of the twentieth century. According to Sloterdijk, there is indeed a specific moment when this occurred for the first time: the German regiment in the First World War using chlorine gas to attack French-Canadian troupes outside of Ypres in Belgium. The newness of this event is that the attack was not carried out on the enemy's body but on the enemy's environment.[10] Analogously, there is another shift that has occurred in the tactics of twenty-first-century terrorism: an attack is performed here on one's own body which in turn becomes a weapon. The expression of animosity toward the enemy has undoubtedly undergone an evolution: today the militant is prepared to destroy herself in order to destroy the other. That this form of intensified destruction occurs now reveals that the enemy, both as a figure and as an actual combatant, has passed from being a person to being a hostile region (still constructed with old imperialist modalities of the unknown, the unmapped, the unconquered, and as such wild and barbarian). The self-other destruction is not a pure gesture of fanaticism but rather one of affective implosion (one implodes inside in order to explode the outside). Hence, humiliation has reached a point where the desperate act of self-destruction becomes politically viable. There is something distinctive here: the performance of self-immolation (suicide-bombing) has reached new ontological heights of phantomality, where becoming a phantom is preferred to remaining a human.

Suspension

Hostage taking, in its ontological sphere, is a matter of suspending, or better yet, a mimicking of the suspension of the divine that occurs with God's withdrawal from the world. In terms of temporality, hostage spacing puts the world in delay; everyone has to stop and focus on the event of terror. To put the world on delay means to take it out of its furrow, to make it delirious, or else to point to its delirious aspect which usually remains hidden under the veil of comfort and safety advertised by the West. Nassir, the militant, lives inside the sphere of suspension all the time; first in the space of his teaching in the backroom of the Parisian projects; then in the bombed neighborhoods of the Middle East; then in the space of the attack in the subway; and finally in the aftermath (as a special category of the hostage space). One could say that the notion of the state of exception is nothing but a state of suspension formed by the movement through hostage spaces; in this world, the suspension of (secular) law corresponds to the simultaneous withdrawal of divine law (which is invisible). Nassir is thus a sovereign in his own world, while also a captive of western humiliation, a sovereign that ultimately must suspend itself and withdraw, like the divine, into its own invisibility (or annihilation). In suspension, one takes a deep breath because it might be one's last.

The suspension of air is also a political gesture of the state (e.g. the air of racism, ethnocentrism, nationalism, populism, etc.). And the physical suffocation comes first from the presence of the walls. This can be seen in the walling around the convent in which young Hadewijch entered, one that represents the suffocation of worldly or earthly desire, and the invisible walls that separate rich from immigrant neighborhoods in Paris where Nassir and Yassin live. Furthermore, walls are the most primitive form of veiling or separation between the territorial inside and the outside (as is the case along national borders, checkpoints, and ports). Walls permeate the psyche of the modern individual and are an essential part of the architecture of the state that materialize in the process of domestication (or civilizing) which secures the citizen from the presumed threat from the outside. Seen from above (as if from an airplane), walls are diagrammatic deliriums of the line, a madness of demarcations, a consolidation of traces, or in other words, the consolidation of an injury. Walling as a process has the impulse to suspend the movement of people, or more specifically that of the stranger and, by extension, the suspect enemy. Of course, the need for containment on the side of the state (and the political subjectivity of the citizen who belongs to it) is viewed as both a social and psychological necessity; without walls, one might get into delirium, for an open horizon induces mirages and hallucinations. One also might be too sensitive to the world outside the furrow which keeps one sane.

The process of walling is equivalent to the building of a second skin (or third, after clothing, or the uniform) that makes the citizen tougher to penetrate by the enemy. In a way, humanitarian psychiatry agrees with the state here, for well-being is hard to imagine outside these "healthy" containments. Writing about the phenomenon of containment by walls, Wendy Brown states: "Containment within an increasingly boundaryless world is one kind of psychic longing animating the desire for walls; the fantasy of impermeability—perhaps even impenetrability—complements it."[11] Today we see a paradox: the global opening of the world (in terms of economic markets) is followed by an increase in the erection of the most primitive walled structures (on the US/Mexico border, Israeli/Palestinian territories, Afghanistan, etc.).

The walls of the militant: it is curious that those that are ready to explode themselves are infinitely sensitive to humiliation even though it does not necessarily come from personal experience. A being-on-the-lookout can sense the air around him; he can distinguish the degrees to which the air is suffocating. Responding to a tremendous political suffocation in America, Malcolm X spoke (half-jokingly, with a gentle grin) of the following realization:

When I was on the pilgrimage, I had close contact with Muslims whose skin would in America be classified as white and with Muslims who would themselves be classified as white in America, but these particular Muslims didn't call themselves white. They looked upon themselves as human beings, as part of the human family and therefore they looked upon all other segments of the human family as part of that same family. Now, they had a different look or a different air or a different attitude than that which is reflected in the attitude of the man in America who calls himself white. So I said that if Islam had done this—done that for them, perhaps if the white man in America would study Islam, perhaps it could do the same thing for him.[12]

"The look," "the air," "the attitude." There are not metaphorical demarcations but bloodlines of the medico-political diagram, the very atmospheric lines of subjugation and resistance. It is not only the proliferation of new walls and technological devices on the borders that stifle the other; it is the construction of the particular "air" that creates walls. It is the air that individuals carry as a set of dispositions (or, as I discussed earlier, as a certain charisma). Ultimately these politics are based on the production of attitudes (toward friendship or enmity). And to be more theoretically inventive, or delirious, one might say that it is God that reveals himself through the air (already in the breath he blew into Adam), invisible outside of the struggle that occurs in life. Is this not what the vulnerability of the militant would reveal? The air brings suffering, or sometimes, in a poisonous form, death, as well as hope and vision (or a message that is like a lost relic that we pick up, that is like a breath of fresh air).

Law

The militant-terrorist is not simply a criminal. Rather, she points to the omnipresence of crime, the world that is in suspension, both as a hostage of the theopolitical and as the consequence of its withdrawal. Hence the paradox of human freedom that occurs only after the absolute sovereign withdraws and the omnipresence of crime remains; and here I include the petty crimes of the everyday as well as those of more exceptional "humanitarian" bombings. In the predicament of the twenty-first century, democracy arrives from the air; first through bombs, then through humanitarian aid (which includes experts on trauma). And so does the theopolitical, compressed and stored between the interior and exterior layers of the air—theopolitical gas bottle.

The ungraspable essence of the law. Unlike the liberal democracy in which she lives, the militant does not forget the origin of the law, or at least she does not forget the original story through which the law emerged. In this sense, it is the secular world that makes law into a form of mystification, forgetting the origins of its foundations, wresting it into its own obscure zero-degree. But again, I want to be clear: law, as far as I see it, leads to enslavement, to a form of suffocation. And yet there are different types of law. For example: the law of desire, the law of the state, and the divine law. The hostage space of the theopolitical is precisely a space (both in the arenas of individual delirium and in specific spatial locations) where these different laws enter into collusion. The difference between the militant and the nonmilitant is simply a degree of sensitivity that each has to this confrontational complicity between different laws; that is to say, the more intensely one feels it, the more militant one becomes. Ultimately, sensitivity, or even sensuality (as much as fanaticism is also related to the love of the divine, or participation in that love), moves one to action.

But this collusion does not always bring divinity to the forefront. The so-called fanatical body is not necessarily transcendent, it is sometimes merely a form of intimacy or passion that relates to nothing but the militant herself. This implies that a new form of masochism, or being-towards-death, could be envisioned, one that runs from the militant toward the divine (and thus changes the image of the divine). Here ecstasy flows from the militant into the divine. Here individual proclivities deviate, the specificity and materiality of the militant's body (her relationship to the hand that pulls the trigger, the chest loaded with explosives, the eyes that flutter shut or stay wide open) becomes an inventory of minor impulses, emphasizing the visceral particularities that occur in the realm of individual sensation.

All religious and political movements were built on the cultivation and disciplining of specific sensitivities; this can be seen in the examples of touching the black stone, in a gaze that humiliates, in the veiling that protects from the outside, etc. To be militant is to be thrown out of the furrow where one acquires different sensibilities for the world.

To repeat differently, for theologically oriented versions of militant thought the object of the law is known: it is the implementation of God's rules. For the militant, the law makes itself known counterintuitively through God's withdrawal, through his visible invisibility, manifested in radical acts of brotherhood and sisterhood and in the violence that this alliance elicits. One can never understand the desire for violence found in militancy without an understanding of the general principle of violence in which the theopolitical is hatched as if from an egg. Of course this coupling of violence and the law is diluted in liberal thought (both Islamic and western), but only to the extent that violence itself becomes diluted as the object of the law becomes unknowable. I think here of the opus of Franz Kafka, but also of Sadeq Hedayat whose writing often takes the form of an image within an image within an image that in turn makes the origin of the prohibition (or morality) unknown or irrelevant. There is no doubt that there lies a certain politics within the delirium of these writers who diagnosed a condition of the law that finds its sinister manifestation in the present democratic states of suspension.

These are two dimensions of the law as it passes from its divine manifestation into that of the secular, embodied concurrently in the militant and in the liberal citizen. In the former, the law is determinate (insofar as God's withdrawal can be characterized as determinacy) and in the latter, it is indeterminate. Both of these dimensions speak to the hostage-like quality of the law as it suspends the individual in his veils, one of invisibility (God), the other of transparency (democracy). But the militant does not transgress the law of the invisible and therefore does not have to develop feelings of guilt in the aftermath of the terrorist act (in this sense, humanitarian psychiatry should extend itself to the perpetrators of the crimes as well). This is also the case because the terrorist act precludes the experience of the aftermath, or the remnant of an affective trace that might lead to trauma, because the militant is prepared to die and often does die, and in this way ends the theological and psychological concerns raised by the notions of guilt and trauma. The militant's self-annihilation is, in this sense, a journey into the sphere of invisibility, a conscious becoming-invisible, resembling an artist of disappearance (as he wants to exist in the inexistent, the unseen, the unknown). At this level of the militant's body, an alternative ontology of melting, incineration, and evaporation oozes out, a body caught up in disintegrative transfiguration.

Important to note is that these two different dimensions of the law (or religious dispositions even), that of the visible and the invisible, are not antithetical. Already in 1929, Schmitt announced the collapse of the antithesis within the struggle that occurs in the sphere of the political: "For life struggles not with death, spirit not with spiritlessness; spirit struggles with spirit, life with life, and out of the power of an integral understanding of this arises the order of human things."[13] The contemporary age, and the theory that diagnoses it, still refuses to believe in this proposition and prefers to see the conflict of militant Islam and the secular West in terms of antithesis (or even more crudely, as a clash of civilizations). In light of this, we can say that the law does not confront illegality, and that delirium does not confront mental health; rather, the law fights the law and delirium fights delirium (albeit of another kind).

When inside the space of the theopolitical, it is not only a matter of governing bodies (beings-toward-hostage) but also of governing the air (the international airspace). For the divine law of the militant is not only internal to her but also unfolds itself into a control of the sky now crisscrossed by planes that fly always higher into the void of space—into the sovereign's delirium.

The New Weapon

Garden

The ontology of the individual is determined by the garden which she chooses (or that is imposed on her): the avant-garde garden, the militant garden, the democratic garden, the totalitarian garden, the garden of delight (and the neoliberal garden as the overlapping quadrant of all the preceding ones). It is this relationship to and existence within a garden (at the same time fictional and real) that determines one's political and aesthetic dispositions. To what extent is the construction of these diverse types of theopolitical dwelling tied to the act of protest? I start with the broken-down, condensed definition tied to the garden of paradise: a first manifestation of harmony and protest (or harmony of protest). One protests by exiting and entering different spheres of thought, justice, instrumentality, freedom, etc. Exiting and entering is of course tied to the experience of the inside and the outside, to being-inside (becoming-friend) or being-outside (becoming-enemy). The complications of these simple strategic moves, themselves gestures of moving (one protests through writing or through walking out), are more intricate today with the figure of the terrorist who invents a new tactical weapon that changes the topology of the insider and the outsider, and with it the topology of otherness. Terrorist: being-inside-as-enemy (inside the crowd, inside the state against which she fights, etc.).

The militant is a being that "exits" the folds of the everyday; or else, her being is enfolded by the ordinariness of the precarious. This is where the horror of the regular citizen toward the militant comes from; the fear of the one who exits the folds of the inside justifies all sorts of violent responses that become part of so-called security procedures. In this sense, for example, when the American soldier in Afghanistan knocks on the door of a house in the middle of the night, he does this under the veil of protecting the nonmilitant regularity of the inside (of his nation that is paradoxically elsewhere). The militant is thus defined as a being that exists because she leaves the tempered atmosphere of the world, a being that exits the world by not exiting the garden (i.e. its story and topography).

In this respect, we can speak of two types of precariousness: one that occurs in exiting the garden of God, or the fold of the prophet's message (the Adamic life of the secular); and the other that arrives with exiting the secular (democratic) world that is intertwined, paradoxically, with violence and tolerance. The terrorist, then, is one who exits in order to stay within the phantomality of the law, the law that follows and carves into the topography of the divine garden. (As a result, one could observe the calligraphic lines, the scriptural lines, of a religious text, or text of the law, as already forging the labyrinthine forms of a garden, or the delineations of an oasis in the desert.) The law that is writing is actually already present in the line, in the very diagram whose lines separate the ordered space from the chaotic.

The contemporary legal status of the Islamic militant as a region unto himself—that is, a space of illegality no matter where he finds himself, a space within space, like a hostage within a hostage space—allows him to appear as a new weapon.[1] The fact of being a region or territory is further intensified because the militant, especially when elevated to the sphere of terrorism, is primarily a phantom territory. This is manifested in three ways: first, by the phantomality of nondistinction in physical appearance, in seeming a civilian, and wearing regular clothes with the hidden purpose of attack and the use of disguised explosives; second, in the fact that the phantom is both visible and invisible, appears disappearing (its divine quality), sets the borders of his regionality through his atmospheric principles (attitudes, temperaments, charisma) which in turn change the borders of his body, namely extend it further into space (the apparitional, chimeric aspect of space); and third, in turning one's own body into a vehicle and a weapon, a body-explosive, a body that is a minefield. Hence, the phantom outline of the terrorist territory: clothes-invisibility-body-bomb.

On the one hand, the militant is pushed into, or else she chooses, a condition of phantom territoriality because of her desire for resistance, her "will to violence," or struggle, which reacts to the sinfulness of the world across two axes: (a) theological, by embodying the unrepentant figure of Adam, reflected in the rejection of the prophet's message and the divine law; (b) political, because of the social injustices performed on the side of western countries, from embedded ordinary discriminations to explicit imperialistic tendencies (the need for oil and so-called world security). In the domain of radical Muslim militancy of the conservative type (which interests me more because it is, in a sense, harder to analyze), we see the theological dimension seeping into the theopolitical.

At the extreme limit of thought, then, *jihad* inaugurates the notion of "absent obligation," as Muhammad 'Abdus Salam Faraj defined it, which consists of three categories:

1. *jihad* of the *nafs* (inner self);
2. *jihad* of the *shaytan* (the Devil); and
3. *jihad* against the disbelievers and hypocrites.[2]

Rather than providing an exegesis of the terms, I want to follow this topography of extreme thought in order to see what kind of hostage space (what type of garden) it constructs. Important to note is that 'Abdus Salam Faraj qualifies these three categories as proceeding "on a straight line,"[3] or, in other words, that they cut through one another, demanding simultaneous action on all three locations. This means that there are no dialectics or teleologies in the primacy of the act, but only tactical topographics (movement through the space of ideas as if they were an actual landscape, a visceral terrain of thought). And, more importantly, as everything returns to the genesis story, the initial story of the garden and the human, Adam himself is the first proof that sin arrives from a failure in the *jihad* of the nafs. Or else: in order to be a true Muslim one needs to go against oneself. This is the logic of the counter-life in militant thought.

On the other hand, phantom territoriality is placed upon the militant in negative terms by the western legal apparatus which allows states to deal with her in any way they desire (primarily as one would treat a non-person, a dangerous mine-field, or indeed, a phantom). In short, phantom territoriality assumes a negative definition and implementation of that definition in the confrontation with someone constructed as other than human, that is without "human" values (secular, Christian, or moderate); at the same time, this is also a condition that the militant assumes in order to construct herself as a new weapon, mixed with expressions of protest, fanaticism, hatred, indifference, and extreme passion (for the God who withdraws). This is the affective province of phantomality that the militant navigates just as she would the city in which she lives. The map of the phantom garden is superimposed on the western or eastern megalopolis. This psycho-geography, or theo-geography, is also what makes a terrorist into a territorial avant-gardist.

Through a radically different type of militancy, the Egyptian writer Georges Henein inspired the pan-Arabic Surrealist movement which consolidated its ideas throughout the 1970s. The Arab Surrealists published their writings in the journal *Le Desir Libertaire* which was censored in Arab countries and worked itself as the hostage space of a minor kind of writing that countered the state inscriptions of nationalism and Islamic theology (the journal as the space of the outside). In 1975, the group wrote a "Manifesto of the Arab Surrealist Movement."[4] The movement itself is worth paying a closer look, for it addressed the questions of protest, radical politics, revolution, and, by extension, terrorism. The members of the group relied on their instincts and despised the intellectual pose of the bourgeoisie (something they had in common with European Futurists) and yet they called for the abolishment of national belongings and the destruction of traditional Muslim architectonics (from family to fatherland to mosque). This rare manifesto is nothing short of a writing against the divine garden; indeed, it is a writing-act that sets the garden on fire. This, however, is a recognizable avant-garde tactic. More important for the present schematic of thought-body weaponry is the fact that the language of the manifesto inspires a sensitivity of the being-in-exit: "we are the enemies . . . embracing the insurrectional dawn."[5]

This terrorist passage of the avant-garde should not be confused with that of the militants, even though both are operating in the ontology of exiting, of rising up (into divine space) or rising down (into a surrealist underground). Rather, it should be recognized that Arab Surrealists provide a lasting resonance in the idea that the enemy, the enemy of the age they wish to exit, is one who "discovers new dimensions," presumably that of life (its vitality and potential for freedom). Being an enemy is thus a critical tool for reaching these dimensions, while the group itself already inhabits an existential stance of a weapon (writing as an infliction). Joyce Mansour (a Jewish-Arab writer who was introduced to French surrealism in Cairo) addresses this ontology of exiting through a series of poems which are, paradoxically, based on the devouring (i.e. incorporation) of the lover or, in fact, the enemy. The devouring speaks to the theme of the body, and the body speaks to the theme of flesh or of body parts. These lines are paradigmatic of her entire opus:

> I opened your head
> To read your thoughts.
> I devoured your eyes
> To taste your sight.
> I drank your blood
> To know your wants
> And made of your shivering body
> My nourishment.[6]

In this logic of eating, the lover is affectively (and effectively) devoured, but so is the enemy (we are not sure who she is addressing). All of this incessant feasting is an articulation of that which emerges out of it—the screams. The body, as it is, has to explode, and it explodes into carefully devised screams. Through the violence of imagery and turbulence of expressions, words turn into bodies and sounds of animals ("the whispered cries of animals without sleep").[7] Now a multitude of animals—zebras, octopus, lions, bears, monkeys, untamed dogs, desert animals—populate the newborn reality (or at least the desire for it). The importance of the image of the animal, or, better described as the carnality of the animal, immediately brings to the fore the primary act of animality which is devouring: turning something or someone from the outside into one's inside. This process of incorporation, however, is accomplished by poetic screams that are her whispers. The words thus exit as utterances of screams, as permutated animals. As such, they change their original territory (being inside the communicable language), and assume a different physicality, that of air (the whisper), or spit (of the octopus, as she says), or decomposed flesh (of a lion).

Hence an unpleasant but useful recognition: there is an immense power in declaring oneself an enemy. Yet there lies another difference between the avant-garde of militancy and the militancy of the avant-garde: namely, that the former is protected by an all-powerful God, while the latter is protected only by their own instincts. These are the two different types of living precariously. Moreover, there is always a confrontation, in all theopolitical plateaus, between the marvelous and the monstrous, the two operational images of surrealists and terrorists alike: the beauty of the divine garden (the marvelous) that is nourished by decapitations of the enemy (the monstrous), the beauty of the veil (the marvelous) and the desperate forms of torment, peril, and subjugation (the monstrous). Again we see here that the theopolitical is a matter of health, of healing or infliction (rather than of morality), of that which minimizes the trauma and increases participation in the sphere of the invisible.

Furthermore, the radicality of Arab Surrealists is to be found in their shamelessness; while the militant is a witness, sometimes a *shahid*, of God's regiment, the Surrealist is a witness of one's own "corruption" of non-belonging to any territory.[8] Still, I raise the question of the surrealists because they expressed the aggressive blow of protest in writing first (through a manifesto, a form of hand-grenade writing). Writing, in the surrealist context, is the initial gesture of protest, the initial push to resistance. One should therefore keep in mind how the notion of protest transforms amidst three different manifestations: in the works of Arab Surrealists, in the manifestos of Islamic militants, and finally in the mass protests recently witnessed throughout the streets and squares of Middle Eastern towns and cities (the Arab Spring of 2011).

Suicide protest

In contemporary Arab protests we see how the body becomes a vehicle for resistance. The protests across Tahrir square in particular showcase the conglomeration of a mass resembling the swirling multitude during hajj, but this time with a different directionality, and with different exits from the theopolitical. The objections of the multitudes in Tahrir square were not written down in declarations. Rather, their act of exiting across the square was their manifesto; the manifesto becoming manifestation and vice-versa. The multitude of Egyptians asserted themselves as the new law, their movement through the streets resembling the guided disorder of writing itself. The multitude of the square protests publicly asserts itself, bearing witness to its own appearance and enunciation. And protests of this (third) kind are immediately viewed as democratic since they are public and transparent, and opposed to those of the avant-garde groups and militants which are shrouded in semi- or absolute secrecy.[9]

The wave of protests that comprised the Arab Spring started with a self-immolation. More precisely, a 26-year-old street vendor named Mohamed Bouazizi set himself ablaze in Sidi Bouzid, Tunisia (consequently, he was named person of the year by *Time* Magazine as well as by several countries, which shows that the figure of the radical protester rose to global recognition). A number of other self-immolations then followed in Algeria, Egypt, Saudi Arabia, Italy, and Holland. A radical act if ever there was one, self-immolation becomes: the taking hostage of one's own body, the destroying of one's topography. Or contemplated otherwise, self-immolation: the scorching of the divine garden that is found to be rotten.

In Sana, Yemen, yet another parallel type of self-immolation, or ontological exiting, occurred: women burned their *burqa*s in protest of the government crackdown on the protesters. The burning of the veil is another way of exiting the dominant theopolitical sphere which has become militarized. The burning of the veil is also a way of going against oneself, against one's own protective layers, and also, let us not be immodest in saying it, against the folds of the divine. By burning *burqa*s, women peel off the intimations of their bodies. With this act, the women did not want to uphold the values of western democracy or modernity, but rather to find a different way of managing the divine garden, excavating another form of theopolitical engagement.

The sphere of protest as a countercurrent to the dominant powers of the state, as an extreme enunciation of bearing witness to one's life, the desired life of freedom, was also posited by Foucault as the micro-politics of resistance. In fact, he speaks even more radically of the ultimate value of self-destruction, that is suicide, or better still of a certain going-against-oneself. This indeed is the culminating radical act of ethics: to instigate a counter-life, against all dictatorship entrenched in one's "land within," in the continuum of one's theopolitical belonging. Foucault was an avant-garde thinker without the need to assert himself as such. Here is the startling excerpt:

> I'm in favor of a true cultural combat in order to teach people again that there is no conduct that is more beautiful, that, consequently, deserves to be considered with as much attention as suicide. On should work on one's suicide all one's life.[10]

It is as if Foucault spoke with the same sensitivity for humiliation that is found in the Islamic militant (or is it the sensitivity of the surrealist instead?); humiliation that asks for a new weapon to counter it: the destruction of one's own body, the deformation of the divine garden, a new monstrous-beautiful dimensionality of the phantom territory. Indeed, he calls the conduct of countering, of self-immolation, "beautiful." Can we say, in light of this, that the site of women burning *burqas* was beautiful, and that beauty itself is already a dimension of ethical conduct? Certainly. For it is through ethics that one disorganizes the inscriptions of the divine garden, or desolates it, an ethical conduct that leads to monstrous beauty (of course, here we need a better definition of the monstrous and a better definition of the beautiful). Can we, in light of this, also say that Adam's "fall," reaching toward the forbidden fruit, was (or is) beautiful? Certainly.

What is more, this suicide, setting oneself on fire, is not a singular act but a lifelong process, always making sure that one does not enter the given garden under the given rules (the rules of God or of the state) with pleasure and comfort, but rather that one enacts the counter-topography of one's body incessantly and thoroughly. This is self-terrorism (opposite of self-reflection). Of course, there is a difference between this conception of suicide and the suicide-bombing that occurs in the sphere of terrorism. The complicated part is that they both speak of self-immolation or the necessity for it. But the garden, or hostage space, that they construct with this act is nevertheless different.

Self-immolation, or the covering of one's body with poisonous gases and flames, is another kind of writing, a writing that subdues the voice and yet is the loudest image fathomable, one that works as a witnessing of the erasure: first, the erasure of all the humiliations amassed on one's body like the branches of dead trees at the entrance of a dam; second, the erasure of the theopolitical garden that has formed what we call one's identity and subjectivity. As a writing of the erasure, self-immolation is also a minor form of speech, one that makes the command and the humiliation (of the command) irrelevant. Suicide appears as a gesture to spite the command. (Bouazizi scorches himself in order to scorch the corruption of the command, tied to the humiliation imposed by the police, since his body was treated as nothing but an inscription of the petty laws of the local police.) In suicide, one therefore turns one's regionality into a phantom territory, the potency of the erased body, through an exertion of one's own will.

Moreover, suicide is the inscription of one's own counterpower, like the beheading of a sovereign, as a denial of the dominant power's ability to assert itself. I recall the scene from Michael Haneke's film *Caché*, also discussed by Talal Asad, where an Arab man, the most gentle character, after a taxing confrontation with a childhood friend (a rich Frenchman) takes out a razorblade and cuts his own throat.[11] There is no explanation as to why, no "reading" of the event, only the stupefaction of the viewer. This is exactly the same approach to suicide, the approach of the everyday, its affective counterpower and sabotage, its erasure of sovereign domination (or of the subjugating law of the other). This never fully explored triple configuration of the law, writing, and the body, was clearly articulated by Pierre Clastres:

> For, in its severity, the law is at the same time writing. Writing is on the side of the law; the law lives in writing; and knowing the one means that the unfamiliarity with the other is no longer possible. Hence all law is written; all writing in an index of law.[12]

Torture is thus only an alternative form of the writing of the law on the body of the enemy, with the various techniques of cruelty being merely a question of stylistics.

If we follow this argument to its finality, then the ultimate form of radical inscription, a forceful inscribing of one's will, that is to say, one's law, through the aesthetic of erasure, is that of ethnic cleansing. How does one define this procedure? In another lapidary enclosure, we encounter a form of genocidal gardening: engraving the rules of base theopolitics on the bodies of others. The garden emerges again, as the etymology of the word relates it to "an enclosure." The first space of enclosure (and a space of discipline, as Foucault would say) is therefore a divine garden. The further one pursues the conceptual transmutations of the word itself, at least as it relates to western languages, one comes to the proto-Slavic "grad," meaning a fortified settlement and by extension a fence. This also shows that the divine garden has to be permeated with experiences of separation, exclusion, security, and legality. In a more disturbing twist, this also makes visible how the hostage space of the divine becomes a militaristic space. Ethnic cleansing is an enclosure and eradication of everyone different inside this enclosure. One contemporary example would be Srebrenica camp where, in 1995, units of the Army of Republika Srpska first held and then killed 8,372 Bosnian Muslims.

Through the erasure of the other, one establishes the archives of one's terror. One drags entire populations across the territory of the state, redrawing the borders around, recomposing the contents of its space. In this sense, it is correct to think of killing and suicide as forms of inscription, albeit of a radically different nature—that is, different, in the bodies that each spree consumes. This is why the figure of the terrorist is such a potent figure for thought (not only for analysis of the political but also for the act of writing).

Arkan

The aesthetics of theopolitical faciality. The divine garden has to remain abstract in its form; the rules and laws cannot be represented, but rather they must be enacted. Yet the faces of the militant fighters are carefully constructed, either as dangerous or as being faceless. And still there are interesting photographs of Taliban men, for example, emerging from clandestine photo-shops (mostly used for taking passport photos) in Kandahar, with dyed hair and beards, ornamented sandals, decorated fingernails, and outlined eyes.[13] The significance of this beautification: the arrangement of one's body, its appearance and enhancement, already bears on the notion of theopolitical. In some respect, it is enough to be "arranged" properly—that is, dressed, veiled, in order to be recognized as part of the community, as if the outward appearance confirms the proclamation of one's faith. This is true of all secret societies and all armies, as can be noted in the way in which they pay attention to the design of their uniforms, as well as in everyday institutional settings (the type of suits one wears to work). These instances show that belonging, including to heretical sects and state paramilitaries, is a matter of one's temperament, or, as I pointed out earlier, of affective intensifications, rather than only or entirely a matter of psychology, poverty, or ideology.

In the garden of confrontation that is ethnic cleansing, which has been set up in eastern Europe these past decades, it is impossible not to address the force of

Muslim extermination. And there is a specific warrior-figure that is necessary to bring to the surface so as to attend to these procedures of eradication.

Ron Haviv captured ethnic cleansing as it was unfolding in Bosnia in 1992 through his exclusive appointment as a photographer embedded in the infamous Serbian paramilitary group known as Arkan's Tigers.[14] Haviv was there at the very beginning of the inscription; he took the photograph of three civilians (a local butcher, his wife, and her sister, all Muslim) lying on the sidewalk next to the three soldiers who had just executed them. It is the life of the pictures, in this instance at least, that gives life to the forces of erasure: the leader of the group, Arkan, loved the photo Haviv took of him and his group weeks earlier, where he is standing in front of a tank, two dozen men in uniforms and balaclavas on their heads behind him, all with covered faces except him, and holding a baby tiger in his raised hand.[15]

There is always an animal in the bosom of the military man—or, more accurately, as is often the case, as an emblem on the uniform. Not even the surrealists would be able to summon this image in all their imagination, a tiger in the Balkans, amidst the delirium of ethnic cleansing. The covering of the face or veiling that is at the core of paramilitary "fashion" could be viewed as part of the procedures of veiling in general. The *balaclavas* and the *burqa*. How immensely different these coverings are from one another. I point this out not because it is obvious but because I suggest that there is in fact a surprising relationship in the folding of the theopolitical which connects the two articles. The question, then: how do these radically disparate concealments operate in the sphere of the theopolitical? Here is how: both serve as protections but with entirely different dispositions. The former is the expression of utmost humility, a response to the Adamic modalities of desire (the possibility of sin), while the latter provides a legitimate right to humiliate (and in extreme cases to rape and kill). One puts the balaclava on and everything is permitted (what one normally would not do). One is not oneself but a mask, without a face, and, just like everyone else in the paramilitary unit, a non-differentiated form of a killing machine. In short, the *burqa* addresses the veils of the theopolitical, whereas the balaclava addresses the suspension of the theopolitical (the space of genocide, the mute space of the wordless, the dark nothingness of indifference).

And yet Arkan's face is uncovered in the photograph; he shows no shame, no fear, no horror. This is precisely what makes him a successful murderer. He is a sovereign of his own hostage space and has the face to prove it. His is also one that proves that "the face" does not always invite responsibility toward the other. On the contrary, his is a proof that, in certain situations, the face is nothing but a war-mask. The face is an image through which the fabulation of "evil" incarnates the enemy. Or, in other words, the image has its own tonalities of sound—that is, whispering (if we think of Satan, the whisperer, as the originator of evil). The aesthetic aspect of "extreme" politics is also visible in Arkan's distantiation from another Serbian paramilitary group, the famous Chetniks, who traditionally wear long beards; namely, Arkan demanded from each of his soldiers to carry a razor and shave daily (which also distances them from Muslim mujahideens).

Arkan's paramilitaries are therefore hostage takers par excellence, as they overtake (and erase) people and territories. After them, nothing remains except the erasure (the tracing or the trauma, in the language of the psychiatrist). Furthermore, their taking hostage is different from the Islamic militant, in that it represents a bastardized version of the theopolitical. Arkan wants the expansion of Serbia, not the instantiation of God's rule or, in spatial terms, God's garden, even though his vision is that of the nation as God's kingdom (of eastern Orthodox Christianity). The profane aspect of his "missions" was further seen in the amassing of war booty, criminal activity (smuggling of arms and oil into Serbia), extortions, etc. Yet even within this there is still a trace of the theopolitical. Namely, he goes to Christian orthodox churches and receives blessings from priests (for what exactly if not the implementation or preservation of divine violence?). It might be too disturbing to qualify ethnic cleansing as a form of divine violence (since it is a matter of the most profane and vulgar enactment of killing), and yet even in this act there are traces of the political, of Church architectonics, of religious incantations, of celebratory ethnocentric singing, and of historical mythmaking. Could not Arkan himself, in fact, be seen as the high priest of ethnic warfare, distributing death to whomever he pleases? Even his uniforms resemble the adoration of the old warriors, with ancient medals, hats, and arms. Furthermore, he wore a large plastic orthodox cross underneath his uniform, and tested the knowledge of each of his volunteers with the basic tenets of the Christian orthodox faith, while carrying an image of Saint Nicolas in his wallet (a potent relic). In line with all of this, he sees Muslims in former Yugoslavia as Turks, and derogatorily calls them as such.

Eighty years prior to these excursions into ethnic cleansing, a secret society was formed by high-ranking members in the Kingdom of Serbs. On May 9, 1911, nine men gathered and formed an organization called "Crna Ruka," or The Black Hand. It had an incantatory subtitle that was also its slogan—"*Ujedinjenje ili Smrt"* (Unification or Death). The society also had its own seal, as article 34 of the official Constitution describes:

> The Organization's official seal is thus composed: In the centre of the seal there is a powerful arm holding in its hand an unfurled flag on which—as a coat of arms—there is a skull with crossed bones; by the side of the flag, a knife, a bomb and a phial of poison. Around, in a circle, there is the following inscription, reading from left to right: "Unification or Death", and in the base: "The Supreme Central Directorate".[16]

Words, weapons, and a reduced body: the drawing-image of extreme politics. The contract with death and illegality is clearly visible in this ceremonial image. The Serbian officials therefore created a paramilitary unit within the official territory of the Kingdom that could operate in a more clandestine way, merging terrorism with piracy. The secret formation of the organization's cells (there were three to five known cells organized at the grassroots level) became a new weapon in the battlefield of Europe. For the Black Hand was formed primarily for terrorist activity and it was indeed one of its young members, Gavrilo Princip, who, together with two others trained in bomb-throwing and marksmanship, killed Archduke Franz Ferdinand, the heir-apparent of Austria, during his visit to Sarajevo. As a result of this assassination, the little war between Serbia and Austria escalated into the First World War.

More importantly, the professed goal of the Black Hand society was the creation of a Greater Serbia, by violent means if necessary. The organization was put to rest six years after its inception in 1917 and its main leaders executed by a firing squad. But immediately in the aftermath, a new offshoot organization was formed (the White Hand) which continued the same insurrectional imperialism and terrorist technique of political engagement. In 1997, in Kosovo, one could hear from the Albanian population that paramilitary units of the Black Hand were traversing their vicinity. The extent to which this is a rumor or an empirical fact is not important. What is significant is the climate of terror that a secret society instantiates through the atmospherics of fear that in turn become a weapon in and of themselves (the horror is already announced in the sight of Arkan's men emerging out of the forested hills of northern Bosnia, before they do anything). And more: Arkan's Tigers, even if they had never heard of the Black Hand (and they most probably have), continue its work, for the machine of ethnic cleansing and purification of the territories has already been put into work by the early acts of their predecessors. It is in their spirit that all later Serbian nationalist secret and semi-secret units operate, through a genocidal chemistry that latched onto individual desires. This is not to say that the Black Hand was the very origin of imperialistic modalities; its constitution is in fact only another manifestation of the theopolitical plateau (i.e. God-law-nation-sovereign body). Hence, the Black Hand is a movement of erasure that transpires throughout history in the formation of hostage spaces as just one molecular detail in the greater machinery of the negation of otherness.

The following question now imposes itself: is not the entire mechanism of eradication, the art of ethnic cleansing, a matter of divine aesthetics—namely, inscribing the topography of the divine garden following the blueprint given by the messenger (prophet) or other sovereign authority? The law and power are both just tools used to carve out this hostage space of the divine. Even freedom, in both secularized and militant form, is only freedom while one is inside the garden and not outside of it. Rather than a clash of civilizations, then, what we are witnessing is a clash of ontological landscape architectures (spatial ways of being, cultivation of one's affects, etc.). In every form, militarism is indeed not only political and economic but also a matter of urban and landscape planning.

Takfiri

Another example of militant chemistry and its transferal: *Takfir wal Hijra* (meaning "anathema and exile" in Arabic), a popular name of the extremist group founded in Egypt in the 1960s. This was a derogatory version of the original name Jama'at al-Muslimin or Society of Muslims, which its founder saw as the only true group of Muslims. The society was known primarily for pronouncing judgment on non-Muslims and liberal Muslims as infidels that could subsequently be executed. The group was destroyed by the Egyptian government but it is believed that its influence seeped into many other militant groups, including al-Qa'eda. For the purposes of the discussion at hand, important to point out is the "new weapon" that Takfir wal Hijra perfected, which is that of a sleeping cell, or of being a civilian in hyper-camouflage, that includes activities which would normally be forbidden to Muslims. In other words, the group initiated a new way of approaching the enemy which radically changed the landscape of combat: living within the enemy.

But what exactly is different about this secret, heretical, or murderous society? It is true that all sects have, in their essence, tactics of dissimulation (pretending not to be who they are), for these are crucial aspects for their survival. For different historical reasons, in Shi'a Islamic doctrine there is a practice that provides legitimacy for denial of one's faith in situations of serious threat: *taqiyya* ("caution" in Arabic, but which has come to mean "dissimulation" in the language of official jurisprudence). The new weapon is precisely the maximization of this article of faith. The militant merges with the civilian, carrying her territory (and its vision of the divine garden) into the crowds of liberal nation-states. The consequence is that the novelty of combat techniques of contemporary militant Islam rests not only in the irregularity of warfare but in the ability to strip itself from ideological identity; for the topography of the garden is internal, "the land within," and hence is accessible only to those who participate in the secret of concealment. Reza Negarestani clarified the effects of this tactic in the undifferentiated space of the contemporary crowd, now marked with the paranoia of the state as well:

> Each individual is potentially a *Takfiri* cell or niche, a site of infestation, a primary military target. So that the most offensive, active phase of a *Takfiri*'s life is not when he or she is on a high-profile mission like 9/11, but rather when he or she becomes a mere civilian, totally unarmed and dissociated from any line of command. A *Takfiri* levels himself with everyone and consequently levels everyone with himself; when it comes to hunting a *Takfiri*, one ineluctably ends up exterminating non-military entities, far away from the battlefield, in the heart of one's own land.[17]

The language of virology feels at home in military vocabulary, that is in the discourse of war, and thus we can speak not only of biopolitics but also of biobellum (bio-war), a phenomenon that encapsulates not only the administration of life but of warring within life, within the folds of life. The above definition of a Takfiri could easily correspond to the one employed by the military apparatus of a western state (which is not to say that it is inaccurate). The terrorist cells do in fact operate as microorganisms, both on the scale of political action and on the scale of theological influence. By extension, a secret society, just like the sect, operates as a gravitational force that attracts the few with select affinities (be it courage, intelligence, allegiance to an idea or faith or territory). It is an orbit of influence that wants to change the "taste" of the world around it. This is its avant-garde character, the main difference being that the avant-garde group (e.g. Egyptian Surrealists) wants to change the taste of the public, while the sect wants to change the population of the territory (its numbers or its theopolitical affinities). This returns us to the idea that all topographies of gardens are a matter of taste, including the divine garden that speaks either to the beauty or to the monstrosity of laws that constitute it.

The relationship between this topography of the theopolitical garden, sects, and mainstream society asks for further investigation. In 1943, Roger Caillois wrote an essay (published 20 years later) entitled "Preamble to the Spirit of Sects." There is a revealing image of the garden in his summary of the problem:

> Indeed, civilization is perhaps nothing other than the difficult enterprise of forcing wild saps and grasses, the origin and source of everything, to become fruitful and excellent. The dialectic that I establish between sect and society tries to define the chief mechanism governing the renewal of the social fabric.[18]

Not all of this is accurate, but the choice to speak of "forcing wild saps and grasses" as the project of civilization, that is the implementation of laws, divine or secular, is telling of the cultivation that occurs in all human affairs. In this regard, the avant-garde is a particular type of cultivation of taste, and so is militancy, starting already with its early religious schooling of incantation and repetition of Qur'anic verses (cultivating the rhythmic folding of the body's tonalities). The militant is of course the fruit of a whole set of forces, from these early incantations to western geopolitics to personal and cultural tastes when it comes to the vision of the divine. But besides this diagram of theological horticulture, there is another essential point that needs to be clarified: that mainstream society and the underground sect are not in a dialectical relationship (as Caillois would say); they are rather in a zone of proximity that can now only be defined as immanent. The molecules of the secret society are dormant in each social institution; this is visible in everyday affinities toward favoritism, friendship, unspoken agreements, sharing of the same taste (which can mean morality), and so on. Indeed, these modalities of the social are not only present in the practices of the religious groups but constitute general aspects of quotidian relationships in public, private, and professional spheres, including that of ordinary friendship.

Secret societies, militant organizations, are thus setting up climates, arranging the world as the garden of God's law. The new weapon (as far as one can speak of newness) is found in the constant transmutations of the climates of taste that disseminate terror, justice, and power, a climate that will then produce a new sap for the divine and monstrous plants. A sap is a fluid, of course, but there is yet another meaning of the term, that of a tunnel that conceals an assailant's approach to a fortified place. Indeed, this meaning is tied to the unusual etymology of the word: sap comes, it is assumed, from the Arabic *sabar*, "underground passage," or *sabora*, "to probe a wound, explore." And so the science of horticulture enters into its own militant modalities.

Shaytan

To what extent is the enemy imagined to be evil by nature, politics, or religion? All of these three metaphysical properties enter into confusion in the construction of an enemy.[19] According to the Qur'an, the devil, or Shaytan (Satan), was made from pure fire while the human being was made from clay. This speaks not only to differing temperaments but to the very materiality of their being, which necessarily influences the modalities of their existence and in turn their ontological status. What is the ontology of Satan? An answer to this question reveals a whole range of problems tied to the notions of the human and the inhuman. Further still: would there be militancy without the figure of Satan? I take this question to be political rather than theological or exegetical. In short, the human being becomes evil when he incorporates the suggestions of Satan (the proclivity toward evil), through the enactment of which he changes his nature (becoming burning clay). Evil is therefore the ontological change that happens in the sphere of rebellion against God, that is in the non-humility of one's affinities or, still differently, in the burning of one's veils that separate the divine from the human.

There is elitism in Satan's outlook. He considers himself higher than Adam, as fire is superior to clay. Because of this, he is thrown out of the divine garden (paradise). All sects in a way bear witness to this story as they make a deal with the devil, so to speak, secretly desiring to transform the garden (or the world) according to their own elitist hierarchies. This might be a heretical definition of the sect but nevertheless exposes a critical complication. What makes things complicated is the fact that all official political parties and religious orders have at their core molecularized proclivities of secret societies. This is the case in the ruling parties of liberal democracies too, with their transparent policies out of which something unwanted always leaks.

According to the tradition, Satan is the whisperer who materializes sin through his whisper. This is also one of the first definitions of desire—namely, that desire is what arrives through a whisper. The emergence of secret societies is a matter of using the whisper as a weapon, as an affective tool that changes the hearts and dispositions of potential members. As such, all loud proclamations first start as whispers, as minor hostage spaces, capturing and directing the desire of the listener. One writes a manifesto first inside a small circle. One has a conversation with an ally. And so on. The whisper also means that evil is a form of contamination, not dualism. The whisper influences the end results of one's actions or dispositions. The enemy is thus one who is influenced by the whisper and who accepts the arrogance of the implementation of the whisper (the implementation of the whisper equals arrogance). This is a serious matter, powerful enough to drive Adam out of paradise. Consequently, this should also mean that there is no such thing as an absolute enemy, and yet this discursive construct exists in contemporary Islamic militancy as well as in western liberalism. This is because the state of suspension always transmogrifies, constantly changing forms depending on the dance it performs with the figure of the sovereign.

The paradox of radical militant thought is that one kills the other because the other lacks humility. This however is not so difficult to imagine. All examples of self-immolation mentioned earlier speak to this same principle: in the act of my explosive humility, I destroy myself in light of your arrogance. Some just decide to destroy others so as to undermine their superiority. But the story that underlies this conflict is straightforward in its fabulation (but not in its manifestation): the affective implosion of humility in light of arrogance. Mahmoud Darwish pushes this sensitivity of the destructive character further into valor: "We die so that you do not prevail! . . . We live our death. This half-death is our triumph."[20] These poetic lines are primarily founded on propensities of the body which reveal experiential and affective qualities of honor, active futility, and the temptation to mortal risk.

Satan is therefore the master of whispering, a primordial hostage taker, who is found overtaking the territory of human desire as a theo-traumatologist, while setting the entire machine of hostaging into motion. If God is the creator, the devil is the supreme horticulturalist, planting seeds through the delirium of air (releasing whispers in proper climates), planting through breaths and murmurs. In this sense, it is hard to say if the hostage taker has a deal with God or with the devil, for the whisper is infinitely more damaging (when it takes the form of corroded healing) than the bullet.

Nickname

Put simply, what is a new weapon in light of terrorism? It is first the invocation of the group (the cell, the paramilitary band, the sect). And the name of the group is already a weapon of fear, a name that contains transmutational properties: The Group of Holy Struggle, The Black Hand, Anathema and Exile. These are already set up with the purpose to haunt the enemy. The phantomality of the name, as we know, precedes the arrival of the group; the horror arrives through the air, before actual militants and mercenaries appear. Then there is the use of the nicknames (Arkan, Fantomas) which themselves carry an atmosphere of horror within them. And are not these war criminals in fact carefully implementing their climatology with systematic acts that instill fear and horror? We say that one is sadistic when one enjoys the instillment of fear into the other. And indeed, these men, and torturers and executioners in general, speak with excitement and pleasure about their terror-adventures. (This is not to confuse ethnic cleansers with Islamic militants, for there is a major difference that arises in the fact of being on the side of conquest versus that of resistance. Arkan is an invader who is part of the society that starts the war, whereas the Bosnian militant is responding from the vantage of self-protection.)

The nicknames, the adventures: this is what takes them back to the unformed world of childhood, where they could experiment on other creatures as they later do on humans (which they still see as "other" creatures). Why is there such pleasure in killing? Without going into reductive psychological definitions, we can say that sadism is a force that underlies the power of the sovereign. This is visible in the lives of recently executed, wounded, or exiled presidents Zine el Abidine Ben Ali, Hosni Mubarak, Muammar Qaddafi, and a few others who have still remained in power but belong to the same type of fabulation of the sadistic.[21] By sadistic, I therefore mean enjoyment in the implementation and containment of the excess of violence; the sadist is primarily the sovereign of the excess of violence, as he contains it with his rule and distributes it with his irony. By fabulation, I mean that the sadist-sovereign lives in his own myth which he attempts to inscribe into the world (i.e. his nation-state), and continues to live inside of it even when the entire state collapses. The fable turned into indefinite nightmare.

It is this "will to violence" that becomes the novelty (without being new historically), the very new weapon which runs both parallel and counter to the evolution of technological weaponry design; it is novel in a way that the will to violence itself becomes a projectile, since it moves bodies into absolute collision with the space of the enemy (a checkpoint, embassy, café, historic landmark, etc.). The new weapon is a tool or technique developed to attack the enemy under new, always evolving, circumstances. In the world of the militant, this will to violence unfolds in three ways: as self-immolation (at the level of the body), as *taqiyya* or dissimulation (at the level of the community in which one lives), and as the inhabitation of peace (at the level of false social harmony). It is also here, in this threefold veil, that the militant turns into the sovereign of a special type: a sovereign outside of oneself, that is, outside of the territory that constitutes him. Or simply, of the outside.

Sovereign, Of the Outside

Speculative undercurrent

One wants to be a sovereign, one's own ruler; and yet there is also the desire to be ruled. The theopolitical garden is an ambiguous space of both physical and abstract proportions whose vectors of power traverse one's body as well as one's environment (from the way one builds cities to the way in which one perceives nature). I often return to the story of Adam because he is the first inhabitant of a theopolitical constellation, and a progenitor of its diagram which reveals affective lines of power, evil, sin, humility, rebellion, love, and so on. I take Adam's emergence in and exile from the divine garden as a narrative event that is implicitly tied to the historical experience of politics, economics, and the everyday.[1] He is a monotheistic molecule that reveals the configuration of theopolitical power within the garden. His body is the terrain across which this power intensifies and spreads further. I am thus primarily concerned with the spatial dimension of the theopolitical, not avoiding its broad questions but instead approaching from unexpected corners so as to catch them in ambush.

And from this, a first guiding point: sovereignty is initially a matter of space and then of power, after which these two dimensions, power and space, become indivisible (and space turns into territory). Indeed, can we imagine a space not traversed by some power? There is a politics of sovereignty already infused in each climate, where a constant overtaking, seizing, rising and falling, swelling and breaking, occurs through atmospheric permutations. Sovereignty is a process of condensation, of becoming more dense, where two or more molecules combine to produce a larger one: a precipitation of politics. (But there is always a by-product in this chemistry of the sovereign: a terrorist, a militant, a revolutionary.) It is therefore hard to imagine the disappearance of sovereignty, its withdrawal, as long as there remains a space inhabited by humans, animals, plants, or minerals. Someone, something, always overtakes something else, like weeds that suffocate the tree.

And from this, a second guiding point: sovereignty is implemented, gestured, and divined into existence through violence. This is already the case in its conceptual momentum, forever driven by the need to overtake and seize, to govern, control, and regulate. Violence is the undercurrent, running like an underground stream in the sovereign's desire, like a complex system of sewage underneath a megalopolis, draining the power yet purifying it, flowing and disposing, as a liquid with a dangerous surcharge. This inextricable relationship of sovereignty and violence also makes it problematic to couple sovereignty with the experience of freedom. Thus, Georges Bataille writes:

> Sovereignty designates a movement of free and internally wrenching violence that animates the whole, dissolves into tears, into ecstasy and into bursts of laughter, and reveals the impossible of laughter, ecstasy, or tears. But the impossible thus revealed is not an equivocal position; it is the sovereign self-consciousness that, precisely, no longer turns away from itself.[2]

Bataille here inadvertently gives a paradoxical definition of both a fanatic and of a free human. In between these two modalities lies the hostage taker who stops being servile (to the state) and yet finds freedom only in the moment of "internally wrenching violence." A condensed equation of militant sovereignty couples such an expression with God. This equation, however, needs to be further complicated, molecularized, and affirmed since there are modes of violence that do not regulate, stabilize, and impose order but rather liberate, explode open, and expand the borders of one's political possibility. The militant does not only look into the violence of the secular or liberal state and confront it. She also stands face-to-face with the violence within her, and in this sense it is death which governs her. All pronouncements of terrorists that say "we love death" respond precisely to this fact of facing not the other but one's own death that is internally wrenching (the confluence of laughter and terror).

This underlying system of violence, the flattening of the divine into a prophetic message and into spatial proportions inhabited by one's body, is the consummate individual ground zero. And where is this zero-degree intensity to be found? The militant who lives in a liberal democracy, in the West or elsewhere, lives in a way outside of it, she approaches it from the outside (even if she is born within it), because she does not recognize the rules that govern its political garden of democracy. The separation between the inside and the outside is thus secretly broken, and only nominally kept as an everyday reality.

The hostage space is precisely the moment, the suspension of time, in which this unfolding of the militant's divine garden occurs, where she shows the irreality of the separation through explosive explications (and whoever survives . . .).

Airport

The definitions surrounding assumptions of who is the enemy and who is the friend, what is humanitarian and what is terrorist activity, have shaped the geopolitical landscape of today's world. This is where the importance of an obscure figure such as the hostage taker lies; it is also where the importance of small fringe postcommunist societies like Kosovo, Bosnia, and Chechnya emerges; for they are new political collectivities that provide their imprint in the global world, and reshaping it in the process. And what is the shape of the world today? A grand question, to be sure, but nevertheless comprehensible spatially. Space has not only shrunk because of globalization but it has also flattened architecturally. In other words, the world, that is, all of its activity, unfolds through and on air terminals and strips. As early as the 1940s, Schmitt precipitated this spatial evolution: "The whole world, our planet, is now only a landing field or an airport, a storehouse of raw materials, and a mother ship for travel in outer space."[3] The entire world as a landing field is basically a description of the world set up for intervention (usually called humanitarian). In this flattening of topography, as a new form of the desertification of space (the airport as both a desert and an oasis), and a dream site for all contemporary architects, the nation-state fulfills its imperative of controlling the departures and arrivals, comings and goings, and, in a sense, the visibility and invisibility, of the passengers and citizens. But the hostage taker too finds the air terminal a most functional weapon, or rather a strategic region for combat. Indeed, guerrilla warfare has since moved from the deserts and forests to the airport. Paul Virilio addresses this condition with usual precision:

> It must be conceded that, after the state of blockade of the City State and of the Nation State, *the state of emergency is the new city*. The end of the world or rather the twilight of sites. It will be Palestinians who will first measure the effect of its weightlessness, "a people without a land", as hijackers are forced to understand the suicidal character of the *air-terminal*. After art, after architecture, here we see the advent of airport politics . . . but this time, of airports that will no longer have the relaxed atmosphere of leisure that the traveling bourgeoisie conferred upon it, instead they will have the tragic character of the extermination camp.[4]

If not in constant emergency, the airport is certainly a site in constant suspension: all citizens are on stand-by for an unknown period of time. They are hostages either of the real hostage takers (rarely), or of the imagination of the hostages (often), or else of the technological glitches caused by overcrowding (most often). The world as a city, or "anti-city" as Virilio calls the airport, is one of prolonged stand-by, where movement is announced, delayed, and finally executed (or rejected for some). Is this "twilight of the sites" a sovereign space? Absolutely. Someone decides who is on stand-by and who is not; this also depends on which country's little booklet (passport) one holds, but also on other arbitrary things. Even though Kafka wrote almost 100 years ago, in central Europe, we are only now seeing before us his micro-political meteorology: the invisible rules of endless suspensions.

One does not have to share the apocalyptic view of Virilio to notice the accuracy of such spatial demarcations, the phantom territoriality of the air terminal, with its new rules of invisible sovereignty. And yet, at the same time, this sovereignty is transparent. Air terminals are cities of the glass, reigned over by the camera and the screen, the ultimate architecture of democracy. They are like galleries, with shops and interrogation rooms all on the same platform. In this new hostage space of the spectacular city, everything unfolds through the screen (all of the information about the people, goods, airplanes). If sovereignty has withdrawn, it no doubt withdraws behind the screen. If the "extermination camp" is too harsh of a notion, one can certainly see the airport as a gallery, a world exhibit, where the people are the objects on display that become mortified just as art objects lose their vitality in the atmospherics of the museum. Everyone mingles in semi-anonymity (a democratic right of moderation), from terrorists to war criminals, from secret service officials to tourists, from maintenance employees to transnational businessmen. It is this quasi-cosmopolitan compound that makes the airport volatile.

If there is a new form of sovereignty, it is one that comes from the outside. The hostage takers are only one instantiation of this outside. There are other figures, however, who are immanently tied to hostage takers and indeed direct the very production of hostage spaces. I mentioned earlier the warrior-democrat (Hashim Taçi). But the sphere of the political, including the theopolitical, has been corporatized as everything else, and this means that there is a businessman behind every warrior (if not within). That is not to say that the economic has overtaken the political; economics, as far as I see it, are only one manifestation of planetary antagonism, a watered-down version of the friend/enemy dichotomy, a more subtle but not less detrimental engagement with the other, often by ways of indifference toward the other and the resources of the planet. In fact, liberal economics take the political back to the theological since they have the entire planet (the whole of creation in theological terms) as their preoccupation and potential agent of exchange (i.e. source of income).

To be more concrete, there is thus another figure of the sovereign from the outside, in direct relation to the figure of the warrior-democrat: that of the businessman-politician-urban planner. I am referring specifically to Behgjet Isa Pacolli, a former president of the Republic of Kosovo (now recognized by 86 countries) and the president and CEO of the highly successful Mabetex group, a Swiss-based construction and civil engineering company. Pacolli works on two levels that tie him to the present discussion. One is his role in the reconstruction of political architectures, the actual built environment of postcommunist cities. In this domain, he reconstructed the former Russian Federation Parliament, Russian Opera House, State Duma, and Moscow's Kremlin. In addition, and more significantly, he is largely credited for the construction of the presidential complex in Astana, Kazakhstan, where he also built a presidential palace. In Tashkent, Uzbekistan, he is involved in the construction of the City Hall. And of course, he has large construction operations throughout Kosovo. The other significant aspect of Pacolli's skills resides in negotiating hostage-taking situations: in 2004 he spent a month in Kabul, Afghanistan, securing the release of three UN workers taken hostage by the Taliban; in 2006 he negotiated the release of an Italian citizen; in 2007 he negotiated the release, after 2 were killed, of 21 South Korean hostages (Christian missionaries) from Afghanistan. Indeed, Pacolli is the figure of the new sovereign that works from the outside, including the outside of nation-states. Since the international community often does not negotiate with terrorists, there are other agencies (of power) that do. Pacolli belongs to one of them. He spends his working time suspended in the air and in stand-by in the international air terminals of Lugano, Prishtina, and Kabul. The CEO is the new humanitarian and the new politician. One of course needs financial privilege to be an active humanitarian in the first place. Nevertheless, this example shows that there is always a hostage space within a hostage space. Kosovo is devastated but also caught up in the fierce reconstruction of infrastructure and political institutions. Pacolli is a spatial force immanent to this devastated reconstructive space, emerging from it, coming and going, as a passenger and as a sovereign—the new sovereign figure of both the airport and of the post-conflict zone.

Post-Conflict

Today we find postcommunist Muslim localities to be post-conflict spaces of this new sovereignty, or, less optimistically a laboratory space for the new sovereignty (that of independent states, enclaves, semi-independent regions, etc.).[5] The reason why NATO forces reluctantly implement their own withdrawal from these locations is because they fear that so-called democratic values have not taken root in the region and that theopolitical weeds of another (ethnocentric) divine garden can take over instead. NATO forces are therefore implementing a political sensitivity (if not the actual figure of a presidential candidate) for a specific type of loose sovereignty. And the state of suspension in the post-conflict zone is one of great anticipation of this implementation. The outline of a post-conflict space proceeds through suspension and anticipation. We see that the entire planet is in a sense becoming this kind of hostage space with a pattern of low-intensity conflict (as Weizman argued) that turns into permanent regularity. The militant is precisely the one that does not accept this regularity and instead pushes the underlying irregularity to the extreme. He makes a home out of this suspension and anticipation.

The post-conflict zone is a space without a stable or monolithic sovereign; it is a temporary space in which the powers of destruction (of hypernationalism, ethnic cleansing, etc.) have withdrawn but are at the same time consolidating in a new phantomal way. Or otherwise, it is a space where the psychiatrists take over the medico-political care of the region. A doctor precedes the sovereign, ushering the way for the future regulator. Sometimes the two collide in one person (as in the case of Radovan Karadić, the psychiatrist-political leader-war criminal). All postcommunist Muslim regions live under this image of the phantomal, or apparitional, procedure of disappearance: first of the communist ideal, then of the hypernationalist and religious interruption that leads to war. What appears in the wake of the disappearance of communism, in the aftermath of NATO interventions, is the image of the neoliberal embodied in the advertising billboards on the highways, positioned amidst the vacuum of the theopolitical.

The post-conflict zone is an image, like a children's drawing with lines incomplete and borders twisted, with colorful hope and the inexplicable horror of formlessness (indeed, why do all children draw like this, as if inside a post-conflict zone, their visual orientations always beckoning toward the suspended?). It is inside the post-conflict experience, then, that one lives in the image which animates reality, from the banal aspects of bare survival to the sacred aspects of the construction of new religious and political infrastructures. More specifically, to live in the image of these war-torn zones is to live under the shadow of a hero-criminal, as the highest degree of sovereign violence finds its territory in the figure of the war criminal. (The only knowledge we have of him, and the entire atmosphere of this type of criminality, the final aberration of war rules, the absolutization of the enemy, comes from those that survive—the witnesses.)

To live under the shadow of the war-criminal: this is the hostage space of former Yugoslavia. It is not uncommon here to hear people say that they are hostages of (their own) criminals, of the political and military elites that emerged in the early 1990s. While this is different from the actual taking of hostages by militants, the implicit violence of the military atmospherics that engulf a person (or what now can be called an individual's own climate), condensed through the figure of the war criminal, participates in the construction of this particular hostage space. Hence, the entire society lives under an influence of the phantom, a general that has withdrawn from the military post but continues to operate through his old climatology of fear. Bosnia: a phantomal state.

The issue of the warrior-hero is a particularly sensitive one. Some generals that are heroes for their own communities (Bosnian, Croat, or Serb) are war criminals in the eyes of the international community; at present there are 15 indicted military leaders at the International Criminal Tribunal from the former Yugoslavia in The Hague.[6] In this fog of war-heroes, it is the international tribunal that determines who turns from a hero into a criminal (this is not to say that there are no objective circumstances based on systematic exterminations of civilians and prisoners of war). As a consequence, the post-conflict territories of the western Balkans live under the shadow of their former generals even though they have withdrawn from public view. They are indeed phantomal characters whose influence, even now when they are completely powerless, shapes the affective space of the new nation-states. This is quite extraordinary. We see the creation of phantom territories in the former lives of generals (warriors-heroes-criminals). In light of this, one of the voices from an online forum discussing war crimes in Bosnia caught my attention: "No one is interested today if Mengele was a doctor, a philosopher, or a hero, everyone sees him as a war criminal. A war criminal is a war criminal, a category beyond nationality or profession."[7] There is a seduction in this straightforward demarcation of the figure of the war criminal. Indeed, war criminality becomes a trait, an essential characteristic. But then again, it is an essence that is created through one's acts; certainly, everyone involved in the aesthetics of eradication, that is ethnic cleansing, assumed a new essence. It is not for nothing that combatants who come back from war say "the war has changed me . . .," thereby giving psychiatrists food for thought and action.

Generals are witnesses to their own criminality; as such, they are the only perfect witnesses; they witness their own violence but also the violence of sovereignty, as they are its direct fulfillments. There is thus a little of the war criminal in every sovereign.

Witness

Crimes against humanity inscribe themselves onto the body of the perpetrator, reconfiguring his relationship to the world. He becomes a prisoner of his own sovereignty. For conflict is at once the most bodily experience (of exhaustion, pain, hunger, longing) and the most ontological (reshaping one's being). It is not only that the person involved in war crimes does not remain the same; rather, nothing remains the same. The world shifts in the delirium of air, in the perception of the physical environment where the eyes swirl; the clouds are different, the trees are different, the rain is different, everything is slightly more monstrous. And yet, with the militant and the terrorist, all of these "characteristics" are secondary; what defines him is the belonging to the divine garden. The militant is indeed a kind of doctor who gives medicine, that is to say poison, to the world, the medico-political infusion that we call terrorism. Is it proper to conjecture that he can heal the world? To understand the ethics of this improper question one has to see him as a form of the witness too. Indeed, from the perspective of the militant, the entire world should be a form of witnessing. In this light, martyrdom is not merely tied to a specific event (that of dying or suicide bombing), but rather to an entire existence that leads to the event of death. Life itself as witnessing and nothing else. To be a witness, furthermore, means to perceive a certain event or reality properly, truly, accurately under the worst conditions. The witnessing is a matter of "seeing" (this is the root of the word "wit" too), and in the context of the Islamic militant it means to see the invisible, or to bear witness to the withdrawal of the divine. The martyr is the one who keeps one's eyes permanently open.

Herein lies the main difference between the avant-garde and the militant movements, for the avant-garde is also a matter of seeing and by extension a reconfiguration of the world through sights and sounds, the creation of new perceptions, a modulation of one's retina, so to speak. This indeed is the "wit" in the witness. But the wit of the avant-garde has humor lodged inside of its expression (we cannot view the slogans of the Egyptian Surrealists without internal laughter), no matter how serious the subject they address or attack. The militant is indeed an avant-garde force without humor. This is not just the case with Islamic militancy. The word witness is usually tied to the gravest forms of violence, and, what is more, to the survival of these catastrophic forms. The witness can barely speak, let alone laugh. A sense of humor of course is also tied to the specificity of a morality, that is it testifies to one's moral grounding and, as such, is not of the divine but of the human (and animal) world.

To return to the martyr, then: even though the notion of sacrifice (giving oneself as an offering) comes easily to mind when discussing martyrdom, it is not accurate enough. When we take the idea of witnessing as a form of living, martyrdom stops being purely sacrificial.[8] Furthermore, the message of the Qur'an, Talal Asad points out, does not make explicit reference to the word *shāhid* (martyr); indeed, the combative techniques of self-death are of modern origins.[9] This of course makes sense since the techniques of combat respond to specific historical situations. It is also questionable if the victim of beheading, for example, could be viewed as a sacrificial victim since the victim is never sanctified in any way, neither through incantations nor through ritual gesture.[10] The victim is in fact treated purely as a body of the enemy, a living corpse. The performativity of the beheading has an exclusively terroristic functionality, that is to instill fear, rather than to give praise to God.

Moreover, suicide bombing is an affective weapon developed and perfected through the careful harnessing and devising of rage. If there were other ways to approach the enemy, there is no doubt that the militant would use them. In the world in which we live, this technique has become the only way in which certain groups find a prospect for the recuperation of their individual sovereignty (through the divine prism). Rage, as we have seen earlier, is first divine, then physical. And, for this reason, suicide bombing and the administration of death to oneself and others is perfectly aligned with the sphere of the theopolitical. By administering death, the hostage taker is a sovereign of the zero-degree: reducing her energy to complete stillness (the concealment of who she really is) and then imploding toward absolute intensity as a weapon of destruction.

More importantly, when viewed from the limits of the extreme, the message of God's law—that is, subjugation to it, the physical and affective folding it enjoins—is not mythological but divine. This is an important distinction, for this means that the violence it necessitates is not sacrificial but constitutive; rather, it is not concerned with a violence that has the power to appease but one that instead has the power to organize space into passageways of divine law (an underground cistern of internal violence). Indeed, suicide bombing, as a radical fractal of divine violence, is secular in a sense that it desires territory and justice but also theological (not only by virtue of its faith) because it desires divine spatiality, a theopolitical patch of land.

This rank of martyr, in the Islamic landscape, is she who has been expiated by the laws of the divine garden. The laws of this expiation are of course the laws of violence (but what is "violence" inside of the divine garden, where a self-immolation becomes a form of love?). We have gone further here than the formula of Walter Benjamin that equates divine violence with sovereign violence.[11] For sovereign violence is only a reduced, concentrated, and qualified violence of the divine. In other words, there is also divine violence outside of the sovereign space, where it indeed stops being "violence." The hostage space is an inkling that takes us closer to sensing this idea and an experience that still lacks its own terminology. Mahmoud Darwish at least provides an entryway to the language of divine violence as embedded in the body of the dead ones:

> When the martyrs go to sleep, I wake to protect them from professional
>   mourners.
> I say: Have a good morning at home, a home of clouds and trees, a
>   mirage of water.
> I congratulate them on their safety from injury, and the generosity of
>   the slaughterhouse.
> I take time so they can take me from time. Are we all martyrs?[12]

In the world where everyone is a martyr (potential or actual), divine violence must exist. In Darwish's language we see that witnessing, or martyrdom is a matter of delirious perceptions ("a mirage"), territorial or climatic peculiarities ("clouds and trees," "water"), and health ("safety from injury"). In this one example, we see a way of addressing the language of the divine with the language of the earthly that has only slightly shifted from the experience of the mundane.

Fear

Terrorists are actors of the extreme, of an extremity that is tied to the celestial. This is precisely what makes them dangerous and fearful—that is, they have an alliance with the divine, or, more accurately, with the extreme edge of this divinity. They exude fear, which changes their essence, for in fear lies the first experience of power (fear being the elementary particle of power). Before rage there is fear. From this perspective, Esposito writes of the human condition (in relation to Hobbes):

> Indeed, what does it mean that we are "mortals" if not that we are subjects above all to fear? Because the fear that traverses us or rather constitutes us is essentially the fear of death; fear of no longer being what we are: alive.[13]

The figure of the hostage taker inverts this definition, or else confirms it with one difference. She fears no death. At least not in the same way that other combatants or civilians fear it. The space of the militant is indeed a double space of fear: (a) the negative fear of neighboring countries (Serbia for Kosovars, Russia for Chechens, Israel for Palestinians) and; (b) the positive fear of the divine. We confront our own mortality; through fear, the militant confronts her own immortality. This relationship to fear is in fact a prerequisite for being-fanatical. It is through certainty of one's immortality that one engages in struggle, not out of mere hope for a better future but because one already lives in the theopolitical garden (internally wrenching) which only needs to be instantiated.

Fear is a primordial affect, one that imbues the individual with the power to live and to die, to move toward death voluntarily. This is a staggering problem: moving toward one's own death. But there is also a positive aspect of fear: it binds together. Radical groups are not just bound by arguments about which they agree, nor exclusively by their faith; more importantly, they are bound by the fear of the one that they admire. The leader or the divine serves his love through fear. As a consequence, fear is not only tied to the perception of the enemy but also to that of the friend, or even that of the lover.

Esposito continues with a further enunciation of fear: ". . . it is we outside ourselves. It is the other from us that constitutes us as subjects infinitely divided from ourselves."[14] It is perhaps more proper to say that the militant is indeed constituted by fear (in addition to saying that he is fearless or fearful). He is the climate of fear itself and arrives as such, since fear is the theopolitical photosynthesis that produces the militant. It is only through this affective corridor that his sovereignty arrives. In militancy, he is the sovereign of his own fear.

The first fear of the human transpires in the depiction of Adam, since he exercised his freedom against the fear that he felt. He conceivably instigated a sovereignty of the outside and was thereafter banished from the inside. The militant, however, is an opposite parallel of Adam even though they both reach for the forbidden and the radical elsewhere of exteriority: namely, the militant that becomes a martyr grasps for the bomb in order to leave the sovereignty of the state, the inside of the nation, and enter the outside of the divine, or simply, the outside of freedom.

The inversion of Adam: Mohammed Atta, now one of the most famous hijackers in the world (the pilot of the American Airlines Flight 11 that crashed into the North Tower of the World Trade Center). Atta is a prime example of the fixation with the theopolitical garden and the fear of the divine. He followed his path of outsider sovereignty with geometrical precision, without much divergence from the pathways of this paradigm: he was trained as an architect in Cairo and Hamburg, his father was a lawyer, his mother came from a wealthy farming family, his sister a medical doctor. The entire plateau of the theopolitical finds itself converged in Atta's family: architecture-law-farming-medicine (the first garden of the family extended and intensified). This is not to suggest that one's most convoluted existential decisions and acts unfold in correspondence to one's nuclear family structure. But this particular case is exemplary: a sensitive and intelligent young man gives himself over to the forces of immense destruction; one cannot speak here only about political, economic, or psychological causes. One can listen to him instead: in his last will he speaks of the "marriage in heaven" that is a union with a beloved. Furthermore, in the final notes directed to his accomplices, he speaks of no less than "gardens of paradise" decorated with the most beautiful ornaments awaiting them (the martyr-witnesses).[15]

The architectonics of the family extends to the architectonics of the garden. Atta criticized western architecture in the Middle East, especially the skyscrapers that destroy community streets and alter the skyline. One could say that his suicide attack was a matter of architectural rage, his final word on the matter.[16] This highlights yet again the importance of the architectonics of the hostage space: skyscrapers take over the view and the streets, just as their destruction leaves the void of the hostage space. In each instance, we are dealing with a "taste" for a particular spatial formation. A short parable of sovereignty that runs parallel to Atta's example: I was told by a former Muslim combatant from Bosnia how much he disliked communism even before it collapsed. I asked why? He answered: "Who wants to live in these bleak buildings?" Indeed, ideology, or the imagination of it, was a matter of shapes (buildings, parades, clothing, etc.). Post-communist Islam emerged, or manifested itself, first through the building of new mosques that now dot the new urban landscape.

There is also a militancy of fearlessness that has been implied here. Engaging the politics of naming before anything else, the very first implementation of the terror of naming, Malcolm X eradicated the political subjectivity (i.e. oppression) that comes with a name, his once imposed name of enslavement, by abstracting it, turning it into a ground-zero, an X, the zero-degree intensity of a new political subjectivity. The first decision was a gesture of eradication of oneself—or, better yet, the creation of a zero-degree atmospherics which do not produce new political subjectivity as much as re-envision political collectivity. Hamid Dabashi gives Malcolm X an exceptional status among Islamic revolutionaries:

> In more than 200 years of encounter with colonial modernity, and literally hundreds of Muslim thinkers, no Muslim revolutionary comes even close to Malcolm X in the liberating, global, and visionary grasp of his faith and its place in facing the barefaced barbarity of economic and military world domination.[17]

Malcolm X did not tolerate, he went against, like a countercurrent, a vitalist counter-life. When Malcolm X says that he has no fear because he died already 20 years ago, it means that he had spent his life preparing for a suicide, preparing to be killed one way or another. A strange form of vitality of the dead. In this respect, he fulfills the beauty of self-death by inscribing himself into the world and into humanity. This is an expert practice of militancy, one that illustrates the sovereignty of the outside. However, the suicide bomber, even though she is a sovereign of the outside, is not a revolutionary of this kind and falls short of the vision and articulation of Malcolm X's force. In the same vein, Henri Bergson speaks of a mystic genius that will appear and

> draw after him a humanity already vastly grown in body, and whose soul he has transfigured. He will yearn to make of it a new species, or rather deliver it from the necessity of being a species; for every species means a collective halt, and complete existence is mobility in individuality.[18]

Not a mystic but a militant genius, Malcolm X delivers not only the vision of freedom but a vision of new humanity. There is something unique in the redefinitions that he performed on the grammar of American politics, something that made him incompatible with the state and with any party; indeed it is the party, the movement that wants to be a nation (The Nation of Islam), which killed him. Coincidently, Malcolm X revealed his new vision in interviews conducted in an airport after he landed, having just returned from his pilgrimage to Mecca—that is, after his encounter with the axiomatics of the black stone.

Decision

The fear that the militant asserts comes from the certainty of his act. The act, the terrorist act, is in turn always infallible. But how does one come to decide for, or give oneself to, the act of hostage taking or suicide bombing? We know the famous formula of the sovereign put forth by Schmitt that has been unfurled, and in some respects flattened, in the last decade: that the "sovereign is he who decides on the exception."[19] The usual interpretations of this statement focus on the state of exception part of the formula. And with good reason; these words provide accurate diagnosis of an entire era, including our own twenty-first century, which has still not foreclosed its exceptionality (and has, in some respects, only aggravated it). But I would like to turn the attention to the more simple term, one that precedes the state of exception—syntagma, which is that of decision. Hence, another definition might be decomposed to read: the sovereign is the one who decides.

Who makes a decision and in whose name? It is the heaviness, the gravity, of the decision that weighs so dominantly in the act of hostage taking. But how does the hostage taker live with her decision? The decision turns the hostage taker into a sovereign, for the overtaking of a space and the people within it is preceded by a decision. This is tied to the militant's critique of the bureaucracies of democracy, a labyrinth in which no one takes a decisive stance. The militant cell, since it works underground, decides quickly. In other words, if there was no decision-making, or the act that determines, there would be no terrorism. Everything starts with a decision: to submit or not submit. If fear is the first affect, the primordial substance of dark space, the decision is the first act. And this act is one of freedom or submission. The act of deciding is therefore the very first gesture of the political (And with his decision to disobey God, Adam instantiates the politics of resistance, which is later intensified into disobedience by his son Cain).

This raises the question as to whether there is politics without sovereignty. The answers abound in the history of political thought, but I instead look to the position of the hostage taker found in the very decision that turns her into one. To reiterate, I see the experience of sovereignty as a form of the hostage space, or a theopolitical garden, similar yet different in essence and intensity from the divine garden. My next point is that the architectonics of this garden produces desire, fear, and attraction that finally lead to a decision (a political act). As a result, freedom, as far as it is tied to sovereignty, is also enslavement. In fact, freedom is one modality of being hostage. Perhaps this is also why violence is imbued in the notion of freedom, or as Asad concludes: "Violence is therefore embedded in the very concept of liberty that lies at the heart of liberal doctrine."[20] Such violence lies at the heart of liberalism only because the theopolitical platform extends itself into so-called secularism. The hostage taker elicits the decision to stand outside of a sovereign state (western or liberal) not in order to become impolitic but rather to assume the position of the sovereign herself: the sovereign of the outside. The peculiar nature of Islamic militant cells is that they operate according to, what could be called, rotating sovereignty, or minor sovereignty. In this context, if a leader is killed another one is immediately instituted. There is no hierarchy in the cells besides the one that is momentary decision-maker. Killing the leader, in this sense, does not make much difference in the operational character of the cell, since one does not abolish the power that circulates and which is not tied to the body of any one individual. In this spherical hierarchy, the visibility of the sovereign, or the leader, changes dramatically, that is becomes more apparitional. In this respect, Devji points out that, for most of his followers, bin-Laden appears only as an image on the television set.[21] Bin-Laden is only an image, a ghost, through whose atmospherics militancy abides, where it finds its comfort.

In short, the hostage taker is the sovereign of the space that she overtakes, for she institutes a rupture in the quotidian constructs of time and space and turns it into an exception—and further, into an administration of life and death. But this administration is by no means on the same plane with that of the head of a state (liberal or despotic), since the discourse is not the same, because the lived material and existential circumstances are vastly different for those who are systematically exterminated first. The legacy of liberal democracy entails a history of slavery, genocide against native peoples, hatred of the immigrant, colonial conquest/warfare, and CIA intervention throughout the world. The question remains whether these assumptions of self-interest, nationalism, and capitalism are the core of liberal democracy or just aberrations of it; and if the latter, how can they be then matters of the everyday? This fact should strike balance in the investigation of two different types of sovereignty: one of the inside, belonging to the powers of the state, and the other of the outside, belonging to the exigencies of injustice and subversion.

The one who speaks decides; the one who decides inscribes. Of course, it is a matter of "proper" speaking and writing, the stylistics and grammar of which will take effect and become the law: writing and speaking with an imprint. For the militant, this can take the form of scriptures or manifestos; for secular states, it is the international law and the governing of its exceptions that takes precedence.

There is a helpful discussion of decisionism and sovereignty in Schmitt, which assumes another turn with the introduction of the notion of infallibility:

> Infallibility was for him the essence of the decision that cannot be appealed, and the infallibility of the spiritual order was of the same nature as the sovereignty of the state order. The two words infallibility and sovereignty were "perfectly synonymous."[22]

This perfects the definition of sovereignty as a form of decision-making. The sovereign is one whose decision is infallible. And the term itself takes us back to the first decision that led to the fall: that of Adam as a free man and an exile, or a hostage of his own freedom. But infallibility also comes from the Latin *in* + *fallere*, "not" + "deceive." The decision of the sovereign is therefore nondeceptive, or at least it pretends to be so. In Bosnian, the term is *nepogrešivost*, meaning "without a mistake" or "unmistakable." In every respect, the sovereign decision is unmistakable. The above quote addresses governmental authority, but one could also see it as describing the law of decision-making that governs hostage taking itself, since it is in this individual gesture, though always related to the group, or cell, or secret society, that we find the very first instance of governing oneself against the government. This is why the problem of guilt is negotiated differently inside the hostage space, for decisions that govern it are presumed to be unmistakable and infallible.[23] And yet, even in this sphere of the infallibility, there is tension, an opening to regret, since fanaticism is not always absent of sorrow and trembling. It is also true that liberalism, as well as historical communism, supposedly elevates a criterion and protocol of discussion, where the decision is born out of a consensus that favors the dispositions of the majority (even though this majority is always under some corruptive influence of the privileged).

The micro-politics of the decision leads to the secret of its definition. The decision too is a question of form, or of boundaries determining whether it will become pregnant with the power of the law (civil or divine), or even become law. The one who decides is the one who defines (the shape, the outline). It is in the aesthetics of the grammar that the decision lies. Again, the solidification of liberal or secular decision-making is tied to the strict formulations of the legal language; for the hostage taker, for the militant, it is a poetic invocation of the prophetic message that crystallizes into law. The confrontation is, first and foremost, grammatical, syntactical, or formal. To redefine grammar is to redefine the world; this is also the first sign of sovereignty, like a stamp that makes the sentences of official documents valid. Grammar, in short, is the imprint of the sovereign. And even if the hostage taker does not define the grammar, he certainly bases his decision, and by extension his act of hostaging, on what he considers the proper definition of the community, nation, paradise, etc. In this respect, the definition has more agency than the hostage taker or the militant. The inscription, invocation, or incantation is the sovereign. But it would be wrong to view the hostage taker as a puppet; by embodying the grammar of *jihad*, the struggle, he disrupts the grammar of the liberal everyday, of secular time and space, in the act of overtaking it and sometimes eradicating it (enlisting wrath against judgment and regulation). In other words, the theopolitical, just like the militant, is temperamental.

If the hostage taker steps out of the ordinary, or civil law, only to fall into the theopolitical space, how can one determine or define the space of complete freedom, one that is not tied to subjugation? As we have addressed, in certain variations of Islam God appears disappearing, he is visible in his withdrawal into invisibility. In this respect, divinity is an infinite movement and not a destination. The theopolitical is, furthermore, that which captures this movement, that which makes the horizon of the infinite static; and yet if it is a territory, then it must be called a phantom territory, an infallible fallacy consisting of delirious materiality.

Can this infinite horizon of the invisible, emblematic of God, also be a space of the impolitical? What the hostage taker announces with a blast is that sovereignty is not staging its act of disappearance yet.[24] States may be dissipating under the new rules of circulatory capital but this does not mean that sovereignty, as a force of condensation, is on the way out. From one perspective, hostage taking might be a phenomenon on the periphery of the neoliberal world, an aberration that is bound to dissolve with the success of the global market economy. But it is also a barometer of the insidious health of this same economy, or more accurately, of the new forms of humanitarian sovereignty that are put into place in all rising and still forthcoming democratic states. We saw how this presumably decreased sovereignty was manifested in Bosnia, Chechnya, and Kosovo through complete devastation of cities and landscapes, monuments and people; all for the sake of being in another hostage space, now of the shadows of former war leaders/criminals, or new CEOs. After this phase, it is not only democracy that will arrive but also another form of hostage economy. To think the impolitical, which would suggest a non-sovereign space, we need to go beyond the concerns of the hostage taker but also beyond (or is it underneath?) neoliberal thought. Where to start?

Faisal Devji suggests that militant groups such as al-Qaeda do not operate as a party and as such have no desire to crystallize into a stately power, which implies that they do not have hierarchies, sovereign constitutions, or implementations of regulated governing. One would think that they are impolitical. To this end, he states: "If certain elements in the communist or fascist parties of the past aimed to destroy the state form, those who go under the name of al-Qaʾeda have destroyed the party form itself, as if recognizing it to be an institution too closely connected with the state and its particular rationality."[25] Perhaps there is a promise in terrorist cells of the flight from the political, but for this flight to take effect the cells would have to remain forever cells; that is, one should always be a terrorist, in perpetual insurgency, since this in a sense prevents the formation of the state. The question that has to be answered at this point in history is: what kind of terrorist exactly would this be? Indeed, this is the old question of the avant-garde as well, to which each movement gave a specific answer. The sovereign of the outside that is to come will no doubt provide her own.

Taking, Seizing, the Event

Message

Does an event necessitate explosion, does it have to arrive through its vibratory expulsions? With all this talk of the aftermath and the post-conflict zone, with all the rubble that surrounds the event, we forget that which precludes these spatio-affective sites: the secrecy of planning and the explosion itself. The aftermath, that which is visible, is horror; what precludes it, the planning and strategy, the invisible, is terror. But every event, terrorist or not, arrives as a micro-explosion, a change of vibrations in the air of the theopolitical, caught in a delirium of its own. Stéphane Mallarmé says it well: "There is no explosion except a book." He is not speaking only of the ideas found in the book but rather of the cracking sound which occurs when one opens up the page (the "carnal" detonation of the book as a body). The vibrations, the soundings, override the ideas; or else, only the explosive ideas (those that create rupture) count. The event arrives not through the idea, not even with the word, but with the sound of the opening, the pre-linguistic vibration.

One is overtaken by an idea, or a message (especially if it is the prophet's articulation). For the message too is an event, especially the message of God's greatness. But the message that overtakes the hostage taker is not tied primarily to communication but rather to inspiration and vision. The message which is an event (even when it is a message of death) is one of revolt, a wave that sends one forth, that spreads to the outside, into space. It is not the ideological aspect of the message that is the most important here, but rather its spatial intimations, its seizing characteristics, and the transformations of space that lead into a hostage space (of the body, territory, building, airplane, etc.). The message turns one into a phantom, then, setting one apart and projecting one into space. The question now arises: how can one endure a humiliation (i.e. historical conditions of injustice) if one lives under the symptom, or an event, that is the message? The message works its way through the space of the body and goes further still. Just like writing, or inscriptions, both of the law and of the divine, it arrives through the projection of thoughts, where a certain exorcism of personal preoccupations occurs, in favor of the event of writing. The event does not meditate, it seizes.

There are thus two types of seizure happening in this symptomatology of the event: the overtaking of the hostage taker first and the overtaking of the hostage space second (sometimes the other way around). The city under siege is a phantom space intensified by the event of death that reveals the vulnerability of life (not just the horror and hardness of violence). Life quivers like a phantom and yet is more palpable and vital than ever before. The hostage space brings life to its bare essentials: life and death. In the case of hostage takers, it is death that is perceived as a form of life. Statements (micro-messages) of the kind "We love death more than you love life" have no other meaning than this: we have reduced life to its final precarious vibration. To step into death as an event, the hostage taker turns herself into that event itself. This is not a case of ideological depersonalization as much as of a metamorphic eventfulness. There is a confusion of life and death, a comingling, in this space, the breaking of the distinction, all of which shatters one's humanity. Of course, not all hostage taking is the same and not all abductions are signs of revolt; on the contrary, some are methods to destroy resistance. Understanding the context of the conflict or the situation is crucial; but so is decontextualizing, which allows for entering that same hostage space, not innocently or naively, but with the same sense of fatality as the one that comes with the message. Or more precisely, the clarification of the message in a journalistic sense, with some description of what is going on, can only go a certain distance. A dangerous thought of counter-life is necessary in order to explore the hostage space on its own terms, not to explain it but to overtake it just as the hostage space overtakes everyone inside of it.

To reiterate: what is at stake here is a double capture, that of the space and that of the people. With hostage taking an invisible membrane, an impenetrable barrier, is created, one that separates the inside world of the event from the outside world of the everyday. The inside becomes the esoteric space qualitatively different from the exoteric space of transparent politics. Norman O. Brown uses the terminology of the *zahir* and the *batin*, or the "external-visible-patent and internal-invisible-latent,"[1] to describe the distinction between materialist and spiritualist meanings, surface and substance, that appears in the analysis of Islamic scriptures (including folktales). What we have in the hostage space, however, is the confusion of these two polarities, that is the substance of war or hostage taking is pulverized into endless particles that now permeate the area under violence, without substance and without surfaces. The event is a form of dusting, history turned into infinitesimal waste matter.

The message therefore constitutes a space, or more precisely a site. It is in the strangeness of the message (loving death) that the event occurs: the hostage space is otherness turned into intimacy, turning (literally) the animosity of the outside (the humiliation of the neoliberal world) into an inside that demarcates one's own sovereign space. The school is not a school anymore; a theater is not a theater; the airplane is not an airplane: they all become sites of negated otherness, an intensified affect in which the hostage taker lives. By shrinking the captured space, the hostage taker turns it into a site (of terror, resistance, struggle); she thus renames the functionality of space. Accordingly, the hostage taker is usually forced to live as a phantom, on the fringes, not only because of her theopolitical dispositions but even more because of her temperamental proclivities. The hostage space is hence the expansion of this forced phantomality into the world (hostage taking is usually a national crisis, even though it happens within a single site, even a single room or vehicle). By way of shrinking, she expands her influence: the site of influence, the archipelago of eruption that finally turns into dust (the post-explosion rubble), is the imposition of her home.

At the heart of otherness, the hostage taker builds a home for herself which is also her tomb. The hostage space is a temporary monument to one's own death, a vitalist tomb, for it is an active death, through one's own power, onto which, in the aftermath, a national monument commemorating the victims lies superimposed (e.g. a large typographic sculpture that reads, in English, "Newborn" in the Kosovo capital of Priština). One is placed on top of the other and through this the site of hostage taking is further intensified. In other words, one hostage space covers the other, only then to turn into yet another hostage space. If the site is luminous or somber in the aftermath of the crisis, it is only so because the event arrives not only as an interruption of everyday time and space but also as an eruption. The event erupts into visibility or audibility; it articulates itself by shaking the foundations. When one approached Ground Zero in the years that followed 9/11, all one could see were the foundations, the gutted-out site, without content except for its own phantomal character, the fullness of the void.

Certainly, I take the theopolitical as the lifeline of the hostage taker, the reason why he can love death more than life, a form of theo-health that is visibly constructed. However, I also need to undermine my thought: this is not to fetishize the divine aspect but simply to distinguish it from other manifestations of the concept of the political, such as medico-political and aesthetic-political. All of these interpenetrate to a certain degree in the forces that carry to the extreme the experiences of life and death; they interpenetrate in what we call political institutions and religious laws. My point is that apparently less important manifestations of these forces such as dust, uniforms, beards, veils, a sentence here and there, a cloak, and so on, are ultimately brimming with energy that is obscured in any pure analysis of political institutions and religious doctrines. These absolutely concrete and at the same time formless appearances impose their force on the experience of terror, resistance, and death with utter precision. In this sense, one has to decipher absolute notions such as life and death while, at the same time ciphering further the intensified materials that compose these larger notions. In other words, death is banal, but dust, which announces it, is not.[2]

In the hostage space, I am bound to become the other. When revolt begins within oneself (the affirmative kind of suicide, against the oppression one endures or instigates), it then leaks into the streets, against the extended self – that is, the nation. We see this today, in February 2012, in the Syrian city of Homs where rebels and Syrian forces backing President al-Assad turned the city into a hostage space (where the post-conflict zoning is yet to come).[3] Rebels construct the event of interruption by making secret spaces of gathering, as for instance they have done in makeshift hospitals. Death smuggles its way into homes. The mother whose son has been tortured and killed says that her heart is burned, it is set on fire, and this is what she wants to happen to the Syrian president as well. The event is precisely this: a heart on fire. There is of course a difference between the grief caused by the immense loss which reduces one's power to act (biopotentiality) and that of the self-arson of the inside, an act which can be defined as a becoming-event which increases one's power to act. There is seemingly no poetry in Homs, the town leveled by clashes where hundreds of people have been killed, except that there is: what is extracted from the destruction is not only a burned-down rubble (of the heart) but also a burning heart, that which makes the event. Wherever the human is eradicated, the inhuman is born. If performed on the other, this is thanatopolitics, crime against humanity; if performed on oneself, it is the opening of the cosmopological, crime against one's own limitations. The hostage taker treads between these two spheres, falling to both sides, getting up and treading again.

Harmony

I am speaking of the event of war, terrorism and counterterrorism, the events that find their excuse in the acts of hostage taking. The event surges forth, disrupts history, reorients it, imposes the need to engage with it, or, in other words, takes hostage the entire world. The event is born of history but does not belong to it. It has its own continuity outside of historical time, an ahistorical vibration or resonance that is in all time at the same time. Hostage taking inverts the creation of the world, where one thing perceives the other in joy and responds with its own vibrations. The fusion of sounds in a symphony, the bodies folding in prayer, the swirling of the mass around black stones: all of these speak of a certain harmony of creation, a vitality of the theopolitical garden, the harmony of the sacred where the sovereign has withdrawn. To take and seize is to put this movement to a halt; through desire and out of love for the movement, the hostage taker destroys all that does not belong to it. Of course hostage taking and suicide bombing occur in large part because of socioeconomic circumstances (which is essentially the subjugation or exploitation of the other, occupation of her territory, and disruption of the other's landscape). All militant groups agree on this. But this is all still essentially a cosmological question, a question of arrangement (not simply the distribution of rights or resources). Arrangement in this sense: a decision on the ways in which the space will be carved out, what paths will be followed, and whose names will be invoked.

I thus speak of the event as a particular form of harmony; but hostage taking is also an interruption, a harmonic rupture, a breaking of the dominant form (or the form of domination). As I mentioned earlier, it is inaccurate to speak of terroristic acts as being purely revolutionary, or militant Islam as a revolutionary force, even though these singular movements emerge out of a similar enclosure and affective space of oppression (slavery, colonialism, neo-feudalism, exploited laborers, corporate indifference to local communities, etc.). But it is also important to note that the atonality of terrorism emerges from the core of liberal values. Even so-called tolerance, for example, harbors an allergic reaction to difference, such that an atonality of otherness is already inscribed in the middle of harmonic sameness.

There is no grasping that does not exert a force—lays hold upon, overcomes, and imposes. To take, to seize, is the first proprietary act: to claim as one's own. The hostage taker is a phantom sovereign, one who overtakes and suspends the procedures so as to lay claim of the territory and the bodies within it. In this sense, like a revolutionary, she imposes her harmony by a force born out of the enforcement to which she has been submitted. To seize is then to already be captured. One is overtaken by an event of freedom, revolt, struggle, etc., by all the atmospheric precipitations of medico-political affects. Indeed, the hostage taker is not a person but an event itself.[4] She brings the event with her arrival. In this respect, she is a set of atmospheric conditions.

The hostage space speaks with a different syntax than a regular space, both through ordinariness and extraordinariness, through the exorbitance of extreme simplicity (just as a god speaks through withdrawal) and through the pulverization of experience. The hostage space is thus paradoxical but not confusing. To give another image: prophecies often occur in the desert. This is to say that the concreteness of the message, even the form of the law, happens in the formlessness of spaces, such as the desert, just as the harmony of the garden arrives on the whirlwind of a nebulous sound (the harmony of the chaos-orbit). Recall here the case of the former US soldier, John Walker Lindh, who joined the Taliban, and who, before embracing this ideology, metamorphosed by the force of a beard and clothes, reconfiguring the temperaments of his body. Of course, it was the ideas, though better construed as poetry, that he read in Northwest Pakistan that led to his overtaking, but the ideas found their materiality in the physical attributes of the Taliban.[5] These transformations cannot be reduced to case studies in traumatology. Rather, they are implementations of new atmospheric conditions, where the climate of the desert spreads unnaturally into foreign microclimates, appearing where it does not belong. This is becoming the other rather than producing the other.[6]

To return to the premise of the absolute event (a problematic term) in the study of hostage spaces is to pose the following question: was 9/11 an event of such proportions, as outlined above, that it ushered in something new in the relations between humans on this planet? Was it cosmopological (both cosmopolitical and cosmological)? The United States seems to believe so—hence the annual commemorations, as well as the main memorial, which turn all the tension (i.e. the post-traumatic stress disorder) into a concrete block of memory. The memorial freezes painful memories, giving anaesthetizing form to affects such as grief, loss, and suffering. The event of hostage spacing also gives rise to that medico-political symptom which now entire nations claim for themselves. Or, stated otherwise, it is after the hostage crisis that the entire national community is traumatized; indeed the entire globe is presumably in a state of threat, captured by its own feelings of terror, now detached from the hostage taker who in any case exists only as dust, or a cell, or an amorphous rage. The medico-political predicament of the twenty-first century: planetary traumatology that comes from within, from the inside. The memorials which commemorate the "event" of hostage taking or terrorist attack are there not only to soothe the trauma but to also keep it alive. The real commemorations, however, the only perfect monuments, are the invisible particles of dust.

The event of 9/11 can indeed be seen in continuity with other events that sent ripples of their collapse throughout the global stratosphere; just as the fall of the Berlin wall announced the end of communism, a collapse of an alternative vision to neoliberalism that held the entire eastern hemisphere hostage (or was it in freedom?), so did the fall of the Twin Towers raise the official animosity of the West toward Islam to planetary proportions. This event is like a wave whose high frequency disrupts the cosmic aspect of the everyday order and the presumed harmonics of the world. But it is not chaos that arrived with the suicidal airplanes but rather another form of harmony—the harmony of a theopolitical garden. In fact, what we have in hostage taking is a combat of harmony against harmony (or else, we could say, a war within a war). Indeed, we could posit that Islamic militancy emerged from within the harmony of the West, that is from a capitalist neurosis that builds crude economic hierarchies. So what we have now is the fractalization of harmony, a war that harmonizes its own tonality into infinity. As such, the fall of the towers does not unfold the violence; rather, it enfolds it, involutes the violence always further into the interior of the harmony, into the borders of its own cosmos. If there are guiding ideas behind terror, words that promote the effort, they do not crystallize into an ideology of any kind. To this end, Baudrillard writes the following concerning the attack on these edifices:

> This is terror against terror—there is no longer any ideology behind it. We are far beyond ideology and politics now. No ideology, no cause—not even the Islamic cause—can account for the energy that fuels terror. The aim is no longer even to transform the world, but (as the heresies did in their day) to radicalize the world by sacrifice.[7]

Despite this precise formulation, one has to note that the radicalization of the world does not in fact not occur through sacrifice (which belongs to religious ideology) but rather through the simple tendency to resist, to exert oneself in spite of the overwhelming power that encapsulates the entire globe (the military and technological power of the West and its capital) and conceivably to generate some possibility that would prove anomalous to its operation.

The hostage taker is thus a negative cosmopologist, engaging the work of a divine harmonics of death. She summons the waves of history to their highest degree and like a surfer rides on them until they crash into nothingness (or, in human and environmental terms, into a catastrophe). Amidst happenings such as 9/11, an incredible amount of molecular configurations (of the political, theological, economic, and affective order) amass and implode (this is their energetic principle). The hostage taker is therefore the conscriptor of a composition—that is, a harmony of death the world hears and sees thanks to the proliferation of media images. But besides the omnipresence of the image that captures this negative cosmopology in its aftermath (or, more precisely, captures the rubble), it is actually the smoke and dust, the materialities of the rubble, that give us knowledge and insight into these negative tonalities of the event.[8] In Kosovo, it was the smoke which operated as a visible sign of ethnic cleansing; photographs of burning houses and villages attest to this. (The extent to which smoke has a life of its own is present in a series of photographs that were rejected by all major newspapers because they were characterized as too beautiful. These were then salvaged by Italian artist Gianni Motti who exhibited them.[9] In this example, we see that the event of terror, as perceived by humanist ethics, is not allowed to inflect itself through the experience of the beautiful image of smoke.)

The hostage takers operate through their inspirations and tendencies. Can the same be said of the western conglomerations of power (what tendencies or inspirations can one extract from democracy)? In other words, the so-called extremists do not have ideology. They only have their bodies that extend the message. The terrorists hide, smuggle, and erupt. They straddle their theopolitical rope. But ultimately they are crossing the abysses of western powers that are like images on the screen—or else, as renaissance paintings which frame the entire world with their lofty titles. The West is nothing but an image, one that is continually framing and capturing. In numerous written statements of the Islamic militants, we see that the inspiration for such attacks comes from the sense of humiliation, occupation, and hurt; the violent attacks could thus be seen as attempts to explode this entrapment of western powers.[10] As a result, a cosmopological dust sets on the surface of this old painting, or world-picture, governed by the exchange of blows, words, and laws. And on the surface, a new diagram of bodily intensities is drawn, visible only as lines in the dust.

Dust

Dust is the imprint, the stamp of the event of terror, since it overtakes the individual and seizes the breathing space, and never leaves the body. One can indeed claim illness from inhaling the dust of the explosion from the towers, a dust that is an implosive molecularization of building materials, human bodies, and endless amounts of objects originally present at the site. The inhalation of this dust forces one to exist immanently, as part of a monstrous inhumanity (containing the material effects of the catastrophe within oneself), departing from the original composition of one's body. The victims of a hostage taking (I speak of 9/11 here but also of countless others, as a shadow that conceals the dust), or those who were in close proximity, suddenly feel like a community. And we see them as a community of sufferers, brought together by a psychological trauma, while in fact they were brought together by being contaminated (one could also say, inappropriately, consecrated) by the materiality of terror in the event—that is, by the dust and smoke. Of course, the survivor of a catastrophe enters another state of being, but the analysis of this state should not merely be reduced to victimology; a certain vitalist epidemiology is necessary for a better understanding of this encounter. It is the encounter with the material substances (including the voice or breath of the other, of the enemy) that initiates new irreparable state of being.

The event comes on the wings of imperceptible particles, carried by the winds that contaminate the bodies with an eruptive dust. What a terroristic explosion announces is indeed infection, a new form of plague, contamination with terror. And it is in fright that everyone, especially the western citizen, feels most vulnerable. Again, the formlessness, and the embrace of it on the part of the hostage takers, makes the western participant horrified. Death is formless (or it is thought to be), except when it is tied to a story, or more precisely, to a kind of architecture, a place, like that of the divine garden. The theopolitical is thus nothing but an implementation of a form, an extension of the idea of death, but also game of the desire, the magnificent tendency of the body to resist. All monotheisms yearn for this procedure of forming and of sculpting. As mentioned earlier, Adam and Eve, the first couple, were sculpted from clay or dust, and gave form to the human; Satan was sculpted out of fire, a much more amorphous material, impossible to capture or delineate completely (yet possible to extinguish). The terms that followed this initial shaping of forms, humanity and sin, have the same characteristics as the bodies of Adam and Satan. One dies, the other extinguishes. These are the ways of their finitude, the essential thing that separates them. But the materiality of form only changes the ways in which it is expressed. This is why dust, the counter-effect of the hostage taker, is so fascinating; because it undermines love of the form, and in fact undermines the insistence on the theopolitical that I have argued for in preceding chapters. The silence of the hostage taker that eventually erupts is theopolitical but it is also that of dusting, or expansion of the desert winds.

Hostage takers are therefore a different type of militant than the partisan, not only because they take the air and the sea and the earth in their implementation of the prophetic message or resistance narrative, but because they operate on both the theo-sphere, as well as in the nebulous clouding of the dust, in the proliferation of the desert climate where one would not usually expect it. (Indeed, it is a known fact that grains of sand from North Africa often arrive to southern and central Europe, disrupting the "purity" of European air, indifferent to the borders between the states. In some sense, one has to view the hostage space precisely like this: the layering and enfolding of territories, both earthly and divine. The thousands of illegal immigrants that yearly set out for the south European shores from North Africa also embody this same climatology.)

To say that the event is a type of dusting might seem incomprehensible, but everyone understands death to be an event. In the hostage-taking events mentioned earlier, death equals terror and terror equals death, but there is more. The most surprising and potent weaponization of the hostage taker is her mutation into death. The words of Clarice Lispector speak a terroristic language: "And I defy death. I—I am my own death. And no one can go further than that. What is barbaric within me seeks the cruel barbarism beyond me."[11] The hostage taker defies death by dying; the suicide bomber that operates in both western and eastern territories is in a permanent state of latency, reducing her vitality, or harnessing her explosive potentials until the encounter with the event occurs, until she assumes the event of death and implements it. Her consciousness is light as air, turbulent as air, delirious as air. The hostage taker thus inscribes the terror of the air. Moreover, the air gains further materiality through the dust that carries the terror of the explosion, the signature of the event. Dust decomposes the world and is also there at the formation of it. No one can go farther than dust. The horror, in the body of the western citizen, arises precisely in the fact that she is not her own death. The horror in the neoliberal West lies in the fact that death arrives through the other, the barbarism beyond her, the barbaric that is not within her but is always in the other.

Being-toward-death. Is this an accurate definition of the hostage taker? Not entirely. The hostage taker imposes her body onto other bodies, just as a hostage space imposes its spatiality on the space of the ordinary, be it private or public. The physicality of the experience takes place on the bodies of those who happen to be there; one turns toward death accidentally, so to speak. Or in other words, in the hostage space, one is not being death but becoming death. How does this happen? In Spinoza we see the conative aspect of bodies (that strive through impulse or desire) erupting most emphatically on the surface of his thought. What makes one alive is the effort that he exerts, a will to power, despite all the obstacles. This is not only a matter of motivation, for this conation refers to a certain stubbornness, a tendency to persist, that which leads to resistance and revolt (all revolutionaries are thus purely conative beings). All organic (and perhaps even inorganic) materials contain this conative aspect: to live despite the odds. This view augments evolutionary theory, which ultimately provides a negative definition of life, defined in terms of the survival of the fittest. Life, or the vitality that runs through it, is in fact nothing but the effort and struggle to live, which can lead to both survival and to death, to both becoming more fit and to contamination or illness. It is not the fittest organism that is necessarily the most vital one. The hostage space has to be seen as part of this vital procedure where the implementation of death is in continuity with life, where the rupture of the event serves as another opening for life (perhaps after death, but also perhaps now, for the others that remain behind). There is continuity in rupture, the continuity of resistance, the tendency to go on, to become death, to turn into event and into a body that exerts itself in struggle, and into dust. Only within this thought, of an effort and resistance through death, can we catch a glimpse of life in the hostage space.

It is therefore in the dust that a new hostage space is constructed, since a little bit of the hostage taker is inhaled by everyone who finds herself at the site. The phantom is interiorized like the death itself. Now, the death of the other installs itself inside of me. The event steals its way in, always in the hands of the hostage takers and turns history into a hostage space. The event does not only simply interrupt the flow of history; since it arrives with an explosion (taking and seizing is itself explosive, even if it is done through stealth) it pulverizes history into dust. With the event, history is, for a moment, immanently spread through space and time into everyone and everything, and as a result it attains new materiality. Thus the dust from the Twin Towers continues to live on in the bodies of everyone who was in lower Manhattan that morning. The victims, the inhalers of dust, are now the monuments, carrying the dust particles within themselves as relics.[12] History is material, tangible but not visible, a floating and imperceptible debris. In the event, the accident and the will collide, coming together in the act of seizing and overtaking. The terror of Ground Zero comes from what we perceive as the chaos of destruction, and chaos denotes chasm, or else a formless primordial matter. Such is the materiality of the hostage space: out of the depths of this chasm rises the mass of dust particles, appearing through withdrawal, through inhalation.

We think in terms of causes and effects, but we should also think in terms of transformations and becomings. Thinking the event is not only diagnosing the situation but also stepping into a qualitative change of one's corporeality. The hostage space can be viewed as either an inserted intensification of a site (against a situation that is aggressively imposed in the American airport, or an Israeli checkpoint, or a Russian school) or as an extracted concept from the particular event of violence (being overtaken by an idea, or a message, or a line that transforms us, revolutionizes us, or else, revelationizes us), and both of these effects are true. Mohamed Bouazizi did not just criticize the humiliation undergone by people like himself (revealing the cause) or shock the onlookers with his suicide (unraveling the effect), but he also transformed into fire and smoke, into a different form of atmosphere, heat, and materiality. He turned into a counter-effect, and hence, into an event. This insertion and extraction leads, finally, to the only possible symptomatology: "Willing war against past and future wars, the pangs of death against all deaths, and the wound against all scars, in the name of becoming and not of the eternal."[13] Even the theopolitical turns to ashes in the counter-effect of the event. It is wrong to ascribe the theopolitical to all hostage takers, and I take a step back here; it is wrong not because the garden does not exist but because sometimes it simply burns down. Not every hostage taker is the same; not every explosion is the same; not every book (that explodes) is the same; not every hand that opens (the explosive, the book) is the same; not every intonation of the dying scream is the same. This fragmentation goes on into infinity (and into the infinitesimal). But it is not in the causes and effects that the terror (of the state, hostage taker, soldiers, passengers, militant and liberal thought) hides. It is also in the counter-effects, the events born out of historical circumstances to which they also do not belong. In light of this, the hostage space could be here defined as the site of atemporal temperaments.

Moreover, the hostage space is a space that speaks, that screams, turning the barbaric into barbarism. Indeed, how is the "barbarian" to respond to the judgment that turns her into a barbarian? Either with humility or with rage. And the space between the two is not of great distance, for they are not binary distinctions yet instead a fold within a fold, both being parts of the same affective veil. Hence, Majid (the character in Haneke's aforementioned film, "Hidden") cuts his throat in front of the figure of his humiliation; the man burns himself in the square; the women burn their burqas. All these acts of barbarism toward oneself are necessary deeds of the political and ethical gesture of the extreme (and "extreme" should be read positively here). The secular and Christian citizen sees these gestures as horror rather than ethical inevitability. This is not barbarism against barbarism, not the old regulatory theopolitical notion of "an eye for an eye" gesture, but rather barbarism in spite of barbarism. A fold explodes within a fold. Negation of oneself (or annihilation of oneself) is a disturbing way to become other: not anymore oneself, not anymore the other as in human, but the otherness of space, a new form of materiality, ashes and dust. This then encapsulates the paradox of militancy but also the everyday of many so-called apolitical individuals. A paradoxical but understandable becoming: one affirms oneself by denying one's life. Fanaticism, militancy, or terrorism is then nothing but the explosion of the affective fold that captures the individual (in the old theoretical language we would say subjectivity).

Outside of the space of political impotence, or power, or indifference, or planetary economical exchanges, there is a barbarian indeed, one that is created and imposed onto the image of oneself but also one that is latent, unfolding, and revolting, no matter the costs. We arrive at a point of further precision: the event is the rupture in the temporality of barbaric history. The cutting of one's throat works as an interruption of political subjectivity and as an opening of one's own barbarity: an explosion of the page that is also an opening, turning a new page, a poem of the barbarian that the western subject does not want to read. In this sense, Mallarme, the poet, is not western or French but rather an immigrant, a foreigner, an other, and also a terrorist of language, negator of the self. This then is a matter of crossing a threshold, for ". . . the pain must have attained a new threshold for so many to prefer destruction to the given evidence of a too humiliating reality."[14] Most of us are, by contrast, negotiators of the self, satisfied with the institutional therapy received or the pill consumed. The event opens up the hostage space in which life is captured (one's everyday life as well as one's spiritual life) by introducing one's own hostage space, infinitely smaller and weaker, but also impenetrable and indestructible (how does one destroy a self-proliferating cell?). The event is part of an ontological biochemistry. And even though its effects are clearly visible in the devastation of bodies, architecture, and political structures, the most important permutations occur as microscopic fissures (the life of the dust).

Fluvial

The crucial point (and a thesis of this book) rests in the observation that the hostage space actualizes itself across three fronts: that of the hostage taker embodied by the rebel or the militant (as a message or blueprint of the theopolitical); that of the space of occupation, in the territory of the state (in the seized building, city, neighborhood, or arena of humanitarian bombing); and finally that of the revolutionary who is yet to come, one untied to any sovereignty but her own intensity. The last iteration makes the first two reel behind like Frankenstein's children. The first two are minefields of the theopolitical, whereas the third is the explosion itself.

Besides the absolute event, one that levels the ground, clears space, raises dust out of the void, the event is characterized by its fluvial erosions (as in debris that flows in the river's meandering contour, or the products of the stream, its crumbled sediments). Fluvial processes operate as counter-effects to the absolute event, for they are seemingly insignificant, passing, and easily rejected. In wake of this, I present below four found images from contemporary mediascape that also work as instances of terroristic micro-vibrations.

First fluvial: The avant-garde has always been in the business of producing disharmonious harmonies, which today can be found in the mainstream. Mathangi "Maya" Arulpragasam (M.I.A.), a British pop musician of Sri Lankan Tamil descent, formulated a veritable terrorist manifesto in her recent video called "Bad Girls." Here M.I.A. managed to extract the terroristic sensibility from the Islamic context and yet depart from that context as well (banalizing theopolitical modalities usually found in militant manifestos). There is a humorous and dangerous plot in the video: men are surfing on the asphalt while holding on to a speeding car, a hand with a knife extending from the driver's seat, sharpening the knife on the asphalt, and M.I.A. herself on top of the car sharpening her nails, while the desert in the background burns in sporadic fires. The general discourse on terrorism gives little significance to these modes of production, just as it gives little significance to terrorist manifestos themselves. Indeed, how does one produce a close reading of a manifesto or a video?[15] A new form of reading, or better to say, burning, is necessary, one of conceptual eruption. The euphoric quality of M.I.A.'s video lies precisely in this: the eruption of indifference toward all categories that tie hostage takers to the theopolitical garden. The law itself has exploded and turned into lines, or messages, that are loose, explosive, and empowering. From the chains of violence a dangerous joy latent in all figures of fright is extracted. The veils suddenly detonate in a liberatory cry without fanaticism, employing the entire weaponry of the old avant-garde: youth, recklessness, terror, and joy.[16] Furthermore, M.I.A. revitalizes the genre of terror videos by removing the terror from it, and, as a consequence, demarcating the hostage space as post-sacred, no longer dependent on the categories of religion or ethnicity. This is done briefly, as a musical intermezzo, where the video is an event because it announces the potentiality of terror as both serious resistance and serious humor. More significantly, M.I.A. deterritorializes, decontextualizes, and re-embodies herself as a toxic figure (a militant).

Second fluvial: "Foreigners everywhere," a neon sign written in Arabic, is the work of a collective going by the name of Claire Fontaine. The sign announces the confusion that otherness poses in the midst of the metropolis. They, foreigners and signs, are everywhere, all around us (a fact that the state uses to increase security and control), but more importantly they are that which constitutes us (though as the stranger). That foreigners are everywhere, including within us, means that everyone is a sovereign, or should be, and that a sovereignty which does not destroy itself and others belongs to the foreigner. The hostage space is the foreigner's space. In this respect, Claire Fontaine is open about her methodological dispositions: "Only two years old, Claire Fontaine uses her freshness and youth to make herself a whatever-singularity and an existential terrorist in search of subjective emancipation."[17] We should note that she refers to herself in third person singular, not as an "I" or as an ego, but as a self that is multiple. Her name has no family tree but is invented, a simple naming of a territory that does not yet exist. She is a foreigner to herself, a singularity which consists of multiplicity (i.e. always pointing outside of herself toward other singularities)[18] in charge of existential and perceptual reconfigurations. The title of her sign produces two feelings: (1) the fear of the state toward foreigners; (2) the joy of affirming the immanent space of foreignness. Like all collectivities, secret societies, mainstream media, and terrorist cells, Claire Fontaine provides a set of glasses to see the reality beneath, revealing cosmopology as the work of an artisanal optometry.

Third fluvial: In 2007, Anahita Razmi was filming Iranian revolutionary guards when they stopped her and escorted her to their headquarters. They then erased 27 seconds of her video by filming the white wall of the room in the station. This new recording, which she entitled "White Wall Tehran," presents a monochrome grey wall with the sounds of the headquarters in the background.[19] Tehran here becomes the space captured by the flow of a white wall. The original event was overridden by an imposed image, such that the captured image was taken hostage itself. In this double capture, or counter-effect, the event comes forth as a void carried on the stream of history: another zero-point, or zero-wall, an emptiness that serves as a witnessing of the event that has been withdrawn from the public eye.

Fourth fluvial: In the documentary *The Making of a New Empire* by Jos de Putter there is a scene in which an old Chechen man invokes the fairytale of the wolf who asks a dog why he is chained. The dog replies "That's how it is . . ." The wolf turns away and says "I prefer to be free, even for a day . . ." Is this childish anthropomorphism or a guide to some secret political ontology? It is both, of course, since a profound message of resistance trickles out of this animal story. In this same spirit, all the intensities of the story are embodied in the intensities of the dance that unravels outside of the house in which the fairytale has been recounted: the Chechen Qadiri Zikr[20] (*zikr*, or *dhikr*, means remembrance or invocation of God). An endless repetition and incantation of names of God and formulas from the Qur'an correspond in unison to a swirling of men in circles, or else swaying in place in the formation of a mystical swarm. Invocation becomes a dance, dance becomes an invocation; as the group of men are taken hostage by the vibration of the rhythm, voice, clapping, turning gradually into eruption. It is the dance that raises one above the ordinariness or the banality of everyday struggle, just as the fairytale injects humor into specific tactics of survival. The opening into the event comes into being with the propulsion of the (dancing, swaying) body. And the manifestation of this propulsion (toward oneself, one's community, or the enemy) transpires through the open mouth, the movement of the voice that unfurls like fluvial amorphous plants that emerge in the river, zigzagging and curving along, and that now has no other option but to turn into a cry.

Cry, the Inhuman

Community

A man sings; a group of men huddle together beating their chests so as to provide a rhythm. To what politics, to what loves, to what echoes? There are no instruments besides the voice and the clapping of the hands upon the chests. This is the underground gathering of a Shi'a brotherhood where Helali (a singer and militant) sings praises to the medieval martyrs Imam Hussein and Imam Ali. These gatherings are enveloped by an atmosphere of semi-secrecy formed by being of the same "profession of faith, profession of fire," which here, in the case of the Shi'a, unites the expression of violence and love. The singing consists of invocations of the martyrs, the endless repetition of their names; repetition that is an opening to ecstasy, a trance which not only confirms the belonging of all those who are present in the fold of the song (a sonic fold that overtakes the room) but which also provides belonging to the sphere of the dead. It is in the beating of the chest that one communes, or shares the same properties of faith (i.e. love), with the dead.

The incantation, however, the singing and swaying, is really a cry—at once a battle cry and a lover's discourse. The group cries out to its masters. By screaming the names of the martyrs, the dead become alive in the economy of intensification: the cry intensifies the name, whereupon these two elements, sound-as-vibration and name-as-relic, exchange severities. The power of this exchange then echoes and trickles down to the individuals that form the gathering, individuals that profess their future sacrifice (the violent modality of this sonic communion). But more importantly, we arrive here to the most surprising aspect of extreme thought and practice: that it is done out of love and in the name of love. Or in other words, the love for the martyrs is a hopelessly neo-romantic turn. The conservative critic from the West who says that the terrorist is enslaved by ideology is only half-right; the militant is indeed enslaved, but by pure love for the one who dies and withdraws. By listening to the words of the song, we quickly realize that the master is also the lover of those that sing. The cry of the militant: *amor thanatos*. The harshness of the voice and of the repetition has a direct political dimensionality, just as the invoked name has a precise concreteness of love's directionality: it is a target for the arrow of the voice, for the voice that is a cry is already a weapon and the ritualistic beating of one's chests already a combat. Militancy is pure performativity, an art of struggle between life and death, or, better to say, of struggle between love and death.

In this gathering through ecstasy, a chasm opens up in the experience of the human; the rupture that arrives on the wings of the spell, the singing and crying, beating and swaying, the unison of the extreme that makes one stand outside of oneself. What is radical about this practice of Shi'a gathering? It forces one to step outside of oneself and thus become another, one that is still within the community but that has also withdrawn, died, as the master and the martyr.

There is a small leap from a being-on-the-lookout to a being-in-ecstasy. The latter is one way of building a community. But this ecstatic community holds a complicated relationship with civil society; that is why it is often called uncivilized by those that place the civil aspect of human relations as the highest value. As far as an ecstatic, militant, heterodoxic, or even terroristic community is concerned, its formation does not begin with sharing affects of love, grief, and rhythm, sharing that leads to participation in the affects of the other. This sharing is in fact only there in order for a certain transmogrification to occur. One loses oneself in the lover and vice-versa.

It is in becoming a rhythmic vibration that participants commune with the sounds that envelop them and with the invisible materiality of the beloved. When Helali sings "we have to go into insanity . . ." which is implied in the grief that surrounds the loss of the beloved, he elevates delirium as a necessary and, in a sense, ethical reaction to the experience of loss. But this ritual of going insane, the becoming-insane of the community, generates a political question too (including the theopolitical, which in this case means desiring the divine qualities of the master). It is political because insanity, or better to term it irrationality, marginalizes one not just from other ethnic and religious communities but from the world of humanity in general. Everyone in the West (and further) still lives under the sign of the ancient Greek notion that the human is, first and foremost, a rational animal.[1] What differentiates the human from the animal is supposedly the capacity to rationalize things (order, categorize, proceed from definitions that make sense, articulate arguments in linear fashion). But the impulses of passion, love, and terror, do not follow these rational differentiations. They interrupt and break, and rely entirely on the senses. The political aspect of this insanity lies in the birth of militancy. For militancy is also tied to one's passions, the temperament with which one articulates a desire, abandoning oneself to the abyss of death (i.e. to the lover). In other words, as emphasized earlier, the economy of the theopolitical is tied to aesthetic perceptions, to the sensations and feelings that arise in the community that resists, and that configures the expression of this resistance through vibrations of singing, longing, and also exploding.

The becoming-insane of the community thus operates as a reaction to the social and economic injustices that it undergoes but also as the experience of a theopolitical love, or simply love of the master, where the master is understood to be the one that provides an inspired vision. The hostage taker is an apprentice of the master, apprentice of the explosive courage, of extreme faith, an uncompromising action. Extreme faith means responding to the physical proximity to God. Being inside the theopolitical orbit, one is naturally attracted to those bodies which are closer to the core of all love and mercy. Through them the divine modalities shine forth. This is the logic behind the love of martyrs and saints which has a direct implication for the experience of death: on the one hand, the militant loves death because she dies out of love for her vision tied to a specific martyr; on the other hand, the western soldier is meant to follow the codes of professionalism and discipline, and is encouraged to die for an abstract notion of country. But things change in the proximity of death, or when one is outside of oneself. As Rilke writes: "Close to death, one no longer sees it, and you gaze steadily ahead, perhaps with an animal's gaze."[2] Or framed otherwise, as Adonis writes in his "Dream of Death": "When I saw death on a road, I saw my face in his. My thoughts resembled locomotives straining out of fog and into fog. Suddenly I felt akin to lightning or a message scratched in dust."[3] Close to death, one loses one's humanity because only a pure sensation of vulnerability remains, a gaze that is not one's own, a precipitation of mortality that positions one ahead of death.

The problem is that insanity is always defined negatively rather than as an opening, for example, onto a formation of community that simultaneously resists and loves. The a-rationality (rather than irrationality) of the hostage space should not be tied only to some "insane ideology" (the conservative view) or to purely socioeconomic injustices (the progressive leftist view), but also to the peculiar expressions of the aesthetic (i.e. sensory and perceptual) temperaments. And while the western subject sees the end of all (the end of perception and sensation, the end of love and belonging) in death, the hostage taker sees an intensification of these experiences (as we hear and see in Helali's song, which should itself be seen as one aspect of the ritual of flagellation, where the cry is the whip). These two diverging responses to the process of dying can be viewed as two different kinds of spells, charms, incantations, enticements that cannot understand each other; one sings of the love of nation and all the images that this notion conjures, and the other sings of death with images of the beloved, injustice, and sacrifice. For this reason, dialogue with militancy is not really possible; one would have to participate in its incantation first. In this respect, western and liberal refusal of negotiation with terrorists is not a sign of integrity but of impotence; impotence to understand the spell of the militant.

To be under a spell means to be inside of it, inside the images of its power: nationalism, militancy, love, these are only some of the manifestations of different images of spells. Moreover, the spell is a message and a narrative that works as a hostage space. Death is thus both a spell (enticement of love) and a hostage space (luring one's body into it). In the case of the militant song, it is the ultimate witnessing of the love for the master. Martyrdom is thus the witnessing of love, the final explosion of one's temperaments. This is what we see in the experience of ecstasy: dying through love, giving oneself through bodily pain. Helali's singing of the extreme thus shows that existence is not only always "with" others but is actually existence inside the other, under the veil of the other, cloaked and protected even and especially in the act of dying.[4]

Once again, in the gathering of men we see them beat their chests and point their arms upwards, all caught within the same movement—giving their heart, the organ of life, to the divine. This is the rhythm of ecstatic exchange. The three elements or materialities of an extreme poetics that form the experience of ecstasy reveal themselves here: hands, heart, the invisible. In secular societies one observes the hand on the chest, crossing one's heart, during official stately ceremonies (especially when hearing a national anthem). One shows belonging to the state with the hand upon one's heart, wherein the nation constitutes the lover. Is this not a similar form of extremism, a simple gesture pointing to the divine aspect of the state in the hearts of its citizens? The heart, the organ of romance, is always related to sacrifice, to giving one's life away, and thus to death. At the heart of sacrifice, one finds simply death.

Hands stretched upwards. (The Bosnian poet Mak Dizdar, who I mentioned earlier, addressed the importance of the motif of hands extended toward the sky that is to be found on medieval tombstones scattered throughout Bosnia and Herzegovina.)[5] The extended arm is an opening for a relationship, a first intimation of friendship between humans, but also an extension into the sky, the open space of the outside, as an intimation with the divine, a form of longing and desire. This motif of the hand is a gesture that differentiates the world in a sense that it instantiates a community, or potentials for a community. There are thus all those toward whom the hand is extended and all those who do not receive it; or, in other words, the differentiation is set up between the community of friends and the community of enemies. The gesture of the extended hand precedes the thought of the extreme and in a sense makes it possible through its spectrum of inclusion and separation. The acceptance of the hand is an engagement with the radical proximity of the touch. In extending oneself, or one's hand, toward the divine, one is "touched" by love, mercy, death, friendship, etc. Being touched is a medico-political (or pastoral) gesture that frees up the vulnerability of the body (in this sense, the American teenager who became a Taliban fighter was "touched" by what he read and heard from their side).

What is touching, which is to say effective, in the gathering that forms Helali's ritual concert is precisely the enumeration, speed, and shortness of the lines sang, coupled with the compulsive repetition of the heart-hand gesture. What is captivating in Dizdar's poetry is his ability to extract and transmit the lapidary, gnomic expressions from medieval tombstones into late-twentieth-century poetry. Both of these speak of the relationship between death and the extended hand, the openness that embraces fatality as a form of love. Dizdar transmogrifies ordinary language through a sacred language of medieval gnomic enunciations. It is a language of the tomb, of the human reduced to the hand pointing upward, and yet not a language of death but of another undisclosed form: cryptic yet direct, elementary yet impenetrable. As such, it is a language of sheer intensification. Similarly, Helali's cries, and the beating hands of the gathered crowd, do not only share the same dispositions toward social and economic conditions of the world, but actually become tetramorphic, turning the entire crowd into a rhythm, into a cry, into humans that stand outside of themselves and thus no longer human but rather vitalized lovers of death. The poetic language of Dizdar and the metaphysical cries of Helali bring bare language, dead names, into life. A language of the tomb, of an enclosed hostage space, that paradoxically dissolves the feelings of territorial and national enclosures.

With the same celerity of language, Albanian poet Visar Zhiti writes about the configuration of the heart and the sun, the core materiality of the body extracted from the human figure as an intensity of the solar force. He calls it the "Second Sun":

So much blood
Has been spent in this world,
But we have not yet built a sun of blood.

Listen, my friend,
To these trembling words:
A second sun will be born
    of our blood
    in the form of a heart.[6]

This signals a solarity yet to come, one that is born out of blood, that is to say, death, which will be nothing but a palpitating beat of the heart. A community of pulsation, no matter how romantic this may sound, is precisely what Helali's audience represents too: a rhythmic manifestation of militant love.

Cloak

The community sways under the veil of secrecy, under a cloak which protects its fire and incubates passion. I would like to address here another materiality of experience, another object that goes beyond itself, into the eternal, and, as such, enters into contemporary significance for those movements binding themselves to Islamic narratives. The cloak of Muhammad, the garment which the prophet wore, is among the first demarcations of a new territory; for some, it is the initial space of governance in Islam and perhaps the first instance of its political spatiality. The cloak is also the origin of the Shi'a dimension of the religion, as the Hadith (a saying or an act ascribed to Muhammad) of the Cloak describes an incident where Muhammad gathered Hassan, Hussein, Ali, and Fatima (his grandchildren, son-in-law, and daughter) under his cloak. This is also an instance of separation of two main denominations, Sunni and Shi'a (Shi'a believe that only these five members under the cloak form the "People of the House," the sinless unit which determines the future governance of the Muslim community based on the direct posterity of Muhammad). Furthermore, the cloak is tied to the idea of purification (protection) from sin, but it is also where its architectural connotations emerge. The cloak determines who remains inside and who stands outside, and its territorial aspect is visible in the gravitational pull exerted by the body of the prophet. One is safe depending on the proximity to his body. The cloak hides but also purifies and makes those that are under it exclusive and therefore elect. At least this is how the story goes for one enclave of the multifaceted faith.[7] What is undeniable here is that a very simple material object—the cloak—summons an entire metaphysical universe: the problem of domestic space, of community, of sin, and of intimacy. And none of this is symbolic. The militant worldview is never symbolic. The cloak is real and the separation it constructs is equally real. Or at least real enough to beat one's chests, to enact self-flagellation (*matam*), and even to die. The cloak is, in a way, the extension of Muhammad's body but also the first "tool" with which he could leave a mark, for it is through this article that the prophetic figure inscribes his diagram of belonging. In short, to conceal is to protect oneself, but it is also to harness one's community, or a community that is yet to come.

The cloak was a gift of the prophet Muhammad to a Yemeni shepherd whom he had never seen before. Until recently, "the cloak used to be folded and put into a silver container and this container would be bundled with fabrics and then placed into another silver container."[8] A veil upon a veil upon a veil. The magnificence of this image of care for the cloak lies in the fact that, at the core of the container (which is also a protective fold), there is only another veil (a cloak). The place of enclosure, the hostage space, has no substance or content unless another veil is seen as the content. The cloak enshrouds and provides a disguise; a cloak turns one into a secret even when there is nothing to hide. But more importantly, secrecy here refers to the undisclosed discourse, a non-understandable chatter; it hides the secret through silence. It turns the individual into silence and into a sign of humility. This brings me back to the question posed previously: if at the core of power lies secrecy, and at the core of secrecy lies silence, what lies at the core of silence? The answer is simple: a cry. Enfolded in the box of silence is the hidden cry of those who cannot articulate themselves. The love and violence that comes through the cry is always one that otherwise lives under the cloak. Or in other words, the cry is not the opposite of silence; on the contrary, they are both different degrees of stillness or noise, of articulated quietude. A cry is silence unveiled, silence with speed. This is the intimate silence of the community of the prophet, the sacred silence, the rapturous silence. All of this has a clear political dimension. Those who cannot speak harness a cry within. All revolutionary movements (such as the Arab Spring most recently) are basically public unfoldings of this core of silence, a reaction to the silencing perpetrated by the governing powers.

Furthermore, according to legend (and the head caretaker of the prophet's cloak while it was in Kandahar, Afghanistan), the mute would start speaking when in front of the inner sanctuary, before even seeing the cloak. The cloak as a relic has, in this respect, fundamentally medicinal properties. This is the original medico-political aspect of all acts of the prophets (or messianic acts)—to heal. Thus, liberation theology is already instituted in the life of the prophets (as they liberate from bondage and provide antidotes to bodily afflictions). The relic, by the law of contagion, or sympathetic magic, carries the pharmakonic powers of the prophet simply by the fact that it has touched his body. There are opposing views concerning the powers of the relic found in different Hadiths, but for those who gather around the relic it is always its materiality that carries liberation and healing, the actual molecules of the body of the blessed which turn molecules of the cloth itself into blissful properties. The relic contains its own "vibrant materiality"[9] through which it affects the materiality of the faithful.

Degrees

A new form of the enemy, one that is ushered through on a planetary level, is a by-product of the winds of power that arrive from the West (though never fully derivative or dialectical). Terrorist: a countercurrent, a turbulence within the civilized, the barbaric will, where the civilized is the barbaric and the barbaric is a necessity. The hostage space receives a new formulation in the act initiated by its forerunners; it receives a new cry, a quick scream of despair, though often masked, the inhuman tonality. In 1978, the eminent African-American writer James Baldwin sides with the terrorist, with the figure nourished to existence by the western powers themselves. Allow me to cite a longer passage:

> I was traveling before the days of electronic surveillance, before the hijackers and terrorists arrived. For the arrival of these people, the people in the seats of power have only themselves to blame. Who, indeed, has hijacked more than England has, for example, or who is more skilled in the uses of terror than my own unhappy country? Yes, I know: nevertheless, children, what goes around comes around, what you send out comes back to you. A terrorist is called that only because he does not have the power of the State behind him—indeed, he has no State, which is why he is a terrorist. The State, at bottom, and when the chips are down, rules by means of a terror made legal—that is how Franco ruled so long, and is the undeniable truth concerning South Africa. No one called the late J. Edgar Hoover a terrorist, though that is precisely what he was: and if anyone wishes, now, in this context, to speak of "civilized" values or "democracy" or "morality," you will pardon this poor nigger if he puts his hand before his mouth, and snickers—if he laughs at you. I have endured your morality for a very long

time, am still crawling up out of that dungheap: all that the slave can learn from his master is how to be a slave, and that is not morality.[10]

The history of the globe can be characterized as an endless application of hostage spaces, since the political nature of human organization necessitates this overtaking (the governing of a specific territoriality and the people within it). This application of power must be a product of the theological aspect which rests at the core of the political, the monotheistic love of the divine manifested through implementation of laws and sacrifices (even in positive terms, one is always a hostage, even in the domain of love). For this reason, all revolutionary movements, uprisings, and rebellions (from Spartacus to the Arab Spring) are found announcing both political and theological rupture, a rupture that hopes to liberate a people from subjugation. In this sense, colonial or tyrannical rulings of different parts of the world are merely formations of hostage spaces in their own right (though different in discourse and orchestration from the radical type which contests them). But to what extent have the revolutionary impulses remained as such, without subjecting a territory or a people to yet another hostage space? The crystallization of power into a tetramorphic state is a constant of the historical process. The revolution is the insertion of the untimely, the transmogrification of historical timelines. The reason for this might reside in the insistence upon remaining human, or humane, in any given society. And still, it is not enough to valorize the animal either, for even the animal is enslaved to its territory, and indifferent to everything else. When this is not the case, when the animal, for example, takes a path that is neither toward the feeding ground nor back toward its colony, but into the open, into certain death, it is deemed an aberration, the confused animal, the schizo-animal, outside of itself, that is, outside of the pack. One therefore has to be inhuman toward oneself, toward one's territory; the discourse of civilization should indeed have become outdated, kept only for the analysis of ancient Empires. Why is there a desire for civilization (and all the miniscule commands of hygiene, knowledge of the official language, technical specializations, etc.) in the first place if not to make one feel good, secure, aligned with the proper manifestation of one's temperament? The life of a temperament is only visible through the application of power as manifested in social relationships, architectures, tastes, and economies of the day. What Baldwin tells us is that the hostage taker, a figure of diagrammatic intensification, is only an infinitesimal fractal of the same national and imperial hostage space which he turns against. And yet, there are complexities in this emergence, a coalescence of estranged outlooks that are leading outside the backlash, even so far as an anti-civilizational consciousness.

The threat of death that we read and experience in the acts (and songs and dances) of the hostage takers are thus only externalized and materialized forms of much larger threats that loom invisibly in the hostage spaces of those who belong to the state. The terrorist yells out the death threat, and hence she acts; it is in the primacy of the act that she becomes a terrorist. Put simply: the human reflects and contemplates, the inhuman acts on impulse and newly contrived instinct. Elias Canetti reveals that every society runs on the "threat of death" and the reactive violence to it. In light of this threat, he develops a curious theory of the command: "Commands are conveyed without human beings perhaps being aware that they are also receiving a death threat. However commands are given, the threat of death stands behind them."[11] Human beings therefore live under the "sting" of the command, or are more accurately held beneath an infinity of commands. We could call this theory of the command the imposition of humiliation on those deemed uncivilized. If throughout the modern history of the West, detention (and extermination) camps were built upon the principle of humanism, its own version of the hostage space of the extreme limit, then the hostage taker overtakes space through her inhumanity. In any case, can one still be human when outside of the state? Illegal immigrants in western countries have to take the form of a phantom, while legal immigrants are given the official title of a resident alien; but none of these figures is properly human. Even second generation minorities in the West, with the right of citizenship, remain on a social fringe. In the case of the hostage taker, the violence of the command becomes palpable, unveiled as pure corporeality, and pushed to grotesque proportions so as to emphasize its omnipresence. While artists employ the same strategy in order to reveal the implicit absurdity of dominant laws, hostage takers do not just reproduce the threat but rather step into it. Becoming-death has no other meaning than this: turning oneself, one's body, into an energy of threat with all of the potentials for eruption.

Nevertheless, as it happens with all distinctions, the threat is itself only an extreme degree of security, and so these two affects or political dispositions belong to the same sphere of influence. In a corresponding way, the inhuman is only a degree of the human. This change of degree, however, is enough to change one's very nature (for instance, degrees of courage determine whether one becomes a hero or remains a coward, and hence a radically different being).[12] Through the singing of Helali, the community of Shi'a participants exchange affects with the dead. It is in this exchange that their degrees of humanity change, like rising temperatures on the thermometer, transforming each individual into an excess of heat rather than a person. Similarly, when they write about different forms of becoming, Deleuze and Guattari speak of exchanging degrees:

> In short, between substantial forms and determined subjects, between the two, there is not only a whole operation of demonic local transports but a natural play of haecceities, degrees, intensities, events, and accidents that compose individuations totally different from those of the well-formed subjects that receive them.[13]

Between the subjects (the people in the gathering) and the human forms that they contain, there is a "play" of different characteristics (of the air, sound, heat, words, grief, rage, love, etc.) which affects them and recomposes them. One becomes inhuman through the interplay of affects that circulate in immediate proximity; this of course only occurs if one is predisposed, either through resistance to injustices or through love of the commands, to embody these new characteristics. For the duration of the songs and cries, the individual becomes inseparable from the waves of the song, from one's beating upon one's heart so as to make it pulsate faster and faster, and thus through this inseparability (between waves and oneself) dissolves into a pulsating speed. The cry of the singer operates as a transporter of imperative affects. It sweeps one's body and imbues it with intensified characteristics: the love of death, which comes from the love of the dead. Death becomes another form of life: the life of the dead, on the same line of faith, but with different degrees of living.

Sacrifice

The act of sacrifice, when coupled with death, turns one either into an animal or into a saint. One is either debased or elevated. In the songs of Helali, we hear intimations of a sacrificial death as the participants profess their willingness to die for their master/lover. It is a sacrifice comprised of adoration and indignation. Helali's performances are already sacrifices in that they initiate the giving up of oneself, abandoning oneself, dying for a moment through the experience of ecstasy. But they are ultimately, as I mentioned above, romantic sacrifices, no matter how frightening, no matter how serious their claims. Through the act of hostage taking, the practitioner becomes a romantic rather than a sacred object intimately bound to his enemy. In other words, no one can call into question the genuine character of his love for God, the prophet, or the martyrs. Sacrifice in this context is simply an "offering that reverses what is inside to the outside."[14] The constitutive formula of sacrifice: in offering one's love and rage (from the inside), one gives death (to the outside). In the final analysis, however, the underground concerts are not there to promote sacrifice but to provide shelter. Community provides shelter and militancy (extremism of one's love) is the glue with which this shelter is held together.

I would like to point to a particular detail in the practice of sacrifice, which is that of anxiety. What is most shattering in seeing someone give her life away is the fact that she wavers, becomes riddled with doubt, sadness, etc. Anxiety lies at the heart of this theopolitical violence (that is also a paragon of love). Hadewijch feels devastated in the aftermath of her bombing, while Nassir's face reveals anguish for a split second in the subway, just before the charges have detonated. The entire world collapses, not just an underground station in Paris. For a moment, sovereignty is empty, justice is empty, sacrifice is empty. In the rage that negates the intimacy between enemies, the extreme act attempts to restore it through pure destruction. If one has already given oneself up, abandoned oneself, one can ask the same of the enemy. The question of one's destructibility, the cry of willful self-destructibility (Helali's songs), is essentially the question of human vulnerability which, when stripped bare to its last thread, reveals the inhuman. In light of this:

> there is no human essence; the human being is a potential being and, in the moment in which human beings think they have grasped the essence of the human in its infinite destructibility, what then appears is something that "no longer has anything human about it." The human being is thus always beyond or before the human, the central threshold through which pass currents of the human and the inhuman, subjectification and desubjectification, the living being's becoming speaking and the logos' becoming living.[15]

The song, the cry, is the extreme threshold between life and death which hostage takers inhabit, and this extreme threshold (from physical barriers in occupied territories to anxieties of terrorist sacrifice) forge the contours of the hostage space. In the above quote, Giorgio Agamben puts his finger on the beating pulse of such happenings. What the rhythmic repetition reveals is the inhuman vulnerability that quivers inside and outside of itself, within and beyond the space of love and terror.

Furthermore, the hostage space is incarnated in the bodies of those who occupy it. To overtake, to be overtaken by a message or by individuals, is closely tied to enfolding (as was discussed earlier), to the extent that to seize is to enfold the space into an event (we see this in every spectacle). Hostage taking is a form of forbidden articulation, a sudden imposition of one's secret power or vulnerability, and this secret imposition is always related to the process of incubation: the act of seizing as the final release of the silent incubation of vulnerability. A scream of powerlessness: the precarious vulnerability that turns one into an event of hostage taking. Accordingly, silence is an expression both of mourning and rage, the expropriation of energy or the harnessing of explosive power. In this monumentalization of experience, the monuments themselves are nothing but frozen cries, mute cries (a martyr or his name is always a monument). Silencing becomes a cry, except that these tonalities find their purpose in the space and time of their elocution, and, further still, in the intensified site of their happening. The procedure of hostaging in light of this proves evident: it is the sacrificial muting of the other. We recall the definition of an enemy clear as an icicle: the negation of otherness (Schmitt). Intimacy here, then, turns either into understanding (Hadewijch and Nassir) or into annihilation (Arkan and the Bosnian mujahideens).

In the war on terror, in the international political engagement with the hostage space and in the official involvement by which it is produced, the western states decided to pursue this negation of otherness to its final frontier, where the other turns into an absolute enemy and thus becomes an abstract mass or a concept of evil, rather than retaining its singularity of otherness. Becoming-other is a counter-procedure to this conservative mentality. The militant sensibilities of the Tiqqun collective speak to these lines:

> When, at a certain moment and in a certain place, two bodies animated by forms-of-life that are absolutely foreign to one another meet, they experience hostility. This type of encounter gives rise to no relation; to the contrary, it bears witness to the prior absence of relation. The hostis can be identified and its situation can be known, but it itself cannot be known for what it is— singular. Hostility is therefore the impossibility for certain bodies to enter into composition with each another, for certain bodies to know each other as singular. Whenever a thing is known in its singularity, it takes leave of the sphere of hostility and thereby becomes a friend—or an enemy.[16]

In actuality, the ending of this otherwise powerful paragraph is inaccurate: "when a thing is known in its singularity" it in fact becomes other and departs not only from the "sphere of hostility" but also from the binary distinction of friend/enemy. This is the difference between the idea of the enemy in the work of Schmitt and the idea of becoming in the work of Spinoza: Schmitt diagnoses an entire psychosocial landscape of the modern European (militant) mind, while Spinoza goes further than a diagnosis and announces new relationships of immanence that are both in place already and yet to come. The hostage space is found traversing both of these conceptions, in its dispersion and capture.

We can also see that the other of today is a stowaway, the illegal migrant arriving to the West from the East and the South, the other that is not anymore a negative projection of oneself but an invisible yet material "threat"—a phantom that crosses borders without permission.

Silhouette

To summarize, there are two ways to grasp the notion of the inhuman. The first is to perceive it as the act of cruelty toward the other, the environment, or the world. The inhuman is thus one that dehumanizes, one that does not recognize basic human (or animal) rights. The second perception, though, is to define it as cruelty toward oneself (to jump outside of oneself no matter the consequences), wherein cruelty becomes a countercurrent to the power that defines one's subjectivity, one that embraces inhumanity and barbarity and turns them into an affirmative politics, or the politics of the aberrant. In this inversion of the law of forms, the inhuman is not a dehumanized figure but an exacerbated silhouette.

But why define the inhuman in this way, with the potential danger of poeticizing violence? Because to write is to bear witness to the violence of the cry, the violence induced and produced. The cry is the trace released into space, a projectile of its own, with a scarring trajectory (upon the regions of one's body and that of the other), one that is incommensurable with the wound (the violence of the West) since the scar is a wound that has withdrawn.

The instance of hostage taking, the violence of the hostage space, is one that emerges from an enveloping of space, even if it is through the cry of a song or the martyr's name. The familiar turns into an explosive device of resistance and destruction. The great process of domestication that occurs through all social institutions (belonging to one's family, clan, nation, etc.) is precisely the process of taming. But the taming of what? It is not merely that humanity is essentially evil and needs the gravitational forces of society or the state in order to control this inherent violence. The domestic and the untamable belong together, as parts of the same fold, just as hostage space is an essential part of the experience of freedom (at least in the sphere of the theopolitical). As Lyotard puts forth:

The violence I am speaking of exceeds ordinary war and economic and social crisis. Conversely, and in spite of their generality, or because of it, crisis and war do not become desperate unless they are infiltrated with the breath and the asphyxia of the domestic.[17]

Forces of subjugation first appear in the sphere of the domestic (where else do the molecules of reactionary conservatism crystallize if not in the homes of strict fathers and mothers?). The untamable lies in the quiver of the voice that creates a rupture, a drift, an affirmation of a schism (e.g. Shi'a and Sunni). Inhuman modalities make themselves visible in turn through this gesture of the untamable. The voice, the rupture: it arrives as an event, an interruption of time and space. It arrives as an anomalous coordinate, a lightning, a zigzag (the gathering of those who beat their chests). There is unison in this rupturing from the mainstream, and inside the militant cry lies liberation too, awakened from its latent state only by the auditory burst. Rupture: a perennial divergence. Inside the theopolitical garden, the first home, the first domestic space of hostaging, lies the untamable (Adam's need to fall from grace is thus properly inhuman, in a sense that it creates the very first schism in the Judeo-Christian and Muslim ontology by separating him from the creator and his original home). The ancient and the futural, the immemorial myth and the forthcoming rumor, are interlaced in a recurring vision: "Here there is no 'I'. Here Adam remembers the dust of his clay."[18] Darwish makes Adam involute and enwrap with the dust that bears witness to no name but rather to a becoming-free. He continues:

On the verge of death, he says:
I have no trace left to lose:
Free I am so close to my liberty. My future lies in my own hand.
Soon I shall penetrate my life,
I shall be born free and parentless,
And as my name I shall choose azure letters . . .[19]

Violence is a form of consumption, exhaustion, and devouring; that is the economy of its sacrificial molecule. This is why many combatants (hostage takers, terrorists, soldiers, civilians caught in conflict) use amulets, images, or little objects that put them in touch with the divine. Through the object's materiality they realize that they are in the sphere of the theopolitical, crossing the space of appearance and disappearance of, most notably, their own body. Violence in this respect is a spell, a magic charm, like the cloak of the prophet, which needs to be broken so that another form can come out and be born. The violent lines of the song carry the analysis into the open sea so as to meet a community without direction. The new hostage space announces a new geography: the phantom territories of the stowaway, the one who floats because she has to.

The medusas arrive silently in the south Adriatic, on the Albanian coast, in the opposite manner of Helali's tonalities. Yet they are both carriers and mediators of a movement, from east to west, into darkness or liberation. The throbbing of the militant hands with which I began writing on the inhuman resembles the swarming fluctuations of medusas on the Albanian Adriatic coast. It is the old man Blendi who has the last word here, who announces the new figure that emerges on the coasts of twenty-first-century Europe and elsewhere. He, the figure, the body of the figure, arrives in the belly of the ship, in shadow, uninvited yet lured either by the exploitations of the past (colonial history) or by the promises of the future (neoliberal exuberance), or by a further aesthetic motion of defiance. There is no more East and West. There is only hiddenness. There is no witness, only a phantom. The anonymous stowaway: part medusa, part shadow. And who will liberate the hostage taker if not the medusas—that is, their foreboding silence, the explosion of the mute, or better to say, the detonation of the unsaid? In the posture of the clandestine migrant, neither hubris nor domestication plays a role; she is a pure line of the untamable. The migrant as a hostage, but also an involuntary phantom, now more a volatile space than anything else.

Medusas arrive silently, perfectly aligned, immanently disposed to the immense sea, just as the stowaway is immanent to the global world which is indifferent to her. The silent vortexes of the medusas create vibrations for the stowaways, as even such creatures, in their swarming, overtake the Adriatic for a month, create a hostage space, their own phantom territoriality, until they withdraw again. Indifferent to the politics of the nation-states whose waters they infest, they still follow the rhythm of planetary gravity, the phases of the moon, constantly returning as a pulsation, a visible movement of life. In the delirium of dehydration and hunger, the stowaway dreams of becoming a medusa, light and transparent, vulnerable but with the electric sting of a miniature lightning. And so there is no space outside of politics, because politics is simply a pulsation, the effort of the heart to throb and cry out.

Notes

Preface

1   Jean-François Lyotard, "*Domus* and the Metropolis," in *The Inhuman*, trans.
G. Bennington and R. Bowlby (Stanford: Stanford University Press, 1992), p. 198.

Chapter 1

1   I am employing Deleuze's definition of the animal that he provides in the filmed
interview with Claire Parnet, *From A to Z*, dir. P. A. Boutang, trans. C. J. Stivale (New
York: Semiotext(e), 2012). This question is taken up by a number of contemporary
authors. Thematically most significant for the present discussion is Derrida's *The Beast
and the Sovereign Volumes I* and *II* (Chicago: University of Chicago Press, 2009).

2   In recent scholarly literature see Faisal Devji, *Landscapes of Jihad* (Ithaca: Cornell
University Press, 2005) and *The Terrorist in Search of Humanity* (New York: Columbia
University Press, 2008); Talal Asad, *On Suicide Bombing* (New York: Columbia
University Press, 2007); Arjun Appadurai, *Fear of Small Numbers* (Durham:
Duke University Press, 2006); Peter Sloterdijk, *Rage and Time: A Psychopolitical
Investigation,* trans. M. Wenning (New York: Columbia University Press, 2010).

3   It is important to note the sense of being different that Muslim minorities experience
today in the western world; even if in possession of the national identification, for
example passports, their belonging is still not properly national since their ethnicity
differs from the "original" inhabitants of a particular European territory (we see
this problem especially arising in today's Germany, France, Spain, England, and
Russia). In the sphere of ethnicity, the notion of the territory is further reduced, or
materialized and concretized, in the images of soil or earth. In this respect, there are
molecules of extremism in every insistence on ethnic belonging since it brings to the
fore the substances of right-wing thought: blood and soil.

4   George Bataille, *Theory of Religion*, trans. R. Hurley (New York: Zone Books, 1989),
p. 19.

5   See Michael Wines, "Chechens Seize Moscow Theater, Taking as Many as 600
Hostages," *New York Times,* October 24, 2002 (www.nytimes.com/2002/10/24/world/
chechens-seize-moscow-theater-taking-as-many-as-600-hostages.html) (accessed
on July 22, 2011); Janna Lelchuk, *Terror in Russia: The Blood of Nord-Ost and Beslan*
(Bloomington: Authorhouse, 2005), especially part 1.

6   La Fura dels Baus, "Boris Godunov," (www.lafura.com/web/eng/obras_ficha. php?o=108) (accessed on July 24, 2011).

7   It is easy to define terrorism in Islam as a purely ideological act of violence, which immediately becomes theological, since behind the idea that leads to action stands, presumably, God. This is the regular equation of conservative and mainstream media in the West. My position is that terrorism is not ideological at all, and that the theology resides in the politics of the act (in rage, humiliation, hope, despair, territoriality, etc.), the theology of otherwise banal and concrete reasons tied to everyday existence. It is not in the confrontations of civilizations that the East and West collide but precisely in the small everyday gestures of power, friendship, and enmity. Or better yet, in the crystallization of this power in the institutions of the state.

8   The Special Purpose Islamic Regiment is on the "U.S. Department of State List of Foreign Terrorist Organizations." See *Military Education Research Library Network*, National Defense University Library, October 21, 2008 (http://merln.ndu.edu/ archivepdf/terrorism/State/103392.pdf) (accessed on July 25, 2011). Virtually all of the organizations on this list are Islamist or communist in their political nature, proving that the so-called global enemy can come only from these two modalities according to the political imagination of the contemporary American state. As we have seen in recent history, the Islamic militants lead the way in radicality ahead of the rebellious communists. It is in the light of this predicament that I investigate the problem of Islamic militancy in former communist countries.

9   See John B. Dunlop, *The 2002 Dubrovka and 2004 Beslan Hostage Crises: A Critique of Russian Counter-Terrorism*, ed. A. Umland (Germany: ibidem-Verlag, 2006).

10 For an account of giving and taking in the Caucasus while being under a sovereign power that spans several centuries, see Bruce Grant, *The Captive and the Gift: Cultural Histories of Sovereignty in Russia and the Caucasus* (Ithaca: Cornell University Press, 2009).

11 I am referring here to the distinction made by Carl Schmitt in his *Theory of the Partizan*, trans. G. L. Ulmen (New York: Telos Press Publishing, 2007), pp. 85–95. By bracketed war Schmitt means war based on agreement between two parties, with all the necessary determinations of duration, location, and extensiveness of conflict; on the other hand, absolute war he calls the eradication of these contractual and conceptual agreements, war fought not against a clearly defined enemy (number of units and troops) but against an idea, or a moralistic concept such as evil, which eventually leads to complete annihilation of the other.

12 An interesting account that addresses animal transformations inside the human group is found in a section titled "Transformation" in Elias Canetti's *Crowds and Power*, trans. C. Stewart (New York: Viking Press, 1962). One of many discoveries that Canetti presents is the fact that transformation is despised by the tyrant, the one who wields the power, unless it is imposed by him. See ibid., p. 378.

13 Deleuze and Guattari, "1227: Treatise on Nomadology—The War Machine," in *A Thousand Plateaus*, trans. B. Massumi (Minneapolis: University of Minnesota Press, 1987), p. 352. Here the idea of the war machine is a surprising one: the war machine is a demarcation of the nomadic movement which is exterior to the state. It is nothing but a countercurrent in the river of sovereignty, manifested in historical nomadic warrior tribes, in guerilla movements, and historical revolutionaries. But the war machine is also a form of thought, one that invents its own syntax, has no "organs," that is, internal properties, and always makes relations with the outside forces.

14 A short terror video by Richard Mosse, "Shahid," ed. T. Tweeten, 2009 (http://vimeo.com/7065282, 2009) (accessed on July 30, 2011).

15 The Beslan school hostage crisis, as it is called, occurred in September 2004 and lasted for three days. It was an act of hostage taking of over 1,100 people and it ended with the death of 380. See Nick Patton Walsh and Peter Beaumont, "When Hell Came Calling at Beslan's School No. 1," The *Guardian*, September 4, 2004 (www.guardian.co.uk/world/2004/sep/05/russia.chechnya) (accessed on July 27, 2011).

16 By negative interiority I mean the internalized forces that transpire within the individuals, or the institutional powers which have been interiorized by the individual and which limit her capacities to engage freely with the world. In other words, negative interiority is the effect of living in the "spaces of enclosure" (to use Foucault's terminology) which become dominant landscapes of one's expression, one's thinking and acting in the world.

17 In 2005 riots erupted in Paris following the death of two teenagers of Maghrebian descent, which consisted of the burning of cars and public buildings. In 2011 a number of London boroughs were caught in rioting and arson in the aftermath of the killing of Mark Duggan by the police. These riots (as well as many others throughout Europe) show the fragile harmony in the metropolis of liberal democracy.

18 Arjun Appadurai writes about this issue thusly: "As some democratic nations incline to create internal minorities whom they perceive as external majorities in disguise, so some within these minorities—often educated, disaffected youth—begin to identify themselves with the cellular world of global terror rather than with the isolated world of national minorities. Thus they morph from one kind of minority—weak, disempowered, disenfranchised, and angry—to another kind of minority—cellular, globalized, transnational, armed and dangerous." In *Fear of Small Numbers: An Essay on the Geography of Anger*, pp. 112–13. Appadurai shows how there is nothing in the essence of Islam that leads it to terrorist activity but that terror emerges out of the violence toward minorities and the reversed accompanying violence of the minorities. However, I would not agree with his diagnosis of the present age as one of "ideological warfare." It is not ideologies that are at war but geographies themselves, not the ideas but the territories of these ideas.

19 Eyal Weizman, "Walking Through Walls: Frontier Architectures," p. 2 (www.broombergchanarin.com/files/walking-through-walls.pdf) (accessed on August 2, 2011).

20 Adam Broomberg and Oliver Chanarin, "Chicago," SteidlMACK (www.choppedliver.info/chicago/, 2007) (accessed on August 1, 2011).

21 For the alliance of the war on terror with surrealist techniques of mimicry see Michael Taussig, "Zoology, Magic, and Surrealism in the War on Terror," in *Critical Inquiry* 34S2 (2008): S98–S116.

22 Schmitt, *Theory of the Partisan*, p. 85, note 89. This short book is still an unsurpassed source for the analysis of irregular combatants, as is his stylistic use of language and lucid historical analysis that is rarely found in contemporary political philosophy.

23 While discussing manuals, treatises, and books, Jean-Luc Nancy employs the term "militate" in an unexpected way: "All works that militate, that are engaged in a cause, that carry demands—manifestoes, squibs, broadsheets, pamphlets, penny dreadfuls, pasquinades—also belong to this register." In a hyper-sensitive fashion, but not inaccurately, we could say that every expression of a demand (legitimate or illegitimate) is somewhat militant—that is, bearing a degree of militancy. See Jean-Luc Nancy, *On the Commerce of Thinking: Of Books and Bookstores*, trans. D. Wills (New York: Fordham University Press, 2009), p. 5.

24 Ibid., p. 70.

25 Carl Schmitt, *Theory of the Partisan*, p. 69.

26 See Barack Obama's 9-minute speech on the death of Osama bin Laden, uploaded on youtube by the White House channel, see "President Obama on Death of Osama bin Laden," Presidential Speech, May 1, 2011 (www.youtube.com/watch?v=ZNYmK19-d0U&feature=relmfu) (accessed on July 22, 2011).

27 Michel Foucault has created the concept of heterotopia (that I employ for the hostage taker) as an embodiment of phantom territoriality: "But it is about external space that I would like to speak now. The space in which we live, from which we are drawn out of ourselves, just where the erosion of our lives, our times, our history takes place, this space that wears us down and consumes us, is in itself heterogeneous." See Michel Foucault, "Of Other Spaces: Utopias and Heterotopias," in *Rethinking Architecture: A Reader in Cultural Theory*, trans. J. Miskowiec, ed. N. Leach (New York: Routledge, 1997), p. 351. Furthermore, for Foucault, the heterotopic spaces are comprised of gardens, cemeteries, psychiatric clinics, prisons, brothels, "a sort of place that lies outside all places and yet is actually localizable." Ibid., p. 352. The hostage space too is heterotopic since it is a space within a space, for example an imposition of the militant's sovereign space inside a nation-state, or the hostage space of the theological and the political.

28 See the explanatory footnote 90 by the translator G. L. Ulmen in Schmitt, *Theory of the Partisan*, p. 89.

29 Devji, *The Terrorist in Search of Humanity*, p. 172.

30 Heller-Roazen, *The Enemy of All: Piracy and the Law of Nations* (New York: Zone Books, 2009).

31 Ibid., p. 171.

32 Quoted in Paul Virilio, *The Administration of Fear*, trans. A. Hodges (New York: Semiotext(e), 2012), p. 13.

33 This is not to say that there is no terrorism, militancy, or radical thought solely fueled by nihilistic indifference or by pure economic subjugation. For an argument that recent events of the Arab Spring are indeed postideological and thus constitute movements beyond identity politics see Hamid Dabashi, *The Arab Spring: The End of Postcolonialism* (London: Zed Books, 2012). This however does not deny that there are different degrees of militancy that in turn generate different dispositions toward the world, oneself, and the other.

34 Heller-Roazen, *The Enemy of All: Piracy and the Law of Nations*, p. 179.

Chapter 2

1 For a thorough political history of global jihad see Fawaz Gerges, *The Far Enemy: Why Jihad Went Global* (Cambridge: Cambridge University Press, 2009) and *The Rise and Fall of Al-Qaeda* (Oxford: Oxford University Press, 2011).

2 Peter Sloterdijk, *Rage and Time: A Psychopolitical Investigation*, trans. M. Wenning (New York: Columbia University Press, 2010), p. 55. Sloterdijk couples political radicalism with therapeutic theology when he insists: "In our religiously illiterate decades, people have almost completely forgotten that to speak of God in monotheism meant always at once to speak of a wrathful God. A wrathful God is the great impossible variable of our age." Ibid., p. 43. But there is also a supplement to rage (one that is its stratum), which is aggressiveness. Roger Caillois is in agreement with Sloterdijk's physics of rage when he states: "The deep, irreducible root of aggressiveness lies in the will to boundless expansion that is inherent to any idea clearly grasped by the intellect and capable as well of exerting effective motor control over the emotions. There is no judgment that does not directly want to pass into action." Caillois, *The Edge of Surrealism: A Roger Caillois Reader,* ed. C. Frank, trans. C. Frank and C. Naish (Durham: Duke University Press, 2003), p. 163.

3 Jason Bahbak Mohaghegh, *The Writing of Violence in the Middle East: Inflictions* (New York: Continuum, 2011), p. 126.

4 An infamous Serbian paramilitary unit "Scorpions," formed in 1991, was responsible for numerous massacres in Kosovo, Bosnia, and Croatia. Military units around the world still use animal names and images as their monikers, cryptonyms,

or official titles. This is an ancient practice of identification with a particular animal whose powers were believed to seep into the warrior that invokes it through the name or image (hence also the practice of tattooing the image on one's arm or neck).

5 Louise Bourgeois, "The Spider, the Mistress, and The Tangerine," a film by Marion Cajori and Amei Wallach (Zeitgeist Video, 2008).

6 The exterminating machinery of Nazi Germany ran on rage against the other (the absolute other being a Jew) but was executed through day-to-day indifference toward the pain and humiliation inflicted on the other. Namely, the victims of the Nazi regime were perceived as insects and vermin and could thus be exterminated passionlessly (and even ethically). We still see this mechanism of reducing the other to an animal in the present-day Israeli attitude toward Palestinians who are spat on by the settlers and their children, and degraded in every encounter with the Israeli institution. Elias Canetti spoke to this image of the exterminated insect: "If I say to someone, 'I could crush you with one hand', I am expressing the greatest possible contempt. It is as though I were saying 'You are an insect. You mean nothing to me. I can to what I like with you and that won't mean anything to me either. You mean nothing to anyone. You can be destroyed with impunity without anyone noticing. It would make no difference to anyone. Certainly not me.'" In *Crowds and Power*, trans. C. Stewart (New York: Viking Press, 1962), p. 205. In the simple phenomenology of crushing that Canetti unravels, we see that contempt is different from rage, that it is indeed a special type of affect; one that makes one indifferent.

7 Al-Tabari, Abu Djafar Muhammad and Franz Rosenthal, trans. W. M. Watt and M. V. McDonald, *The History of al-Ṭabarī* (New York: State University of New York Press, 1989): 1. See also, Hafiz Ibn Kathir, *Stories of the Prophets* (London: Dar-us-Salam Publications, 2003).

8 Peter Sloterdijk, *Rage and Time: A Psychopolitical Investigation* (New York: Columbia University Press, 2010), p. 64.

9 See Fidel Castro and Ignacio Ramonet, *My Life: A Spoken Autobiography* (New York: Scribner, 2009).

10 Esposito, *Bios: Biopolitics and Philosophy*, trans. T. Campbell (Minneapolis: University of Minnesota Press, 2008), p. 84.

11 Tariq Ramadan, "The Global Ideology of Fear," in *New Perspectives Quarterly* 23.1 (2006): 16.

12 See Gilles Deleuze on the difference between "molding" and "modulating" in "Postscript on the Societies of Control," *October* 59 (Winter, 1992): 3–7.

13 Georges Bataille, "Formless," in *Visions of Excess: Selected Writings, 1927–1939*, trans. A. Stoekl (Minneapolis: University of Minnesota Press, 1985). For an interpretation of Bataille's paragraph on the formless see Yve-Alain Bois, "F—Figure" in Yve-Alain Bois and Rosalind Krauss, *Formless: A User's Guide* (New York: Zone Books, 1997).

14 Roberto Esposito, *Bios: Biopolitics and Philosophy*, trans. T. Campbell (Minneapolis: University of Minnesota Press, 2008), p. 90.

15 Ramadan, "The Global Ideology of Fear," in *New Perspectives Quarterly* 23.1 (2006), 12:17.

16 Ibid., p. 13.

17 Appadurai, *Fear of Small Numbers: An Essay on the Geography of Anger* (Durham: Duke University Press, 2006), p. 32.

18 Ibid., p. 33.

19 Gilles Deleuze and Felix Guattari, "Treatise on Nomadology: The War Machine," in *A Thousand Plateaus: Capitalism and Schizophrenia*, trans. B. Massumi (Minneapolis: University of Minnesota Press).

20 Paul Virilio, *Bunker Archeology* (Princeton: Princeton Architectural Press, 2008), p. 23.

21 Nietzsche, *Frammenti Postumi (1888–1889)*, quoted in Esposito, *Bios: Biopolitics and Philosophy*, p. 92.

22 See "Anders Behring Breivik Indicted on Terror and Murder Charges" in the *Guardian* (www.guardian.co.uk/world/2012/mar/07/anders-behring-breivik-indicted-norway) (accessed on March 12, 2012). The assessment of Breivik's psychological condition can still change during his trial scheduled in April 2012.

23 See "Norway Massacre: Breivik Declared Insane," in *BBC,* November 29, 2011 (www.bbc.co.uk/news/world-15936276) (accessed on December 2, 2011).

24 There is an alternative view to this. Toscano writes about Gabriel Tarde's position: "It is not in the individual that the sources of insurrectionalism are to be sought, but in a particular circulation of affects and ideas, aided and abetted by their material support in communication." See Toscano, *Fanaticism: On the Uses of an Idea* (New York: Verso, 2010), p. 21.

25 See Gilles Deleuze and Felix Guattari, "1914: One or Several Wolves?", in *A Thousand Plateaus*. Deleuze and Guattari follow the line of critique developed by writers of the anti-psychiatric movement, especially that of R. D. Laing. However, they go further than Laing by creating a highly original conception of schizophrenia which they, on the one hand, critique as a form of social illness produced by capitalist society and, on the other, as a liberatory procedure that leads to multiplicity (in thought, in the everyday, in politics, etc.). This second, affirmative version of schizophrenia then becomes a tool for reading and writing—a schizoanalysis. For the first instance of employment of schizoanalysis see "Introduction to Schizoanalysis," in *Anti-Oedipus: Capitalism and Schizophrenia*. For a recent critique of biomedical diagnostics and treatment and its entanglement with the liberal state, see Joao Biehl, *Vita: Life in a Zone of Social Abandonment* (Berkeley: University of California Press, 2005).

26 Walter Benjamin, "The Destructive Character," in *Reflections* (New York: Schocken, 1986), p. 302.

27 A segment of this video can be seen here uploaded on youtube by the debejica channel, see these kinds of skirmishes had been going on back and forth daily, where one group would capture members of the other, in an odd triangular pattern: Croats (bearers of Catholicism) vs Serbs (bearers of Eastern Christianity) vs Bosniaks (bearers of Islam) (www.youtube.com/watch?v=J18jPBy72Eg&feature= related) (accessed on August 10, 2011).

28 Devji, *Landscapes of the Jihad: Militancy, Morality, Modernity* (Ithaca: Cornell University Press, 2005). For the idea that "the jihad itself can be seen as an offspring of the media," see p. 88. While this is an undoubtedly provocative idea, I find it somewhat reductive of the experience of jihad; the technologies of cruelty have been around for much longer than the technologies of modern mass media; one needs to see a consistency of the will to cruelty that spans different eras, that has been instituted in different times and infects the present; ideas, systems of belief, inspirations, and charismas, operate through an affective chemistry, so to speak, as much as they work through the forces of modernity, mass media, and globalization.

29 Asad, *On Suicide Bombing* (New York: Columbia University Press, 2007), p. 90. Asad rightly argues that the interrogation of the terrorist's motives is an impossible task since suicide bombers do not know all the reasons why they do what they do. My focus however is on the affective forces that underlie the acts of hostage takers. For me, motives are affects and vice-versa.

30 Giorgio Agamben, "Witness," in *Remnants of Auschwitz: The Witness and the Archive,* trans. Heller-Roazen (New York: Zone Books, 2002).

31 This surprising idea comes from the Italian criminal anthropologist Cesare Lambroso who investigated, that is, "treated," cases of political criminals at the end of the nineteenth century. The quote is from Alberto Toscano, *Fanaticism: On the Uses of an Idea* (New York: Verso, 2010), p. 20.

32 Caillois, "Aggressiveness as a Value," in *The Edge of Surrealism*, trans. C. Naish (Durham: Duke University Press, 2003), p. 164.

33 Igor Dobaev writes: "After the end of the 1994–1996 war in Chechnya, Mullah Bagautdin began setting up, in Daghestan, Wahhabi cells—'Islamic Societies' (*jamaats*)—leading, in mid-1997, to the formation of a public-political organization, the Islamic Community of Daghestan (Jamaat ul-Islamiyun, or Islamic Djamaat of Degestan, IDD), which was officially registered by the republic's Ministry of Justice." See Igor Dobaev, "Islamic Radicalism in the Northern Caucasus" CA & CC Press, International Conference, 2012 (www.ca-c. org.online2000/journal/eng-06–2000/09.dobaev.shtml) (accessed on March 3, 2012).

34 Paul Virilio, *The Administration of Fear*, trans. A. Hodges (Los Angeles: Semiotext(e), 2012), p. 35.

Chapter 3

1 Taqi-ud-deen ahmad ibn taymiyyah, *The Religious and Moral Doctrine of Jihaad* (England: Maktabah al-Ansaar, 2001).

2 Yuri Kozyrev, "Belsan, Osteria," Noor (www.noorimages.com/photographers/ yurikozyrev/stories/slideshows/beslan-osetia/slideshow/) (accessed on August 22, 2011).

3 Paul Virilio, *War and Cinema: The Logistics of Perception*, trans. P. Carniller (New York: Verso, 1989), p. 61.

4 Roger Caillois, "Mimicry and Legendary Psychasthenia," in *The Edge of Surrealism*, p. 100.

5 Ibid., p. 100.

6 Ibid., p. 101.

7 Hence the subtitle "Capitalism and Schizophrenia" of Deleuze and Guattari's book *A Thousand Plateaus* which addresses the delirium of the capitalist machine not through the analysis of political economy but through the investigation of space, animality, becomings, war, writing, etc.

8 For a description of the contemporary practice of veiling in Cairo see Saba Mahmood, *Politics of Piety: The Islamic Revival and The Feminist Subject* (Princeton: Princeton University Press, 2005). Mahmood says: "Women who wear niqab understand their practice to accord with a strict interpretation of Islamic edicts on female modesty, and often see themselves as more virtuous than women who wear the khimar (the veil that covers the head and torso) or the hijab (headscarf)" (p. 43). The veiling, both as a specifically feminine practice and as a phenomenon in Islamic cosmology, is therefore a question of modesty, but also, I would add, of power and divine architectonics.

9 Cyril Glasse, *The New Encyclopedia of Islam* (Walnut Creek, CA: AltaMira Press, 2001), pp. 179–80.

10 Guy Debord, *The Society of the Spectacle*, trans. D. Nicholson-Smith (New York: Zone Books, 1994), p. 136.

11 See the drawings and models of the master-plan, as well as the simulations of the future site, see Daniel Libeskind, "Ground Zero Master Plan," Studio Daniel Libeskind (http://daniel-libeskind.com/projects/ground-zero-master-plan/ images) (accessed on August 24, 2011). See also the images (that reveal "the communication of the incommunicable") by Joel Meyerowitz, "World Trade Center Archive," Phaidon (www.phaidon.com/agenda/photography/picture-galleries/2011/ september/08/joel-meyerowitzs-world-trade-center-archive/?view=thumbs) (accessed on August 24, 2011).

12 Philippe Petit, *Man on Wire,* dir. J. Marsh, 2008. The events in the book are the subject of a documentary with the same name.

13 Zainab Bahrani, *Rituals of War: The Body and Violence in Mesopotamia* (New York: Zone Books, 2008), p. 160.

14 Ibid., p. 164.

15 Ibid., p. 181.

16 Ayman Al Zawahiri, "Knights Under the Prophet's Banner," in *Voices of Terror*, ed. W. Laqueur (New York: Reed Press, 2004), p. 429. This speech was delivered in London on December 12, 2001.

17 Ibn Qayyim, *Zad al-Mitad* (http://web.youngmuslims.ca/online_library/books/milestones/hold/chapter_4.htm).

18 Susana Lopez and Carlos F. Arias, "How Viruses Hijack Endocytic Machinery," *Nature Education*, 3.9 (2010): 16. Lopez and Arias proceed to speak about the study in terms of warfare: "As part of our war against viruses, scientists have tried to understand all they can about these tiny, but complex, enemies." The study of endocytosis started when zoologist Ilya Metchnikoff collected the larvae of a starfish on the northeastern coast of Sicily and then pierced them with a rose thorn; he then "observed how the tiny amoeboid cells covered the thorn in an attempt to ingest the invading menace," p. 2.

19 Eyal Weizman, "Frontier Architectures," Steidl, 2007 (www.choppedliver.info/files/walking-through-walls.pdf) (accessed on August 27, 2011).

20 Ibid., p. 3.

21 I reference here the prophetic last sentence of Gilles Deleuze's piece "Postscript on the Societies of Control," which reads: "The coils of a serpent are even more complex than the burrows of a molehill." See Deleuze "Postscript on Societies of Control," *October 59* (Winter 1992) (www.n5m.org/n5m2/media/texts/deleuze.htm) (accessed on August 29, 2011).

22 The quote is from the back cover of the book, Hamid Dabashi, *Shi'ism: A Religion of Protest* (Cambridge: Belknap Press of Harvard University Press, 2011).

23 "Al-Qa'eda Manual," in *Voices of Terror*, ed. W. Laquer (New York: Reed Press, 2004), p. 403.

24 Carl Schmitt, *The Concept of the Political*, trans. G. L. Ulmen (New York: Telos Press Publishing, 2007), p. 79.

25 Fassin and Pandolfi, *Contemporary States of Emergency* (New York: Zone Books, 2010), p. 22.

26 Sebastian J., "Open Parliament of Albania/Coop Himmelb(l)au," *Archdaily*: 2011 (www.archdaily.com/124058/the-open-parliament-of-albania-coop-himmelblau/) (accessed on August 31, 2011).

27 Some examples of the destroyed churches include the Holy Trinity Monastery near Musutište, the Church of St Basil of Ostrog at Ljubovo, and the Dolac Monastery of the Holy Virgin near Klina. See "Desecrated Icons in Post War Kosovo and Metohia," in *Life of the Orthodox Church, Serbian Orthodox Diocese of Raska and Prizen* (www.kosovo.net/icons.html) (accessed on September 2, 2011).

Chapter 4

1 Francis R. Jones, the English translator of Dizdar, writes in his diary in 1998: "And yet each state must crumble to the dust of which it is made. The Ottoman empire is no more, and the live-and-let-live pragmatism of Balkan Islam has no place in the age of terrible purity. Twice this century have the heretic-killers come again with fire and the knife and the one true faith, to harry the folk of Bosnia and Herzegovina from their homes, to drown and stab and rape and burn." In Mak Dizdar, *Stone Sleeper*, trans. F. R. Jones (London: Anvil Press Poetry, 2009), p. 116.

2 Ibid., p. 111. This is a term Jones employs in describing Dizdar's approach to writing poetry.

3 Ibid., p. 34.

4 Mamdouh Mohamed, *Hajj & Umrah: From A to Z* (Amana Publications, 1996); Francis E. Peters, *The Hajj: The Muslim Pilgrimage to Mecca and the Holy Places* (Princeton: Princeton University Press, 1994).

5 Francis R. Jones speaks of the same thematic during his visit "to the magnificent Aladža mosque in Foča, built around a sacred meteoric stone," in Mak Dizdar, *Stone Sleeper*, p. 112.

6 John J. Saunders, *A History of Medieval Islam* (London: Routledge, 1978).

7 It is precisely the cosmopolitical character of Islam that Malcolm X, for example, realized when he made the pilgrimage to Mecca, one year before he was assassinated. It was only after his return from this trip to America that he changed his positions regarding racially exclusivist politics (which were not in and of themselves inaccurate in terms of social justice); it is only then that he openly proclaimed that the message of Islam includes everyone, that is, all races, which by extension means that identitarian politics are limiting and ultimately nonrevolutionary. In fact, he came to this realization precisely while being inside the multitude of pilgrims from all over the world, while being in the swirl and letting his body be taken by the gravitational pull of a being-toward-hostage which simultaneously calls for submission to the One and for the inclusion of all (under the condition that they submit). See Malcolm X, *The Autobiography of Malcolm X* (London: Penguin Books, 2010). Interestingly, he was also a prisoner in jail for many years, an experience that radicalized him but did not provide an ecstatic cosmology, which shows that the hostage space is not equivalent or reducible to a pure imprisoning.

8 Carl Schmitt, *The Concept of the Political*, trans. G. L. Ulmen (New York: Telos Press Publishing, 2007), p. 58.

9 See "Saudi Arabia's Top Artist Ahmad Bin Ibrahim Passes Away," *Khaleej Times*, November 9, 2009 (www.khaleejtimes.com/DisplayArticleNew.asp?col=&section=middleeast&xfile=data/middleeast/2009/November/middleeast_November268.xml) (accessed on September 12, 2011).

10 It would be interesting to think and analyze the sacred climatology of the Ka'ba and the black stone through the concepts developed by ancient and medieval theories of *kalam* (an atomist form of theology, cosmology, and metaphysics), especially as it is related to the question of occupied and empty spaces. I see this as one of the fundamental questions in the investigation of the hostage space. A great historical and philosophical analysis of this school of thought is Alnoor Dhanani's, *The Physical Theory of Kalām: Atoms, Space, and Void in Basrian Muʿtazilī Cosmology* (Brill Academic Publishing, 1993). Dhanani discusses a remark by one of the kalam commentators: "It follows then that occupied space is not inherent in empty space, or in other words, occupied space does not interpenetrate empty space. Rather, these two kinds of space are contiguous regions of space such that occupied spaces are embedded in, and surrounded by empty space" (p. 66). The hostage space is a void of the political space but it is obviously occupied (by hostage takers and hostages). It treats all space around itself as empty, which is only possible because it is contiguous with it – that is to say, it is "in-touch" with the empty space of the state, or in a strange proximity that is revealed as the intimacy of death.

11 For problems related to textual interpretations of the rituals surrounding the experience of hajj, see Abdellah Hammoudi, "Textualism and Anthropology: On the Ethnographic Encounter, or an Experience in the Hajj," in *Being There: The Fieldwork Encounter and the Making of Truth*, ed. J. Borneman and A. Hammoudi (Berkeley: University of California Press, 2009).

12 Mak Dizdar, *Stone Sleeper*, trans. F. R. Jones (London: Anvil Press Poetry, 2009), p. 44.

13 Nick McDonell, *The End of Major Combat Operations* (San Francisco: McSweeney's Books, 2010), p. 88.

14 Mak Dizdar, *Stone Sleepers*, trans. F. R. Jones (London: Anvil Press Poetry, 2009), p. 36.

15 Reza Negarestani, *Cyclonopedia: Complicity with Anonymous Materials* (Melbourne: Re.press, 2008), p. 91.

16 Elias Canetti, *Crowds and Power*, trans. C. Stewart (New York: Macmillan, 1984), p. 290.

17 Martin Heidegger, *Being and Time*, trans. J. Macquarrie and E. Robinson (New York: Harper, 1962), p. 265.

18 Ibid.

19 Ibid., p. 91

20 See James George Frazer, *The Golden Bough: A New Abridgment of the Classic Work*, ed. T. H. Gaster (New York: Criterion Books, 1959).

21 Jean-Pierre Vernant, "Dim Body, Dazzling Body," in *Fragments for a History of the Human Body, Part One*, ed. M. Feher, R. Naddaff, and N. Tazi (New York: Zone Books, 1989).

22 Mak Dizdar, *Stone Sleepers*, trans. F. R. Jones (London: Anvil Press Poetry, 2009), p. 34.

23 Concerning the primacy of the tactile in ancient Greek thought, Heller-Roazen writes of Aristotle's theory of sensation: "One can understand, therefore, how the Philosopher could explain in passing that by the term 'sensible' he meant simply 'tactile,' and how, for him, 'tangible qualities' were ultimately equivalent to 'the qualities of the body as a body.'" In Heller-Roazen, *The Inner Touch: Archeology of Sensation* (New York: Zone Books, 2007), p. 30.

Chapter 5

1 In this sense, Deleuze and Guattari are closer to the genius of the East than to the western political thought when they say, in their discussion of literature, that "There is no ideology and never has been." See *Thousand Plateaus: Capitalism and Schizophrenia,* trans. B. Massumi (Minneapolis: University of Minnesota Press, 1987), p. 4.

2 Bruno Dumont studied philosophy and religious studies, not film or directing, and writes the stories for his films himself. In fact, his stance is that films are another, in his words, "more fun," way of doing philosophy. So the reflections and problems raised by his characters should be seen as his own questions. As such, my addressing the trajectories from the film marks a conversation with the problems raised within the work that also move beyond it: the nature of mysticism, love, terror, and violence found in the everyday. By the term "nature," I mean the transmutable essence of a thing, or the nonessential core that changes with the change of degrees with which it connects to any other thing. Or, more simply, the capacity to change which is provoked by the relationship with the outside. The nature of film changes with its relationship to philosophy. The nature of things, in a Deleuzian sense, has to do with their internal properties that transform and change their essence as soon as they enter into relation with something else.

3 See D. Fassin and M. Pandolfi, eds. *Contemporary States of Emergency: The Politics of Military and Humanitarian Interventions* (New York: Zone Books, 2010).

4 I take this concept from the title of Paul Mommaers' book *The Land Within: The Process of Possessing and Being Possessed by God According to the Mystic Jan van Ruysbroeck*, trans. D. N. Smith (Chicago: Franciscan Herald Press, 1975).

5 Didier Fassin and Richard Rechtman, *The Empire of Trauma: An Inquiry into the Condition of Victimhood*, trans. R. Gomme (Princeton: Princeton University Press, 2009), p. 2.

6 Ibid., p. 1, ft. 2.

7 Fassin and Rechtman speak of their methodology as "constructionist": "The reading we propose in the book might be described as constructionist, in the sense that it explores the ways in which trauma is produced through mobilizations of mental health professionals and defenders of victims' rights, and more broadly by a restructuring of the cognitive and moral foundations of our societies that define our relationship to misfortune, memory, and subjectivity." See *The Empire of Trauma: An Inquiry into the Condition of Victimhood*, pp. 6–7. There is one additional disposition that needs to be mentioned in the discussion of trauma: namely, that trauma is also constructed by the negative reading of delirium which places it only on a psychological plateau of disorders without recognizing its theopolitical aspect.

8 Quoted in Marjory Jacobsen, "Anri Sala," in *Sensorium: Embodied Experience, Technology and Contemporary Art*, ed. C. A. Jones (Cambridge: MIT Press, 2006), p. 91.

9 Vaclav Havel, "Stories and Totalitarianism," in *Open Letters: Selected Writings 1965—1990*, ed. P. Wilson (New York: Knopf, 1991), p. 329.

10 See Peter Sloterdijk, *Terror from the Air*, trans. A. Patton and S. Corcoran (Los Angeles: Semiotext(e), 2009). Sloterdijk opens the argument of the essay in this way: "Anybody wanting to grasp the originality of the era has to consider: the practice of terrorism, the concept of product design, and environmental thinking. With the first, enemy interaction was established on a post-militaristic basis; with the second, functionalism was enabled to reconnect to the world of perception; and with the third, phenomena of life and knowledge became more profoundly linked than ever before." In *Terror from the Air*, p. 9. The significance of this analysis is that it poses an "atmoterrorist model" as a decisive form of explication for the first time.

11 Wendy Brown, *Walled States, Waning Sovereignty* (New York: Zone Books, 2010), p. 119. In line with this fear of openness and being outside of containment, Brown accurately includes the vestiges of psychoanalysis (a precursor of psychotherapy), but inaccurately Nietzsche's writings. When Nietzsche says that one can only be alive when bounded by a horizon, he means that one is free (or, absolutely free) only when surrounded by a circular boundary that ignores all obstructions, the space open on all sides. This position is understandable considering that Nietzsche was himself, in a way, a philosophical terrorist, a man who took delirious breaths and wrote in delirious bursts, a writer who planted gas bottles on the tracks of the main philosophical railroad.

12 See and hear: Malcolm X, "Malcolm X After Mecca," Youtube.com (www.youtube.com/watch?v=wgqIek2TYvg) (accessed on October 15, 2011).

13 Carl Schmitt, "The Age of Neutralizations and Depoliticizations," in *The Concept of the Political*, trans. G. Schwab (New Brunswick: Rutgers University Press, 1976), p. 96.

Chapter 6

1   See Heller-Roazen, *The Enemy of All: Piracy and the Law of Nations* (New York: Zone Books, 2009), p. 180. Heller-Roazen provides a helpful analysis of legal determinations that turn the pirate into an "enemy of all" as a result of his complicated spatiality. I pursue this idea by thinking of this undefined spatiality as a form of new weaponry (being a region instead of defending one) in terrorist activity. In other words, the legal demarcation that makes the pirate (or a terrorist) into an absolute enemy is appropriated in militancy as a tactic of maneuvering.

2   Mohammad 'Abdus Salam Faraj, "Jihad, The Absent Obligation," in *Voices of Terror*, ed. W. Laqueur (New York: Reed Press, 2004), p. 401. Faraj was one of the most important modern theorists and organizers for Islamic militant movements. In 1981, he wrote *Al Farida al Ghaiba*, "The Neglected Obligation" (or "Forgotten Duty," "Missing Commandment"); he was also the founder of Jama'at al-Jihad (Group of Holy Struggle), an underground movement which was crushed the same year it was founded. Faraj himself was executed by Egyptian authorities in 1982. For detailed information, see Gilles Kepel, *Muslim Extremism in Egypt: The Prophet and Pharaoh*, trans. J. Rothschild (Berkeley: University of California Press, 1985).

3   Ibid., p. 401.

4   The introduction to the manifesto, the names of all participants, and the manifesto itself can be found at "Surrealism in the Arab World," Libcom.org (http://libcom. org/history/surrealism-arab-world) (accessed on October 23, 2011). Surrealism started as a European modernist movement and was, in a sense, imported into Arab and Persian worlds. But this does not mean that it is authentically European. The fact that artists in Cairo could appropriate the surrealist sensibilities to their ends speaks to their own "authentic" inventiveness that rises above geopolitical context. In addition, there is a long history of experimentation with fantasy, hallucinations, dreams, the paranormal, and the unreal in Arabic and Persian literature, from romanticism to epic genres to mysticism, which demonstrates surrealist affinities in certain Middle Eastern traditions. For this argument see Adonis, *Sufism and Surrealism*, trans. J. Cumberbatch (Beirut: Saqi Books, 2005).

5   See "Manifesto of the Arab Surrealist Movement," Libcom.org (http://libcom.org/ history/surrealism-arab-world) (accessed on October 23, 2011).

6   Joyce Mansour, *Screams*, trans. S. Gavronsky (Sausalito: Post Apollo Press 1995), p. 43.

7   Ibid., p. 27.

8   Michel Surya points to the important distancing in the French Surrealist movement between Andre Breton and Georges Bataille which bears resemblance to the distinction that I am making between the militant and the surrealist: "Andre Breton made Surrealism the instrument of the *marvelous*; he wanted retribution for the hatred in which it was held and the ridicule which, he claimed, everyone cast on it: 'Let's speak plainly: the marvelous is always beautiful, anything

marvelous is beautiful, it is even only the marvelous that is beautiful', he wrote in the *First Manifesto*. At the other extreme, Georges Bataille made *Documents* the instrument of the *monstrous*." See *Georges Bataille: An Intellectual Biography*, trans. K. Fijalkowski and M. Richardson (New York: Verso, 2002), p. 124. Bataille was ultimately antagonistic toward surrealism and for good reason. Surrealism is indeed creatively the most overrated western avant-garde movement of the twentieth century.

9 The assertion of such new dimensions, to use the term of the Arab Surrealists, has not been fully met; in the aftermath of the 2011 revolution in Egypt, for example, the military has consolidated its power, reinstating in many important political positions men close to former dictator Hosni Mubarak. Indeed, the political landscape of the country is suspended in the confrontation between three forces: the secularized youth, the old military, and the conservative Muslim Brotherhood. The revolution was indeed an exit from the prison of the theopolitical, of the extreme version of political theology where the president of the country becomes the absolute sovereign. But this exit seems only to lead into another entrance in the hallway of the same theopolitical predicament, with only slightly better proclivities than the last one. For the most recent commentary on the politics of the square, see Robert Fisk, "Back to Tahrir Square," The *Independent*, December 2, 2011 (www.independent.co.uk/opinion/commentators/fisk/robert-fisk-back-to-tahrir-square-6270756.html) (accessed on December 17, 2011).

10 See Michel Foucault, *Security, Territory, Population: Lectures at the College de France 1977–1978*, ed. M. Senellart, trans. G. Burchell (New York: Palgrave Macmillan, 2007), p. xxxi. The quote is taken from an introduction to this volume by Arnold I. Davidson.

11 Talal Asad, *On Suicide Bombing* (New York: Columbia University Press, 2007), pp. 81–2.

12 Pierre Clastres, "Of Torture in Primitive Societies," in *Society Against the State: Essays in Political Anthropology*, trans. R. Hurley (New York: Zone Books, 1987), p. 177.

13 Thomas Dworzak, "The Enemy," *Cabinet: A Quarterly of Art and Culture* 12 (Fall/Winter 2003): 74–7.

14 See Ron Haviv, *Blood and Honey: A Balkan War Journal* (New York: TV Books, 2000). Also see Haviv's online archive at Ron Havi, "Blood and Honey: A Balkan War Journal" (www.ronhaviv.com/#s=0&mi=2&pt=1&pi=10000&p=14&a=0&at=0) (accessed on November 28, 2011).

15 Arkan is the nickname of Zeljko Raznjatović, a powerful figure in the former Yugoslav criminal milieu and later in the political and military world of Serbia. Throughout the 1970s, Raznjatović was imprisoned in Sweden, Holland, Belgium, Switzerland, Serbia, and Croatia for numerous criminal activities. He managed to escape from all of them (prisons and countries). His paramilitary unit was

initially formed by a group of extreme fans of the Serbian soccer team "The Red Star" from Belgrade. His paramilitary guard was in full operation from 1991–6, but it is plausible to speculate that a number of its members participated in the war in Kosovo from 1998–9. Raznjatović was shot to death in 2000 under unclear circumstances. For an interview in Serbian done while he was still on the battlefield in Bosnia, see Zeljko Raznjatović, "Warrior Steeped in Sacredness: An Interview" (www.dadavujasinovic.com/Arkan.htm) (accessed on October 22, 2011). The title of this interview ("Warrior Steeped in Sacredness") could easily be the title of the present chapter.

16 The entire 37 articles of "The Constitution of Unification of Death" that indeed read like an avant-garde manifesto can be found here: The Black Hand, "Constitution of the Black Hand: Unification or Death," Brigham Young University (http://wwi. lib.byu.edu/index.php/Constitution_of_the_Black_Hand) (accessed on October 28, 2011). The useful historical details which inspired my writing were compiled by Michael Shackelford at (http://wwi.lib.byu.edu/index.php/The_Black_Hand) (accessed on October 28, 2011).

17 Reza Negarestani, "The Militarization of Peace: Absence of Terror or Terror of Absence?" in *Collapse Vol. 1: Numerical Materialism*, ed. R Mackay (United Kingdom: Urbanomic, 2006), p. 62. Negarestani's essay is an excellent analysis of "underground heretical Islamic societies." I also took his term "hypercamouflage" from this essay.

18 Roger Caillois, *The Edge of Surrealism*, ed. C. Frank, trans. C. Frank and C. Naish (Durham: Duke University Press, 2003), p. 205. I take this quotation from a splendid introduction to the essay by Claudine Frank. Caillois provides indispensable explorations of difficult issues in the anthropology of power, aggressiveness, and schizophrenia. It is also impressive that in 1938 he instituted the College of Sociology (with Georges Bataille and Michel Leiris), an institution "exclusively devoted to the study of closed groups."

19 For a description of different ontologies of the enemy in the West, see the interview by Sina Najafi with Peter Galison "The Ontology of the Enemy," in *Cabinet: A Quarterly of Art and Culture* 12 (Fall/Winter 2003), pp. 63–7. Their discussion differentiates between (a) racialized, (b) anonymous, and (c) indifferent-mechanized visions of the enemy developed in the last 100 years in the West. The interesting point that Galison makes is that the scientificity of war changes once it becomes irregular—namely, western countries today have to respond to the enemy that is prepared to kill herself, which they ultimately cannot do. The intense proliferation of technological surveillance is, in a way, an attempt to respond to a new vision of the enemy, a confused and unclear vision at that.

20 Mahmoud Darwish, *Unfortunately, It Was Paradise: Selected Poems,* trans. M. Akash, C. Forche, S. Antoon, and A. El-Zein (Berkeley: University of California Press, 2003), p. 18.

21 The sadistic aspect of political figureheads is not to be confused with the writings of Marquise de Sade. The ousted presidents are only caricatures of Sade's writing; or else, they are actual reflections of the inscriptions of tyranny that he evoked while himself being absolutely against them.

Chapter 7

1 I approach the problem of sovereignty (and the accompanying concepts of power and the political) from the position that religion and politics intertwined still make an institutional couple, no less than an amalgamated force of the everyday. The term sovereignty of course has a long history in both East and West, whose theoretical implications are matter of intense debate. Antonio Negri and Michael Hardt, for example, critique, what they call, "apocalyptic visions" in scholarly and popular discourses that tie theology with politics at the expense of dominant legal and economic structures. In contrast to this, they propose that: "The primary form of power that really confronts us today, however, is not so dramatic and demonic but rather earthly and mundane. We need to stop confusing politics with theology. The predominant contemporary form of sovereignty—if we still want to call it that—is completely embedded within and supported by legal systems and institutions of governance, a republican form characterized not only by the rule of law but also equally by the rule of property." In *Commonwealth*, p. 5. While it is good to bring the analysis to the "earthly and mundane," it would be naïve not to see the detritus of the sacred, the divine flotsam and jetsam, all over the daily banality in which contemporary individuals finds herself. In light of this critique, it is strange that Negri and Hardt, who actually do admirable work, end their *Empire* (Cambridge: Harvard University Press, 2001), with sacred tonalities, by saying that the new communist militant should emulate Saint Francis of Assisi (i.e. his values of poverty and joy) while ignoring from the "space," the terrain, from which Saint Francis draw on these powers (p. 413). Similarly, in their last book, *Commonwealth*, they aptly use mystical visions of Meister Eckhart for defense of queer politics (p. 62). Radical leftist militants in the West are thus expected to be nontheological mystics (who nevertheless absorb their inspiration from certain strands of Christianity). For opposite views, where theology plays a constitutive role in present politics see Simon Critchley, *The Faith of the Faithless: Experiments in Political Theology* (New York: Verso, 2012); Giorgio Agamben, *The Kingdom and the Glory: For a Theological Genealogy of Economy and Government*, trans. L. Chiesa (Stanford: Stanford University Press, 2011).

2 Georges Bataille, *Theory of Religion*, trans. R. Hurley (New York: Zone Books, 1989), pp. 110–11.

3   Carl Schmitt, *Writings on War*, ed. and trans. T. Nunan (Malden, MA: Polity, 2011), p. 23. These lines were taken from the translator's introduction.

4   Paul Virilio, *Negative Horizon: An Essay in Dromoscopy*, trans. M. Degener (New York: Continuum, 2005), p. 97.

5   See Mariella Pandolfi, "From Paradox to Paradigm: The Permanent States of Emergency in the Balkans," in *Contemporary States of Emergency: The Politics of Military and Humanitarian Interventions*, ed. D. Fassin and M. Pandolfi (New York: Zone Books, 2010).

6   International Criminal Tribunal in the Hague was established by the UN Security Council acting under chapter VIII of the UN Charter.

7   See Elvir Padalović, "Interview with T. Klauški," *Buka* (www.6yka.com/index.php/klauskiintervju) (accessed on November 1, 2011).

8   Talal Asad has taken up the problem of witnessing and corrected a number of recent arguments, all of which were unsatisfactory: suicide bombing as a sacrifice, as a secular tactic, and as a compulsive neurosis. The most interesting theory of martyrdom that Asad engages is that of May Jayyusi who addresses Palestinian suicide operations: "Jayyusi's conclusion is a neat inversion of Agamben: 'If homo sacer is he who can be killed and not sacrificed', she writes, 'then the martyr here inverses this relation to sovereignty, transforming himself into he who can be sacrificed but not killed.'" In *On Suicide Bombing* (New York: Columbia University Press, 2007), p. 48.

9   Ibid., pp. 51–2.

10   Concerning this point, Arjun Appadurai writes: "In some ways, we see a return here to the simplest form of religious violence, the sacrifice, about which Rene Girard (1977) has written so eloquently. Starting with the videotaped beheading of Daniel Pearl in Pakistan soon after 9/11, the public sacrifice has grown into a more systematic tool of political expression." In *Fear of Small Numbers: An Essay on the Geography of Anger* (Durham: Duke University Press, 2006), p. 12.

11   See Walter Benjamin, "Critique of Violence," in *Reflections: Essays, Aphorisms, Autobiographical Writings*, ed. P. Demetz, trans. E. Jephcott (New York: Schocken Books, 1986).

12   Mahmoud Darwish, *Unfortunately, It Was Paradise*, trans. M. Akash, C. Forche, S. Antoon, and A. El-Zein (Berkeley: University of California Press, 2003), p. 22.

13   Roberto Esposito, *Communitas: The Origin and Destiny of Community*, trans. T. Campbell (Stanford: Stanford University Press, 2010), p. 21.

14   Ibid., p. 23.

15   See the full document written by Atta and found in his luggage, "Last Words of a Terrorist," trans. I. Musa, the *Observer* (September 30, 2001) (www.guardian.co.uk/world/2001/sep/30/terrorism.september113) (accessed on November 3, 2011).

16 See Jarett Kobek, *Atta* (Los Angeles: Semiotext(e), 2011), a courageous fictional biography of the militant.

17 Hamid Dabashi, *Islamic Liberation Theology: Resisting the Empire* (New York: Routledge, 2008), p. 243. It is important to note that Malcolm X was indeed a militant, affirming violence as a valid form of defense. He was certainly not a tolerant or moderate Muslim, as Dabashi seems to portray him, perfecting his radicality with a Levinasian phenomenology of responsibility. Malcolm X went much further than Levinas: first in his primacy of the act and second in his ethics of resistance (vs tolerance).

18 Henri Bergson, *The Two Sources of Morality and Religion*, trans. R. Ashley Audra and C. Brereton (Garden City: Doubleday Anchor Books, 1935), p. 311.

19 Carl Schmitt, *Political Theology: Four Chapters on the Concept of Sovereignty*, trans. G. Schwab (Cambridge: MIT Press, 1985), p. 5.

20 Talal Asad, *On Suicide Bombing*, p. 59.

21 Faisal Devji, *Terrorist in the Search of Humanity: Militant Islam and Global Politics* (New York: Columbia University Press, 2009), p. 200.

22 Carl Schmitt, *Political Theology: Four Chapters on the Concept of Sovereignty*, trans. G. Schwab (Cambridge: MIT Press, 1985), p. 55.

23 The last sentences of his four chapters on sovereignty read: "Every claim of a decision must be evil for the anarchist, because the right emerges by itself if the immanence of life is not disturbed by such claims. This radical antithesis forces him of course to decide against the decision; and this results in the odd paradox whereby Bakunin, the greatest anarchist of the nineteenth century, had to become in theory the theologian of the antitheological and in practice the dictator of an antidictatorship." In *Political Theology: Four Chapters on the Concept of Sovereignty*, p. 66.

24 In contrast to my argument, Brown writes about postsovereignty: "However, far from instancing state sovereignty, this activity revealed the degree of state subordination to capital. Indeed, states' status as neoliberals actors—and as neoliberalized (or in Foucault's lexicon 'governmentalized') themselves—is one index of their loss of political sovereignty." In *Walled States, Waning Sovereignties* (New York: Zone Books, 2010), p. 67.

25 Faisal Devji, *Terrorist in Search of Humanity: Militant Islam and Global Politics* (New York: Columbia University Press, 2008), p. 140. Devji provides a concrete set of questions which undoubtedly emerge in the light of global Islamic militancy: "What is the future of sovereignty in such a global arena? How might it be attached to a set of institutions and a form of politics that does not as yet exist there? Why has religion come to provide the only vocabulary we have to describe these new worlds? Such are the questions that militancy poses and will in all likelihood proceed to answer. About these questions the moderates have nothing to say." Ibid., p. 200.

Chapter 8

1 N. O. Brown, *Apocalypse and/or Metamorphosis* (Berkeley: University of California Press, 1991), p. 81.

2 Jane Bennett has recently valorized the vitality of ordinary matter with approaches that correspond to those of the present book: "A primordial swerve says that the world is not determined, that an element of chanciness resides at the heart of things, but it also affirms that so-called inanimate things have life, that deep within is an inexplicable vitality or energy, a moment of independence from and resistance to us and other bodies: a kind of thing-power." In *Vibrant Matter: A Political Ecology of Things* (Durham: Duke University Press, 2010), p. 18. The exposition of dust performed here should be viewed in light of this theoretical sensitivity.

3 See "Al Jazeera Reports on Torture Inside Homs," Al Jazeera (February 5, 2012) (www.aljazeera.com/news/middleeast/2012/02/2012241845783949.html) (accessed February 15, 2012).

4 In conversation with Raymond Bellour and François Ewald, Gilles Deleuze revealed: "Félix and I, and many others like us, don't feel we're persons exactly. Our individuality is rather that of events, which isn't making any grand claim, given that haecceities can be modest and microscopic." In Gilles Deleuze, *Negotiations, 1972–1990*, trans. M. Joughin (New York: Columbia University Press, 1995), p. 141. Rather than persons, Deleuze is speaking of the non-personal individualities of things, people, times of day, streams, and so on.

5 See "John Walker Lindh: Profile—The Case of the Taliban American," People (2008) (www.cnn.com/CNN/Programs/people/shows/walker/profile.html) (accessed on November 15, 2011).

6 Ibid.

7 Jean Baudrillard, *The Spirit of Terrorism*, trans. C. Turner (New York: Verso, 2003), pp. 9–10.

8 In the clouds that emerged from the pulverized Twin Towers: "The inorganic analysis identified radionuclides, ions, and asbestos; and the organic analysis identified numerous dangerous types of compounds, including: polycyclic aromatic hydrocarbons (PAHs); polychlorinated biphenyls, dibenzodioxins, and dibenzofurans; phthalate esters; and brominated diphenyl ethers. Unfortunately for those affected, the study's discovery of carcinogenic materials was not disclosed until a summary of the findings were published in *EHP* in November of 2001." See "World Trade Center Dust," 911 Research (http://911research.wtc7.net/wtc/evidence/dust.html) (accessed on November 17, 2011). The inorganic matter here mixes with the organic, making it another type of explosive. Through pulverization, the terrorist act enters the bodies of victims without destroying them, while at the same time reconfiguring the composition of their organic bodies.

9   Gianni Motti, "Collateral Damage" series "consists of 10 landscape photographs that are showing columns of smoke between houses and flowering fruit trees. These photographs are presented without any explanation or narrative. They are photographs the artist bought from an agency. What they depict are the columns of bomb smoke. Shot in the Kosovo, Macedonia and Palestine wars, they were considered inappropriate for press purposes and thus remained unused." See Gianni Motti, "Collateral Damage," (www.kw-berlin.com/english/archiv/production6.htm) (accessed on November 17, 2011). The code of phantom territoriality thus lies in that which is unsaid. The smoke itself is the phantom which permeates those present in it without providing the possibility of an objective explanation of the event (in this case the event of war, ethnic cleansing, and territorial conflict).

10 See especially "Jihad Against Jews and Crusaders, World Islamic Front Statement," in *Voices of Terror*, ed. W. Laquer (New York: Reed Press, 2004).

11 Clarice Lispector, *The Stream of Life*, trans. E. Lowe and E. Fitz (Minneapolis: University of Minnesota Press, 1989), p. 30.

12 On ancient Middle Eastern demonology and dust clouds see Reza Negarestani, *Cyclonopedia: Complicity with Anonymous Materials* (Melbourne: Re.press, 2008), p. 113.

13 Gilles Deleuze and Felix Guattari, *What is Philosophy?*, trans. H. Tomlinson and G. Burchell (New York: Columbia University Press, 1994), p. 160.

14 Claire Fontaine, "Dear R," (Paris, 2005) (www.clairefontaine.ws/pdf/dear_r.pdf) (accessed on November 20, 2011).

15 The video "Bad Girls" was directed by Romain Gavras, shot in Ouarzazate, Morocco: see M.I.A., "Bad Girls," dir. R. Gavras, perf. M.I.A. (www.youtube.com/watch?v=2uYs0gJD-LE) (accessed on February 12, 2012).

16 M.I.A.'s activism comes to the fore with ethnographic honesty: "The fact that I saw it in my life has maybe given me lots of issues, but there's a whole generation of American kids seeing violence on their computer screens and then getting shipped off to Afghanistan. They feel like they know the violence when they don't. Not having a proper understanding of violence, especially what it's like on the receiving end of it, just makes you interpret it wrong and makes inflicting violence easier." See "M.I.A.,"interview with N. Denver, *Complex*, May 24, 2010. Her childhood as a refugee still informs her activist engagements. This also shows that theory, and the rise of an alternative political disposition, is a matter of sensitivity, of a trained temperament, of the ability to cross territories and inhabit different gardens of suffering.

17 Claire Fontaine, "Short Biography," (Paris, 2006) (www.clairefontaine.ws/pdf/bio_eng.pdf) (accessed on November 24, 2011). She problematizes the position of the current artist as one of political impotence. In other words, the contemporary artist can have luxury of being terroristic since she remains in the sphere of the art world; once she steps out of it, she is no longer an artist but a terrorist. In art, terrorism is only an epiphenomenon; in terrorism, art is an epiphenomenon.

18 On the description of singularity and the important difference between multiplicity and identity see Antonio Negri and Michael Hardt, *Commonwealth* (Cambridge: Belknap Press of Harvard University, 2009), pp. 338–9.

19 Anahita Razmi, "White Wall Tehran," (www.anahitarazmi.de/whitewall.php) (accessed on December 1, 2011).

20 See Jos de Putter, "The Making of a New Empire" (Jura Films, 1999).

Chapter 9

1 Daniel Heller-Roazen maps out in detail the ancient Greek, Roman, and medieval Arabic interpretations of the notion of "common sense" (or the "sense of sensing") in both the human and the inhuman: "Setting a clear boundary between human and inhuman beings, the classical definition of man as a rational animal clearly aimed, among other things, to dispel this undifferentiated dimension of all animal life." See Heller-Roazen, *The Inner Touch: Archeology of Sensation* (New York: Zone Books, 2007), p. 92.

2 Rainer Maria Rilke quoted in Paul Virilio, *Bunker Archeology*, trans. G. Collins (New York: Princeton Architectural Press, 2009), p. 89.

3 Adonis, *The Pages of Day and Night*, trans. S. Hazo (Marlboro Press, 2000), p. 21.

4 For the opposite view see Esposito, *Communitas: The Origin and Destiny of Community*, trans. T. Campbell (Stanford: Stanford University Press, 2010), p. 93.

5 See Mak Dizdar, *Stone Sleeper*, trans. Francis R. Jones (London: Anvil Press Poetry, 2009).

6 Visar Zhiti, *The Condemned Apple: Selected Poetry*, trans. R. Elsie (København, Denmark: Green Integer, 2005), p. 175. This poem, among others, was used as a piece of evidence by Albanian authorities in the 1970s to accuse Zhiti of anticommunist activity (wanting a "second sun" instead of the "socialist sun"). As a result, he was sentenced to ten years in prison.

7 See *Sahih Muslim*, "Book 031, Number 5955," (www.cmje.org/religious-texts/hadith/muslim/031-smt.php#031.5955) (accessed on March 2, 2012).

8 See (www.lastprophet.info/prophet-muhammads-cloak-on-display-for-visitors) (accessed March 2, 2012).

9 See Jane Bennett, *Vibrant Matter: Political Ecology of Things* (Durham: Duke University Press, 2010).

10 James Baldwin, *Just Above My Head* (London: Michael Joseph, 1979), p. 342.

11 Elias Canetti: "Discussion with Theodor Adorno," trans. D. Roberts, *Thesis Eleven* 45 (1996): 14. This is a transcription of a radio discussion from 1962.

12 In the introduction to a collection of articles found in the volume *In the Name of Humanity: The Government of Threat and Care* (Durham: Duke University Press, 2010), editors Ilana Feldman and Miriam Ticktin write: "As we have already

seen, the unhuman—as inhumanity, animality, materiality, technology—is in fact foundational for the constitution and elaboration of the category of humanity itself" (p. 19). The limits of the analytical form "humanity" have thus been acknowledged by recent studies in critical anthropology as well.

13 Gilles Deleuze and Felix Guattari, *A Thousand Plateaus: Capitalism and Schizophrenia*, trans. B. Massumi (Minneapolis: University of Minnesota Press, 1987), p. 253. Similarly, Faisal Devji announces the "practices of Muslim militants" as one instance of overcoming the pitfalls of humanist subjectivity: "And men can take on animal forms in this way because they represent abstract virtues like courage and fearlessness that have been freed from humanist subjectivity as much as from humanitarian statistics to offer us another vision of the world and our place in it. Frightening though this vision might be, it tells us that our traditional notions of humanity are becoming meaningless in a global arena where the humanist subject is being replaced by a statistical aggregate on the one hand, and by posthuman politics on the others." In *The Terrorist in Search of Humanity: Militant Islam and Global Politics* (New York: Columbia University Press, 2008), p. 212.

14 Roberto Esposito, *Communitas: The Origin and Destiny of Community*, trans. T. C. Campbell (California: Stanford University Press, 2010), p. 145.

15 Giorgio Agamben, *Remnants of Auschwitz: The Witness and the Archive*, trans. D. Heller-Roazen (New York: Zone Books, 2000), pp. 134–5.

16 Tiqqun, *Introduction to Civil War*, trans. A. R. Galloway and J. E. Smith (Los Angeles: Semiotext(e), 2010), p. 18. The term "Tiqqun" primarily applies to a French ultra-left journal created by various writers which was in operation from 1999 to 2001.

17 Jean-Francois Lyotard, "*Domus* and the Megalopolis," in *The Inhuman*, trans. G. Bennington and R. Bowlby (Stanford: Stanford University Press, 1991), p. 196. Lyotard's impenetrable but rewarding essay continues the thinking of domesticity in a way that is aligned with my discussion of the hostage space and the inhuman: "Homo re-domesticus in power kills in the street shouting 'You are not one of ours.' He takes the visitor hostage. He persecutes anything that migrates. He hides it away in his cellars, reduces it to ashes in the furthest ends of his lowlands. It is not war—he devastates. Hybris break apart the domestic modus. And the domestics remodeling will have served to unleash hybris." Ibid., p. 197. It is in the hostage sphere of the "homo re-domesticus" that the hostage taker finds her ground. For the western power she is inhuman because she is not domesticated (a barbarian, a Muslim). But this inhumanity is an effect of being subjugated to the pride and arrogance of the other. And after this, it flows in a song, externalized as the untamable that bridges love and death, and ultimately becomes love as death.

18 Mahmoud Darwish, "Under Siege," trans. M. De Jager (www.poemhunter.com/poem/under-siege/) (accessed March 25, 2012).

19 Ibid.

Bibliography

Adonis. *The Pages of Day and Night*. Translated by S. Hazo. Evanston: Marlboro Press, 2000.

—. *Sufism and Surrealism*. Translated by J. Cumberbatch. Beirut: Saqi Books, 2005.

Agamben, Giorgio. *Remnants of Auschwitz: The Witness and the Archive*. Translated by D. Heller-Roazen. New York: Zone Books, 2000.

—. *The Kingdom and the Glory: For a Theological Genealogy of Economy and Government*. Translated by L. Chiesa. Stanford: Stanford University Press, 2011.

"Al Jazeera Reports on Torture Inside Homs." Al Jazeera (February 5, 2012) (www.aljazeera.com/news/middleeast/2012/02/2012241845783949.html).

Al Zawahiri, Ayman. "Knights Under the Prophet's Banner." In *Voices of Terror: Manifestos, Writings, and Manuals of Al Qaeda, Hamas, and Other Terrorists from Around the World and Throughout the Ages*. Edited by W. Laquer. New York: Reed Press, 2004.

"Al-Qaʿeda: Manual." In *Voices of Terror: Manifestos, Writings, and Manuals of Al Qaeda, Hamas, and Other Terrorists from Around the World and Throughout the Ages*. Edited by W. Laquer. New York: Reed Press, 2004.

Appadurai, Arjun. *Fear of Small Numbers: An Essay on the Geography of Anger*. Durham: Duke University Press, 2006.

Asad, Talal. *On Suicide Bombing*. New York: Columbia University Press, 2007.

Atta, Mohamed. "Last Words of a Terrorist." Translated by I. Musa. The *Observer*, 2001.

Bahrani, Zainab. *Rituals of War: The Body and Violence in Mesopotamia*. New York: Zone Books, 2008.

Baldwin, James. *Just Above My Head*. London: Michael Joseph, 1979.

Bataille, George. *Visions of Excess: Selected Writings, 1927–1939*. Translated by A. Stoekl. Minneapolis: University of Minnesota Press, 1985.

—. *Theory of Religion*. Translated by R. Hurley. New York: Zone Books, 1989.

Baudrillard, Jean. *Spirit of Terrorism and Other Essays*. Translated by C. Turner. New York: Verso, 2003.

Benjamin, Walter. *Reflections: Essays, Aphorisms, Autobiographical Writings*. Edited by P. Demetz. Translated by E. Jephcott. New York: Schocken Books, 1986.

Bennet, Jane. *Vibrant Matter: A Political Ecology of Things*. Durham: Duke University Press, 2010.

Bergson, Henri. *The Two Sources of Morality and Religion*. Translated by R. Ashley Audra and C. Brereton. Garden City: Doubleday Anchor Books, 1935.

Biehl, João. *Vita: Life in a Zone of Social Abandonment*. Berkeley and Los Angeles: University of California Press, 2005.

Black Hand, The. "Constitution of the Black Hand: Unification or Death." Brigham Young University. (http://wwi.lib.byu.edu/index.php/Constitution_of_the_Black_Hand).

Bois, Yve-Alain and Rosalind Krauss. *Formless: A User's Guide*. New York: Zone Books, 1997.

"Book 031, Number 5955 of Sahih Muslim." Center For Muslim-Jewish Engagement (www.cmje.org/religious-texts/hadith/muslim/031-smt.php#031.5955).

Bourgeois, Louise. "The Spider, the Mistress, and The Tangerine." Director Marion Cajori and Amei Wallach. Zeitgeist Video, 2008.

Broomberg, Adam and Oliver Chanarin. "Chicago." SteidlMACK (www.choppedliver.info/chicago/).

Brown, N. O. *Apocalypse and/or Metamorphosis*. Berkeley: University of California Press, 1991.

Brown, Wendy. *Walled States, Waning Sovereignty*. New York: Zone Books, 2010.

Callois, Roger. *The Edge of Surrealism: A Roger Caillois Reader*. Edited by C. Frank. Translated by C. Frank and C. Naish. Durham: Duke University Press, 2003.

Canetti, Elias. *Crowds and Power*. Translated by C. Stewart. New York: Macmillan, 1984.

—. "Elias Canetti: Discussion with Theodor W. Adorno." Translated by D. Roberts. *Thesis Eleven* 45 (1996).

Castro, Fidel and Ignacio Ramonet. *My Life: A Spoken Autobiography*. New York: Scribner, 2009.

Clastres, Pierre. *Society Against the State: Essays in Political Anthropology*. Translated by R. Hurley. New York: Zone Books, 1987.

Critchley, Simon. *The Faith of the Faithless: Experiments in Political Theology*. New York: Verso, 2012.

Dabashi, Hamid. *Islamic Liberation Theology: Resisting the Empire*. New York: Routledge, 2008.

—. *Shi'ism: A Religion of Protest*. Cambridge: Belknap Press of Harvard University Press, 2011.

—. *The Arab Spring: The End of Postcolonialism*. London: Zed Books, 2012.

Darwish, Mahmoud. "Under Siege." Translated by M. De Jager (www.poemhunter.com/poem/under-siege/).

—. *Unfortunately, It Was Paradise*. Translated by M. Akash, C. Forche, S. Antoon, and A. El-Zein. Berkeley: University of California Press, 2003.

De Putter, Jos. "The Making of a New Empire." Jura Films, 1999.

Debord, Guy. *The Society of the Spectacle*. Translated by D. Nicholson-Smith. New York: Zone Books, 1994.

Deleuze, Gilles. *Spinoza: Practical Philosophy*. Translated by R. Hurley. San Francisco: City Lights Books, 1988.

—. "Postscript on the Societies of Control." *October* 59 (Winter 1992) (www.n5m.org/n5m2/media/texts/deleuze.htm).

—. *Negotiations, 1972–1990*. Translated by M. Joughin. New York: Columbia University Press, 1995.

—. "Gilles Deleuze from A to Z." Interview with C. Parnet. Directed by P. A. Boutang. Translated by C. J. Stivale. Semiotext(e), 2011.

Deleuze, Gilles and Felix Guattari. *A Thousand Plateaus: Capitalism and Schizophrenia.* Translated by B. Massumi. Minneapolis: University of Minnesota Press, 1987.

—. *What is Philosophy?* Translated by H. Tomlinson and G. Burchell. New York: Columbia University Press, 1994.

Derrida, Jacques. *The Beast and the Sovereign, Volume I.* Translated by G. Bennington. Chicago: University of Chicago Press, 2009.

—. *The Beast and the Sovereign, Volume II.* Translated by G. Bennington. Chicago: University of Chicago Press, 2011.

Devji, Faisal. *Landscapes of the Jihad: Militancy, Morality, Modernity.* Ithaca: Cornell University Press, 2005.

—. *The Terrorist in Search of Humanity: Militant Islam and Global Politics.* New York: Columbia University Press, 2008.

Dhanani, Alnoor. *The Physical Theory of Kalām: Atoms, Space and Void in Basrian Mu'tazilī Cosmology.* New York: E.J. Brill, 1994.

Dizdar, Mehmed Alija Mak. *Stone Sleeper.* Translated by F. Jones. Sarajevo: Did, 1999.

Dobaev, Igor. "Islamic Radicalism in the Northern Caucasus." *CA & CC Press: International Conference,* 2012 (www.ca-c.org/journal/eng-06–2000/09.dobaev.shtml).

Dumont, Bruno. "Hadewijch." 3B Productions, 2009.

Dunlop, John. *The 2002 Dubrovka and 2004 Beslan Hostage Crises: A Critique of Russian Counter Terrorism.* Edited by A. Umland. Germany: ibidem-Verlag, 2006.

Dworzak, Thomas. "The Enemy." *Cabinet: A Quarterly of Art and Culture* 12 (Fall/Winter 2003).

Esposito, Roberto. *Bíos: Biopolitics and Philosophy.* Translated by T. Campbell. Minneapolis: University of Minnesota Press, 2008.

—. *Communitas: The Origin and Destiny of Community.* Translated by T. Campbell. Stanford: Stanford University Press, 2010.

Faraj, Mohammad 'Abdus Salam. "Jihad, The Absent Obligation." In *Voices of Terror: Manifestos, Writings, and Manuals of Al Qaeda, Hamas, and Other Terrorists from Around the World and Throughout the Ages.* Edited by W. Laquer. New York: Reed Press, 2004.

Fassin, Didier and Mariella Pandolfi, editors. *Contemporary States of Emergency: The Politics of Military and Humanitarian Interventions.* New York: Zone Books, 2010.

Fassin, Didier and Richard Rechtman. *The Empire of Trauma: An Inquiry into the Condition of Victimhood.* Translated by R. Gomme. Princeton: Princeton University Press, 2009.

Feldman, Ilana and Miriam Iris Ticktin, editors. *In the Name of Humanity: The Government of Threat and Care.* Durham: Duke University Press, 2010.

Fisk, Robert. "Back to Tahrir Square." *The Independent* (December 2, 2011) (www. independent.co.uk/opinion/commentators/fisk/robert-fisk-back-to-tahrir-squar e-6270756.html).

Fontaine, Claire. "Dear R." Paris: 2005 (www.clairefontaine.ws/pdf/dear_r.pdf).

—. "Short Biography." Paris: 2006 (www.clairefontaine.ws/pdf/bio_eng.pdf).

Foucault, Michel. "Of Other Spaces: Utopias and Heterotopias." In *Rethinking Architecture: A Reader in Cultural Theory*. Edited by N. Leach. Translated by J. Miskowiec. New York: Routledge, 1997.

—. *Security, Territory, Population: Lectures at the Collége de France, 1977–78*. Edited by M. Senellart. Translated by G. Burchell. New York: Palgrave Macmillan, 2007.

Frazer, James George. *The New Golden Bough: A New Abridgment of the Classic Work*. Edited by T. H. Gaster. New York: Criterion Books, 1959.

La Fura dels Baus. "Boris Godunov." (www.lafura.com/web/eng/obras_ficha. php?o=108).

Gerges, Fawaz. *The Far Enemy: Why Jihad Went Global*. Cambridge: Cambridge University Press, 2009.

—. *The Rise and Fall of Al-Qaeda*. Oxford: Oxford University Press, 2011.

Glassé, Cyril. *The New Encyclopedia of Islam*. Walnut Creek, CA: AltaMira Press, 2001.

Grant, Bruce. *The Captive and the Gift: Cultural Histories of Sovereignty in Russia and the Caucases*. Ithaca: Cornell University Press, 2009.

Hammoudi, Abdellah. "Textualism and Anthropology: On the Ethnographic Encounter, or an Experience in the Hajj." In *Being There: The Fieldwork Encounter and the Making of Truth*. Edited by J. Borneman and A. Hammoudi. Berkeley: University of California Press, 2009.

Hardt, Michael and Antonio Negri. *Empire*. Cambridge: Harvard University Press, 2001.

—. *Commonwealth*. Cambridge: Belknap Press of Harvard University, 2009.

Havel, Václav. *Open Letters: Selected Writings, 1965–1990*. Selected and Edited by P. Wilson. New York: Knopf, 1991.

Haviv, Ron. *Blood and Honey: A Balkan War Journal*. New York: TV Books, 2000.

—. "Blood and Honey: A Balkan War Journal." (www.ronhaviv.com/#mi=2&pt=1&pi=1 0000&s=0&p=15&a=0&at=0).

Heidegger, Martin. *Being and Time*. Translated by J. Macquarrie and E. Robinson. New York: Harper, 1962.

Heller-Roazen, Daniel. *The Inner Touch: Archaeology of Sensation*. New York: Zone Books, 2007.

—. *The Enemy of All: Piracy and the Law of Nations*. New York: Zone Books, 2009.

Ibn Qayyim, *Zad al-Mitad* (http://web.youngmuslims.ca/online_library/books/ milestones/hold/chapter_4.htm).

Jacobsen, Marjory. "Anri Sala." In *Sensorium: Embodied Experience, Technology, and Contemporary Art*. Edited by C. Jones. Cambridge: MIT Press, 2006.

"John Walker Lindh: Profile." *People* (www.cnn.com/CNN/Programs/people/shows/ walker/profile.html).

Kathir, Ibn, Hafiz. *Stories of the Prophets.* London: Dar-us-Salam Publications, 2003.

Kepel, Gilles. *Muslim Extremism in Egypt: The Prophet and Pharaoh.* Translated by J. Rothschild. Berkeley: University of California Press, 1985.

Khaleej Times. "Saudi Arabia's Top Artist Ahmad Bin Ibrahim Passes Away." (www. khaleejtimes.com/DisplayArticleNew.asp?col=&section=middleeast&xfile=data/ middleeast/2009/November/middleeast_November268.xml).

Kobek, Jarett. *Atta.* Los Angeles: Semiotext(e), 2011.

Kozyrev, Yuri. "Beslan, Osetia." Noor (www.noorimages.com/index.php?id=7621).

Lelchuk, Janna. *Terror in Russia: The Blood of Nord-Ost and Beslan.* Bloomington: Authorhouse, 2005.

Libeskind, Daniel. "Ground Zero Master Plan." Studio Daniel Libeskind (http:// daniel-libeskind.com/projects/ground-zero-master-plan/images).

Lispector, Clarice. *The Stream of Life.* Translated by Elizabeth Lowe and Earl Fitz. Minneapolis: University of Minnesota Press, 1989.

Lopez, Susana and Carlos F. Arias. "How Viruses Hijack Endocytic Machinery." *Nature Education* 3.9 (2010).

Lyotard, Jean-Francois. *The Inhuman: Reflections on Time.* Translated by G. Bennington and R. Bowlby. Stanford: Stanford University Press, 1991.

Mahmood, Saba. *Politics of Piety: The Islamic Revival and the Feminist Subject.* Princeton: Princeton University Press, 2005.

Malcolm X. *The Autobiography of Malcolm X.* London: Penguin Books, 2010.

—. "Malcolm X After Mecca." (www.youtube.com/watch?v=wgqIek2TYvg).

Mansour, Joyce. *Screams.* Sausalito: Post Apollo Press, 1995.

McDonell, Nick. *The End of Major Combat Operations.* San Francisco: McSweeney's Books, 2010.

Meyerowitz, Joel. "World Trade Center Archive." Phaidon (www.phaidon.com/agenda/ photography/picture-galleries/2011/september/08/joel-meyerowitzs-world-trade-center-archive/?view=thumbs).

M.I.A. "MIA" Interview with N. Denver. *Complex* (May 24, 2010) (www.complex.com/ music/2010/05/mia-cover-story).

—. "Bad Girls." Directed by R. Gavras (www.youtube.com/watch?v=2uYs0gJD-LE).

Mohaghegh, Jason Bahbak. *The Writing of Violence in the Middle East: Inflictions.* New York: Continuum, 2011.

Mohamed, Mamdouh. *Hajj & Umrah: From A to Z.* Beltsville: Amana Publications, 1996.

Mommaers, Paul. *The Land Within: The Process of Possessing and Being Possessed by God According to the Mystic Jan van Ruysbroeck.* Translated by D. N. Smith. Chicago: Franciscan Herald Press, 1975.

Mosse, Richard. "Shahid." Edited by T. Tweeten (2009) (http://vimeo.com/7065282).

Motti, Gianni. "Collateral Damage." (www.kw-berlin.com/english/archiv/production6. htm).

Najafi, Sina and Peter Galison. "The Ontology of the Enemy." *Cabinet: A Quarterly of Art and Culture* 12 (Fall/Winter 2003).

Nancy, Jean-Luc. *On the Commerce of Thinking: Of Books and Bookstores*. Translated by D. Wills. New York: Fordham University Press, 2009.

Negarestani, Reza. "The Militarization of Peace: Absence of Terror or Terror of Absence?" In *Collapse Vol. 1: Numerical Materialism*. Edited by R. Mackay. United Kingdom: Urbanomic, 2006.

—. *Cyclonopedia: Complicity with Anonymous Materials*. Melbourne: Re.press, 2008.

Obama, Barack. "The Death of Osama bin Laden." Presidential Speech. White House (May 1, 2011) (www.youtube.com/watch?v=ZNYmK19-d0U&feature=relmfu).

Padalović, Elvir. "Interview." Interviewed by T. Klauški. *Buka* (www.6yka.com/index.php/klauskiintervju).

Pandolfi, Mariella. "From Paradox to Paradigm: The Permanent States of Emergency in the Balkans." In *Contemporary States of Emergency: The Politics of Military and Humanitarian Interventions*. Edited by D. Fassin and M. Pandolfi. New York: Zone Books, 2010.

Peters, Francis E. *The Hajj: The Muslim Pilgrimage to Mecca and the Holy Places*. Princeton: Princeton University Press, 1994.

Petit, Phillippe. "Man on Wire." Director J. Marsh. Magnolia Pictures, 2008.

"Prophet Muhammad's Cloak on Display for Visitors." LastProphet.info (www.lastprophet.info/prophet-muhammads-cloak-on-display-for-visitors).

Ramadan, Tariq. "The Global Ideology of Fear." *New Perspectives Quarterly* 23.1 (2006).

Razmi, Anahita. "White Wall Tehran." (www.anahitarazmi.de/whitewall.php).

Raznjatović, Zeljko. "Warrior Steeped in Sacredness: An Interview." (www.dadavujasinovic.com/Arkan.htm).

Saunders, John J. *A History of Medieval Islam*. London: Routledge, 1978.

Schmitt, Carl. *Political Theology: Four Chapters on the Concept of Sovereignty*. Translated by G. Schwab. Cambridge: MIT Press, 1985.

—. *The Concept of the Political*. Translated by G. Schwab. Chicago: University of Chicago Press, 2007.

—. *Theory of the Partisan: Intermediate Commentary on the Concept of the Political*. Translated by G. L. Ulmen. New York: Telos Press Publications, 2007.

—. *Writings on War*. Edited and Translated by T. Nunan. Malden, MA: Polity, 2011.

Sebastian J. "The Open Parliament of Albania/Coop Himmelb(l)au" (www.archdaily.com/124058/the-open-parliament-of-albania-coop-himmelblau/).

Shackelford, Michael. "The Black Hand." Brigham Young University. (http://wwi.lib.byu.edu/index.php/The_Black_Hand).

Šimić, Marinka. "Jezik Boljunskih Natpisa." (www.post.ba/download/boljuni.pdf).

Sloterdijk, Peter. *Terror from the Air*. Translated by A. Patton and S. Corcoran. Los Angeles: Semiotext(e), 2009.

—. *Rage and Time: A Psychopolitical Investigation*. Translated by M. Wenning. New York: Columbia University Press, 2010.

"Surrealism in the Arab World." Libcom.org (http://libcom.org/history/surrealism-arab-world).

Surya, Michel. *George Bataille: An Intellectual Biography*. Translated by K. Fijalkowski and M. Richardson. New York: Verso, 2002.

Tabari, Al, Djafar, Abu Muhammad, and Franz Rosenthal. Translated by W. M. Watt and M. V. McDonald. *The History of al-Tabari*. New York: State University of New York Press, 1989.

Taqi-ud-deen ahmad ibn taymiyyah. *The Religious and Moral Doctrine of Jihad*. Birmingham, England: Maktabah al-Ansaar, 2001.

Taussig, Michael. "Zoology, Magic, and Surrealism in the War on Terror." *Critical Inquiry* 34.S2 (2008).

Tiqqun. *Introduction to Civil War*. Translated by A. R. Galloway and J. E. Smith. Los Angeles: Semiotext(e), 2010.

Toscano, Alberto. *Fanaticism: On the Uses of an Idea*. New York: Verso, 2010.

"U.S. Department of State List of Foreign Terrorist Organizations." *Military Education Research Library Network*. National Defense University Library (October 21, 2008) (http://merln.ndu.edu/archivepdf/terrorism/state/103392.pdf).

Vernant, Jean-Pierre. "Dim Body, Dazzling Body." In *Fragments for a History of the Human Body, Part 1*. Edited by M. Feher, R. Naddaff, and N. Tazi. New York: Zone Books, 1989.

Virilio, Paul. *War and Cinema: The Logistics of Perception*. Translated by P. Carniller. New York: Verso, 1989.

—. *Negative Horizon: An Essay in Dromoscopy*. Translated by M. Degener. New York: Continuum, 2005.

—. *Bunker Archeology*. Translated by G. Collins. New York: Princeton Architectural Press, 2009.

—. *The Administration of Fear*. Translated by A. Hodges. Los Angeles: Semiotext(e), 2012.

Walsh, Nick Patton and Peter Beaumont. "When Hell Came Calling at Beslan's School No. 1." *The Guardian* (September 4, 2004) (www.guardian.co.uk/world/2004/sep/05/russia.chechnya).

Weizman, Eyal. "Frontier Architectures." *Steidl* (2007) (www.choppedliver.info/files/walking-through-walls.pdf).

Wines, Michael. "Chechens Seize Moscow Theater, Taking as Many as 600 Hostages." *New York Times* (October 24, 2002) (www.nytimes.com/2002/10/24/world/chechens-seize-moscow-theater-taking-as-many-as-600-hostages.html?pagewanted=all&src=pm).

"World Trade Center Dust." 911 Research (http://911research.wtc7.net/wtc/evidence/dust.html).

World Islamic Front. "Jihad Against Jews and Crusaders, World Islamic Front Statement." In *Voices of Terror: Manifestos, Writings, and Manuals of Al Qaeda, Hamas, and Other Terrorists from Around the World and Throughout the Ages*. Edited by W. Laquer. New York: Reed Press, 2004.

Zhiti, Visar. *The Condemned Apple: Selected Poetry*. Translated by R. Elsie. København, Denmark: Green Integer, 2005.

Index

16804598R00115

Printed in Great Britain
by Amazon